TOP STOCKS 2006

12th YEAR of PUBLICATION

TOP STOCKS 2006

12th YEAR of PUBLICATION

MARTIN ROTH

Wrightbooks

The author and publisher would like to thank Aspect Huntley for permission to include the five-year shareholder return figures, and Alan Hull (author of *Active Investing and Active Retirement*) for generating the five-year share price graphs <www.alanhull.com>.

This twelfth edition first published 2006 by Wrightbooks
an imprint of John Wiley & Sons Australia, Ltd
42 McDougall Street, Milton Qld 4064

First edition published as *Top Stocks* by Wrightbooks in 1995
New edition published annually

Typeset in 10.6/12.7 pt Garamond

ISBN: 0 731 403452

Cover design by Rob Cowpe

Printed in Australia by Ligare

10 9 8 7 6 5 4 3 2 1

Disclaimer

The material in this publication is of the nature of general comment only, and does not represent professional advice. It is not intended to provide specific guidance for particular circumstances and it should not be relied on as the basis for any decision to take action or not take action on any matter which it covers. Readers should obtain professional advice where appropriate, before making any such decision. To the maximum extent permitted by law, the author and publisher disclaim all responsibility and liability to any person, arising directly or indirectly from any person taking or not taking action based upon the information in this publication.

Contents

Preface vii

Introduction xiii

Part I: the companies

Adcorp Australia Ltd 3
Adelaide Bank Ltd 4
Adelaide Brighton Ltd 5
Alesco Corporation Ltd 6
Amalgamated Holdings Ltd 7
Angus & Coote (Holdings) Ltd 8
ARB Corporation Ltd 9
Australand Property Group 10
Australia and New Zealand Banking Group Ltd 11
Australian Gas Light Company (The) 12
Australian Stock Exchange Ltd 13
AV Jennings Homes Ltd 14
AXA Asia Pacific Holdings Ltd 15
Bank of Queensland Ltd 16
Bendigo Bank Ltd 17
BHP Billiton Ltd 18
Billabong International Ltd 19
Blackmores Ltd 20
Boral Ltd 21
Brickworks Ltd 22
Cabcharge Australia Ltd 23
Campbell Brothers Ltd 24
Candle Australia Ltd 25
Cellnet Group Ltd 26
Central Equity Ltd 27
CMI Ltd 28
Coates Hire Ltd 29
Cochlear Ltd 30
Coffey International Ltd 31
Coles Myer Ltd 32
Collection House Ltd 33
Colorado Group Ltd 34
Commander Communications Ltd 35
Commonwealth Bank of Australia 36
Computershare Ltd 37
Corporate Express Australia Ltd 38
Count Financial Ltd 39
CSL Ltd 40
CSR Ltd 41
CVC Ltd 42
David Jones Ltd 43
Downer EDI Ltd 44
Fairfax (John) Holdings Ltd 45
Fantastic Holdings Ltd 46
FKP Property Group 47
Fleetwood Corporation Ltd 48
Flight Centre Ltd 49
Foodland Associated Ltd 50
Funtastic Ltd 51
Gazal Corporation Ltd 52
Great Southern Plantations Ltd 53
GUD Holdings Ltd 54
Gunns Ltd 55
GWA International Ltd 56
Harvey Norman Holdings Ltd 57
HGL Ltd 58
Hills Industries Ltd 59
Housewares International Ltd 60
Incitec Pivot Ltd 61
Infomedia Ltd 62
Institute of Drug Technology Australia Ltd 63
Integrated Group Ltd 64

Contents (cont'd)

IRESS Market Technology Ltd 65
K & S Corporation Ltd 66
Leighton Holdings Ltd 67
Macquarie Bank Ltd 68
Magna Pacific (Holdings) Ltd 69
MaxiTRANS Industries Ltd 70
McGuigan Simeon Wines Ltd 71
Metcash Ltd 72
Monadelphous Group Ltd 73
National Australia Bank Ltd 74
Oakton Ltd 75
OAMPS Ltd 76
Origin Energy Ltd 77
OrotonGroup Ltd 78
Pacifica Group Ltd 79
Patrick Corporation Ltd 80
Perpetual Trustees Australia Ltd 81
Portman Ltd 82
Primary Health Care Ltd 83
Pro Medicus Ltd 84
Programmed Maintenance Services Ltd 85
Publishing and Broadcasting Ltd 86
QBE Insurance Group Ltd 87
Rebel Sport Ltd 88
Reece Australia Ltd 89
Rinker Group Ltd 90
Rio Tinto Ltd 91
Rock Building Society Ltd (The) 92
Rural Press Ltd 93
Santos Ltd 94
Select Harvests Ltd 95
Sigma Company Ltd 96
Sims Group Ltd 97
St George Bank Ltd 98
STW Communications Group Ltd 99
Suncorp-Metway Ltd 100
Tasmanian Perpetual Trustees Ltd 101
Technology One Ltd 102
Timbercorp Ltd 103
Toll Holdings Ltd 104
Treasury Group Ltd 105
Troy Resources NL 106
Trust Company of Australia Ltd 107
United Group Ltd 108
Washington H. Soul Pattinson & Company Ltd 109
Wesfarmers Ltd 110
Westpac Banking Corporation 111
Wide Bay Australia Ltd 112
Willmott Forests Ltd 113
Woodside Petroleum Ltd 114

Part II: the tables

Tables index 117
A Market capitalisation 119
B Revenues 120
C Year-on-year revenues growth 121
D EBIT margin 122
E Year-on-year EBIT margin growth 123
F After-tax profit 124
G Year-on-year growth 125
H Return on equity 126
I Year-on-year return on equity growth 127
J Debt-to-equity ratio 128
K Current ratio 129
L Price-earnings ratio 130
M Price-to-NTA-per share ratio 131
N Dividend yield 132
O Year-on-year dividend growth 133
P Five-year share price return 134
Q Non-interest income to total income 135
R Cost-to-income ratio 135
S Return on assets 135

Preface

It's been another bumper year for Australian companies, and 112 have qualified for entry to this 12th edition of *Top Stocks*, nearly as many as the 115 that were in *Top Stocks 2005*, which was the most ever. It is a testament to the continuing strengths of the domestic economy and of the stock market.

When I wrote the first edition of *Top Stocks*, back in 1995, the goal was to find roughly 100 companies to write about. Only eighty made the cut. And, because entry criteria were much looser in those days, seventeen of those eighty would not have made it into the present edition. It is a clear indication of how Australian corporations have become so much more profitable and financially stable over the past decade.

Some highlights of this edition of the book include:

- Twenty-three new companies, of which eighteen have never appeared previously in any edition of *Top Stocks*.
- I used to think it a weakness of *Top Stocks* that it seldom contained high-tech companies —because so few could make a profit and pay a dividend for five consecutive years—but after the dotcom 'meltdown' of 2000 I realised it was a strength. But now high-tech stocks are starting to flow into the book. In *Top Stocks 2005* there were four. In the latest edition there are six.
- Health care is another steadily expanding sector. In *Top Stocks 2006*, there are seven health care stocks, one more than in the previous edition.

Who is *Top Stocks* written for?

Top Stocks is written for every investor who has ever wondered:

> *There are 1700 companies on the stock exchange—where do I start?*

These investors know that there are many excellent companies out there—companies that seem to prosper through good times and bad—but they are just not sure which ones they are, apart from some obvious names.

For, whatever may be happening in the market, the fact remains that there are plenty of good, solid companies with excellent long-term records of regular dividends and capital growth. They may not double or triple in price within the space of months. But so long as a company's business continues to flourish its shares should certainly come to represent good value.

This book is for investors seeking out these stocks.

It is not a how-to book. It does not give step-by-step instructions to 'winning' in the stock market. Rather, it is an independent and objective evaluation of leading companies, based on rigid criteria, with the intention of yielding a large selection of stocks that can become the starting point for investors wishing to do their own research. A large amount of information is presented on each company, and another key feature of the book is that the data is presented in a common format, to allow readers to make easy comparisons between companies.

It is necessarily a conservative book. All stocks must have been listed for five years even to be considered for inclusion (which is why earlier editions missed the dotcom boom entirely). It is especially suited for those seeking value stocks for longer term investment.

Yet, perhaps ironically, the book is also increasingly being used by short-term traders seeking a good selection of financially sound and reliable companies whose shares they can trade.

In addition, there are many regular readers, who buy the book each year, and to them in particular I express my thanks.

What are the entry criteria?

The criteria for inclusion in *Top Stocks* are strict:

- All companies must be included in the All Ordinaries Index, which comprises Australia's 500 largest stocks (out of approximately 1700). The reason for excluding smaller companies is that there is often little investor information available on many of them and some are so thinly traded as to be almost illiquid. In fact, the 500 All Ordinaries companies comprise, by market capitalisation, around 98% of the entire market. (One stock, Portman, is not now in the All Ordinaries Index, but was in *Top Stocks 2005*, so remains in this latest edition of the book.)
- It was necessary that all companies be publicly listed since at least the end of 2000, and have a five-year record of profits and dividend payouts. An exception is companies

de-merged from another company in the All Ordinaries Index. These require just a two-year record of profits and dividend payouts. The only such company in this edition is Rinker Group, formerly part of CSR.

- All companies were required to post a return-on-equity ratio of at least 10% in their latest financial year (a slight tweaking from the 9% benchmark of *Top Stocks 2005*).
- No company should have a debt-to-equity ratio of more than 70% (75% in *Top Stocks 2005*).
- It must be stressed that share price performance is *not* one of the criteria for inclusion in this book. The purpose is to select companies with good profits and a strong balance sheet. These may not offer the spectacular share-price returns of a biotech start-up, but they should also present far less risk. To use an Olympics analogy, the stocks in this book are more like marathon runners than sprinters. They should last the distance, providing solid—if un-flashy—performance over the long term.
- There are several notable exclusions. Investment trusts like Australian Foundation Investment Company are out, as these mainly buy other shares or investments. Also omitted are property trusts.
- A further exclusion is the foreign stocks listed on the Australian Stock Exchange. There is sometimes a lack of information available about such companies. In addition, their stock prices tend to move on events and trends in their home countries, making it difficult at times for local investors to follow them.

Changes to this edition

A total of 26 companies from *Top Stocks 2005* have been omitted from this new edition. One, car parts maker Ion, went into voluntary administration after banks withdrew its line of credit. Another, Macquarie Goodman Management (now renamed Macquarie Goodman Group) has been designated a property trust by the ASX. Three companies, National Foods, Pacific Hydro and Wadepack, have been acquired and delisted.

The following ten companies from *Top Stocks 2005* were excluded because they had debt-to-equity ratios that rose higher than 70%:

- Brazin
- Cedar Wood Properties
- Foster's Group
- McPherson's
- Orica
- Plaspak Group
- Schaffer Corporation
- Sydney Aquarium
- West Australian Newspapers
- Woolworths.

A further eleven companies (listed below) had return-on-equity figures that fell below 10%:

- AJ Lucas
- Amcor
- Equigold
- Iluka Resources

- Auspine
- Coventry Group
- Crane Group
- Danks Holdings
- Miller's Retail
- SDI
- Volante Group.

As noted, there are twenty-three new companies in this book (five of them have appeared in earlier editions of the book, but were not in *Top Stocks 2005*). The companies are:

- Adelaide Brighton#
- Amalgamated Holdings
- Billabong International#
- CMI
- Collection House#
- Commander Communications#
- Count Financial#
- CSL
- CVC#
- David Jones
- Funtastic#
- Infomedia#
- IRESS Market Technology#
- Magna Pacific#
- MaxiTRANS#
- Metcash#
- Oakton#
- Patrick Corporation#
- Pro Medicus#
- Rinker Group#
- Treasury Group#
- Trust Company of Australia
- Willmott Forests#.

(#Companies that have not appeared in any previous edition of *Top Stocks*.)

Companies in every edition of *Top Stocks*

The following twelve companies have appeared in every edition of *Top Stocks*:

- ANZ
- Commonwealth Bank of Australia
- CSR
- Harvey Norman
- Hills Industries
- Incitec Pivot (formerly just Incitec)
- National Australia Bank
- QBE Insurance
- Santos
- Suncorp-Metway
- Wesfarmers
- Westpac Banking.

Woolworths had previously appeared in every edition of the book, but was dropped from *Top Stocks 2006* due to its debt-to-equity ratio rising above 70%, following its acquisition of Australian Leisure and Hospitality Group.

Australian International Financial Reporting Standards

New international reporting standards have been introduced for Australian companies, for reporting periods that begin on or after 1 January 2005. Thus, in *Top Stocks 2006*, only fourteen companies have so far reported using the new rules. Some of these companies expect the new standards to make quite a difference to their results. In many cases, profits are higher, because of rules changing the way that amortisation can be applied to goodwill.

As an example of the impact of the changes, Australand Property announced that the new rules had added 'significant volatility to reported results'. The main reason is that revenue and profits on the development of apartments and residential property are now only recognised on settlement of the sale of the property, rather than progressively on a percentage of completion basis, as under the previous Australian Accounting Standards.

In moving to the new standards, all companies are obliged to restate the previous year's results. In *Top Stocks 2005*, Australand Property had a June 2004 debt-to-equity ratio of 66.7%. However, restating its results under the new standards meant that this ratio became 109.2%. Had the new standards been in effect a year ago, Australand would not have qualified for *Top Stocks 2005*.

Woodside Petroleum noted in its interim results announcement that, under the new rules, gains or losses on embedded derivatives within sales contracts are now recognised as part of profit. This added $63.7 million to the company's June 2005 after-tax profit. In future years the rule could easily reduce profits by a similar—or even larger—amount.

It will be interesting to see what happens in February 2006, when most of the companies in this book report for the first time under the new standards. A few companies that have made some major acquisitions—and thus have seen their earnings held down, because they have been amortising the goodwill—might see a sharp rise in profits. An example is Computershare, which has announced that, had it been required to report its June 2005 results under the new rules, its after-tax profit would have been $127.1 million, instead of the reported $101.5 million (which became $92.3 million after stripping out significant items).

Indeed, *Top Stocks 2007* could see some interesting developments. Until then, I hope that *Top Stocks 2006* will serve you well.

Martin Roth
Melbourne
September 2005

Introduction

The 112 companies in this book have been placed as much as possible into a common format, for ease of comparison. Please study the following explanations in order to get as much as possible from the large amount of data.

Each page begins with a brief introduction to the company and its activities. The highlights of its latest business results follow. For the majority of the companies, these are their June 2005 results, most of which were issued during July and August 2005. Finally, there is a section on the outlook for the company, sometimes including comment on the performance of the shares.

Tables

The tables have been made as concise as possible, though they require careful consideration, as they contain large amounts of information. Note that the tables for the banks have been arranged a little differently from the others; details of these are later in this introduction.

At the top of each page is a small table with the following data.

Share price

This is the closing price on 16 August 2005. Also included are the twelve-month high and low prices, as of the same date.

Market capitalisation

This is the size of the company, as determined by the stock market. It is the share price (again, as of 16 August 2005) multiplied by the number of shares in issue. All companies in this book must be in the All Ordinaries Index, which comprises Australia's 500 largest stocks, as measured by market capitalisation.

Price-to-net-tangible-assets-per-share ratio

The NTA-per-share figure expresses the worth of a company's net tangible assets—that is, its assets minus its liabilities and intangible assets—for each share of the company. The price-to-NTA-per-share ratio relates this figure to the share price.

A ratio of one means that the company is valued exactly according to the value of its assets. A ratio below one suggests that the shares are a bargain, though usually there is a good reason for this. Profits are more important than assets.

Four companies in this book, Cochlear, Computershare, John Fairfax Holdings and Metcash, have a negative NTA-per-share figure—as a result of having intangible assets valued at more than their remaining net assets—and a price-to-NTA-per-share ratio cannot be calculated.

See table M, in the second part of this book, for a little more detail on this ratio.

Five-year share price return

This is the total return you could have received from the stock in the five years to 2005. It includes reinvested dividends, bonus stock, rights issues and capital gain from the stock's appreciation. It is expressed as a compounded annual rate of return (four-year figures are used for six companies that had not been listed for a full five years). These figures have been supplied by Aspect Huntley.

Price-earnings ratio (PER)

The price-earnings ratio is one of the most popular measures of whether a share is cheap or expensive. It is calculated by dividing the share price—in this case the closing price for 16 August 2005—by the EPS figure. Obviously, the share price is continually changing, so the PER figures in this book are for guidance only. Many newspapers publish each morning the latest PER for every stock.

Dividend yield

This is the latest full-year dividend expressed as a percentage of the share price. Like the PER, it changes as the share price moves. It is a useful figure, especially for investors who are buying shares for income, as it allows you to compare this income with alternative investments, such as a bank term deposit or a bond fund.

Sector comparisons

It is often useful to compare a company's price-earnings ratio and its dividend yield with those of its sector. Often the stocks in a sector move together. Thus, if a particular stock is lagging the averages, this may—depending on the reasons—be a buying opportunity.

Figures used in this book are those of the S&P/ASX sectors, again as of 16 August 2005.

Share-price chart

Also at the top of each page is a five-year share-price chart, provided by Alan Hull (author of *Active Investing* and *Active Retirement*, both published by Wrightbooks).

Website

Most public companies now have websites, and the website addresses of companies in this book are placed under the share-price chart.

Be aware that some sites are little more than corporate brochures for the company, with glossy photos and beat-up prose. A few are wildly out of date. But increasingly, public companies are using the internet as a means of providing timely data to shareholders.

Thus, you may now find all the latest ASX company announcements—often placed on the site simultaneously to their ASX release—along with media releases and even, sometimes, speeches and presentations to stock market analysts.

If you are following a particular company, it is highly recommended that you become familiar with that company's website.

Main tables

In the main tables you will find the following.

Revenues

These are the company's revenues from its business activities (generally the sale of products or services). It does not usually include additional income from such sources as investments, bank interest or the sale of assets. If the information is available, the revenues figure has been broken down into the major product areas.

Earnings before interest and taxation

Earnings before interest and taxation (EBIT) is the firm's profit from its operations before the payment of interest and tax. This figure is often used by analysts examining a company. The reason for this is that some companies have borrowed extensively to finance their activities, while others have opted for alternative means. By expressing profits before interest payments, it is possible to compare more precisely the performance of these companies. The net interest figure—interest payments minus interest receipts—has been used for this calculation.

EBIT margin

EBIT margin is the company's EBIT expressed as a percentage of its revenues. It is a gauge of a company's efficiency. A high EBIT margin suggests that a company is achieving success in keeping its costs low.

Gross margin

The gross margin is the company's gross profit as a percentage of its sales. The gross profit is the amount left over after deducting from a company's sales figure its cost of sales: that is, its manufacturing costs or, for a retailer, the cost of purchasing the goods it sells. The cost of goods sold figure does not usually include marketing or administration costs.

As there are different ways of calculating the cost of goods sold figure, this ratio is best used for year-to-year comparisons of a single company's efficiency, rather than for comparing one company with another. Not all companies present a cost of goods sold figure, so a gross margin ratio is not given for every stock in this book. The revenues for some companies include a mix of sales and services. Where a breakdown is possible, the gross profit figure will reflect sales only.

Profit before tax/profit after tax

The profit before tax figure is simply the EBIT figure minus net interest payments. The profit after tax figure is, of course, the company's profit after the payment of tax, and also after the deduction of minority interests. Minority interests are that part of a company's profit that is claimed by outside interests, usually the other shareholders in a subsidiary which is not fully owned by the company. Many companies do not have any minority interests and, for those that do, it is generally a tiny figure.

As much as possible, I have adjusted the profit figures to exclude non-recurring profits and losses, which are called significant items. It is for this reason that the profit figures in *Top Stocks* sometimes differ from those in the financial media or on financial websites, where profit figures normally include significant items.

The significance of significant items

Significant items are those that have an abnormal impact on profits, even though they happen in the normal course of the company's operations. Examples are the profit from the sale of a business, or losses from a business restructuring, the write-down of property, an inventory write-down, a bad-debt loss or a write-off for research and development expenditure.

They were formerly called 'abnormals', and were part of the statement of financial performance. Now they are simply included among the notes to the statement.

Significant items are controversial. It is often a matter of subjective judgment as to what is included and what is excluded. The relevant reporting standard states:

> *When a revenue or an expense from ordinary activities is of such a size, nature or incidence that its disclosure is relevant in explaining the financial performance of the entity for the reporting period, its nature and amount must be disclosed separately in the notes in the financial report.*

But, after analysing the accounts of hundreds of companies, while writing this book, it is clear that different companies use quite widely varying interpretations of what is significant.

Further, when they do report a significant item, there is no consistency as to whether they use pre-tax figures or after-tax figures. Some report both, making it easy to adjust the profit figures in the tables in this book. But difficulties arise when only one figure—generally pre-tax—is given for significant items. A telephone call to the company usually elicits the other figure, but not always.

Fortunately, most companies do not report significant items. But investors should be aware of this issue. It sometimes causes consternation for readers of *Top Stocks* to find that a particular profit figure in this book is substantially different from that given by some other source. In virtually all cases, the reason is that I have stripped out a significant item.

Earnings per share

Earnings per share (EPS) is the after-tax profit divided by the number of shares. Because the profit figure is for a twelve-month period, the number of shares used is a weighted average of those on issue during the year. This number is provided by the company in its annual report and its results announcements.

Cash flow per share

The cash flow per share ratio tells—in theory—how much actual cash the company has generated from its operations.

In fact, the ratio in this book is not exactly a true measure of cash flow. It is simply the company's depreciation and amortisation figures for the year added to the after-tax profit, and then divided by a weighted average of the number of shares. Depreciation and amortisation are expenses that do not actually utilise cash, so can be added back to after-tax profit to give a kind of indication of the company's cash flow.

By contrast, a true cash flow—including such items as newly raised capital and money received from the sale of assets—would require quite complex calculations based on the company's statement of cash flows.

However, many analysts use the ratio as I present it, because it is easy to calculate, and it is certainly a useful guide to how much funding the company has available from its operations.

Dividend

The dividend figure is the total for the year, interim and final. It does not include special dividends. The level of franking is also provided.

Net tangible assets per share

The NTA per share figure tells the theoretical value of the company—per share—if all assets were sold and then all liabilities paid. It is very much a theoretical figure, as there is no guarantee that corporate assets are really worth the price put on them in the balance sheet. Intangible assets such as goodwill, newspaper mastheads and patent rights are excluded because of the difficulty in putting a sales price on them, and also because they may in fact not have much value if separated from the company.

As already noted, four companies in this book—Cochlear, Computershare, John Fairfax Holdings and Metcash—have a negative NTA, due to the fact that their intangible assets are so great, and no figure can be listed for them.

Where a company's most recent financial results are the half-year figures, these are used to calculate this ratio.

Interest cover

The interest cover ratio indicates how many times a company could make its interest payments from its pre-tax profit. A rough rule of thumb says a ratio of at least three times is desirable. Below that and fast-rising interest rates could imperil profits. The ratio is derived by dividing the EBIT figure by net interest payments. Some fortunate companies have interest receipts that are higher than their interest payments, which turns the interest cover into a negative figure, and so it is not listed.

Return on equity

Return on equity (ROE) is the after-tax profit expressed as a percentage of the shareholder's equity. In theory, it is the amount that the company's managers have made for you—the shareholder—on your money. The shareholder's equity figure used is an average for the year.

Debt-to-equity ratio

This ratio is one of the best known measures of a company's debt levels. It is total borrowings minus the company's cash holdings, expressed as a percentage of the shareholders' equity. Some companies have no debt at all, or their cash position is greater than their level of debt, which results in a negative ratio, so no figure is listed for them.

Where a company's most recent financial results are the half-year figures, these are used to calculate this ratio.

Current ratio

The current ratio is simply the company's current assets divided by its current liabilities. Current assets are cash or assets that can, in theory, be converted quickly into cash. Current liabilities are normally those payable within a year. Thus, the current ratio measures the ability of a company to repay in a hurry its short-term debt, should the need arise. The surplus of current assets over current liabilities is referred to as the company's working capital.

Where a company's most recent financial results are the half-year figures, these are used to calculate this ratio.

Banks

The tables for the banks are somewhat different from those for most other companies. EBIT and debt-to-equity ratios have little relevance for them, as they have such high interest payments (to their customers). Other differences are outlined below.

Operating income

Operating income is used instead of sales revenues. Operating income is the bank's net interest income—that is, its total interest income minus its interest expense—plus other income, such as bank fees, funds management fees and income from businesses such as corporate finance and insurance.

Net interest income

Banks borrow money—that is, they accept deposits from savers—and they lend it to businesses, homebuyers and other borrowers. They charge the borrowers more than they pay those who deposit money with them, and the difference is known as net interest income.

Operating expenses

These are all the costs of running the bank. Banks have high operating expenses, and one of the keys to profit growth is cutting these expenses. Add the provision for doubtful debts to operating expenses, then deduct the total from operating income, and you get the pre-tax profit.

Non-interest income to total income

Banks have traditionally made most of their income from savers and from lending money. But increasingly this is becoming a commodity business, with a growing number of entrants offering higher interest rates to savers and lower rates to borrowers. In response, the big banks are working to diversify into new fields, and this ratio is an indication of their success.

Cost to income ratio

As noted, the banks have high costs—numerous branches, expensive computer systems, many staff, to name a few—and they are all striving to reduce these. The cost to income ratio expresses their expenses as a percentage of their operating income, and is one of the ratios most often used as a gauge of efficiency. The lower the ratio drops, the better.

Return on assets

Banks have enormous assets, in sharp contrast to, say, a high-tech start-up whose main physical assets may be little more than a set of computers. So the return on assets—the after-tax profit expressed as a percentage of the year's average total assets—is another measure of efficiency.

Part I: the companies

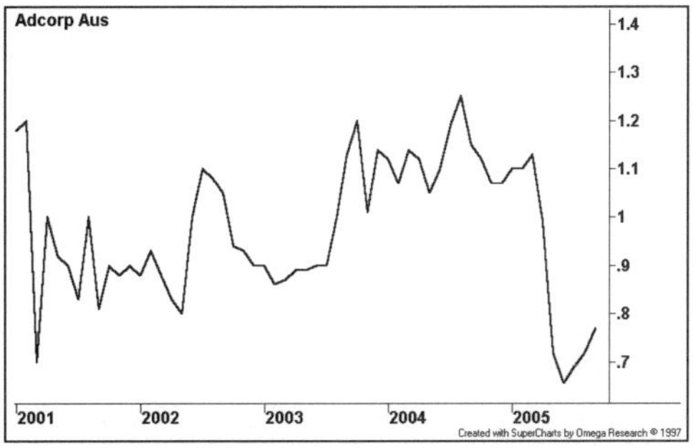

www.adcorp.com.au

ADCORP AUSTRALIA LTD

Share price ($)	0.74	
12-month high ($)	1.25	
12-month low ($)	0.62	
Market capitalisation ($mn)	45.6	
Price-to-NTA-per-share ratio	4.9	
5-year share price return (% pa)	–7.8	
Sector: Consumer discretionary	**Company**	**Sector**
Price-earnings ratio (times)	9.1	24.2
Dividend yield (%)	8.8	1.2

Sydney-based advertising agency services provider Adcorp has its origins in recruitment advertising. It has since grown (by acquisition) into a leading provider of a wide range of advertising and communications services, specialising in human resources, education, real estate, motor vehicles and autioneering. The company's technology division is involved in website- and database-development services. Adcorp operates from six offices in Australia and four in New Zealand.

Latest business results (June 2005, full year)

Profits fell again, due to flat sales, with particular weakness in Adcorp's core NSW operation. By contrast, New Zealand and Queensland reported strong growth, and Western Australia and South Australia also did well. A big restructuring of its Victorian operation led to an improved performance in that state. The company was also hurt by a decline in property advertising, which fell from 23% of the total to 17%. New Zealand was a particular stand-out during the year; revenues there jumped 21%, with EBIT up 14%. Though New Zealand was responsible for only about 20% of total company turnover, it contributed a full 40% of company profit. During the year, Adcorp concluded its relationship as technology provider to News Interactive's CareerOne website.

Outlook

Adcorp has undertaken a major shake-out of its NSW and Victorian operations, involving redundancies and the hiring of new senior executives. Victoria is now performing well, but the company has said that repositioning the NSW business has taken longer than expected, though it had recently secured a number of key new clients and was beginning to gain momentum. With more than $14 million in net cash holdings, the company is actively seeking acquisitions and new business opportunities. It is also embarking on a restructuring of its technology services, and has formed strategic alliances with a number of technology providers, including an updated applicant tracking system in partnership with software company nga.net. It has also entered into an alliance with the leading British advertising software company, Simply D'nA. The company has reported weakness in its residential property, motoring and print recruitment businesses, and it has been exiting some marginal accounts, while boosting its retail advertising business. It has said that, based on this weakness, it does not envisage profit growth in the June 2006 year.

AAU Year to 30 June	2004	2005
Revenues ($mn)	33.6	33.8
EBIT ($mn)	7.2	6.2
EBIT margin (%)	21.4	18.2
Profit before tax ($mn)	7.5	6.7
Profit after tax ($mn)	4.9	4.3
Earnings per share (¢)	8.1	6.8
Cash flow per share (¢)	12.6	10.9
Dividend (¢)	6.5	6.75
Percentage franked	100	100
Net tangible assets per share ($)	0.15	0.19
Interest cover (times)	~	~
Return on equity (%)	20.3	16.3
Debt-to-equity ratio (%)	~	~
Current ratio	1.2	1.3

Adelaide Bank Ltd

Share price ($)	12.30	
12-month high ($)	12.60	
12-month low ($)	8.65	
Market capitalisation ($mn)	1279.6	
Price-to-NTA-per-share ratio	1.8	
5-year share price return (% pa)	26.6	
Sector: Financials	**Company**	**Sector**
Price-earnings ratio (times)	14.6	14.3
Dividend yield (%)	4.3	4.5

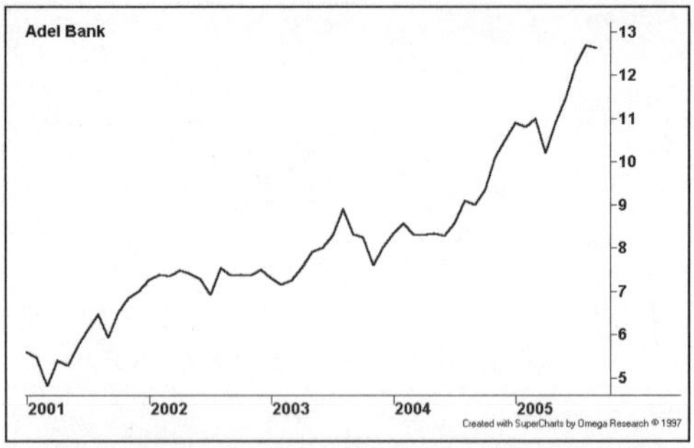

www.adelaidebank.com.au

Adelaide Bank dates back to its establishment as the Cooperative Building Society of South Australia in 1900. It achieved bank status in 1994. It occupies a strong position within South Australia, and is also a prominent home lender in other states. Its Leveraged Equities subsidiary specialises in margin lending, and was boosted in 2005 with the acquisition of Goldman Sachs JBWere Equity Finance, making Adelaide Bank Australia's second-largest margin lender.

Latest business results (June 2005, full year)

Adelaide Bank overcame a slowing home construction market to post another excellent result, powered by record levels of residential lending. Home loan approvals jumped 15% to $8.5 billion, and the bank claims that its share of the national mortgage market rose from 3.2% to 3.9%. Loans under management soared 34% to $19 billion. Excluding the loans that came with the Goldman Sachs JBWere Equity Finance portfolio, growth was still 28%, significantly higher than the national average. Business loans grew 33% to $1.6 billion. Retail deposits were up 19% to $9.2 billion. The bank's margin lending business generated a pre-tax profit of $12.8 million, up 48% from the previous year. Thanks to the Goldman Sachs JBWere Equity Finance acquisition, Adelaide Bank's total margin lending portfolio jumped 84% to $2.6 billion.

Outlook

Its strong base in its home state, its ability to contain costs and its emphasis on the national mortgage market have handed Adelaide Bank some impressive growth, as well as making it one of the most efficient of the regional banks. It has developed close ties with leading national mortgage brokers, and these are delivering significant amounts of new business. Around 75% of mortgage lending now derives from outside South Australia. Despite this growth, home lending now accounts for 51% of profit, down from 56%, and is expected to fall further to 40% by 2008. In its place, the bank predicts a greater stream of profit from such activities as margin lending and business banking, with the latter focused on its areas of expertise, notably aged care, rural lending, commercial property and asset finance. Adelaide Bank has set itself a target EPS growth of at least 10% per year for the coming three years, with the cost to income ratio falling from 53.6% to 46% by 2008.

ADB Year to 30 June	2004	2005
Operating income ($mn)	234.9	282.5
Net interest income ($mn)	216.5	252.0
Operating expenses ($mn)	133.0	151.5
Profit before tax ($mn)	94.0	116.3
Profit after tax ($mn)	65.1	80.4
Earnings per share (¢)	74.1	84.1
Dividend (¢)	44	53
Percentage franked	100	100
Non-interest income to total income (%)	7.9	10.8
Net tangible assets per share ($)	5.49	6.69
Cost to income ratio (%)	56.6	53.6
Return on equity (%)	14.0	13.1
Return on assets (%)	0.7	0.7

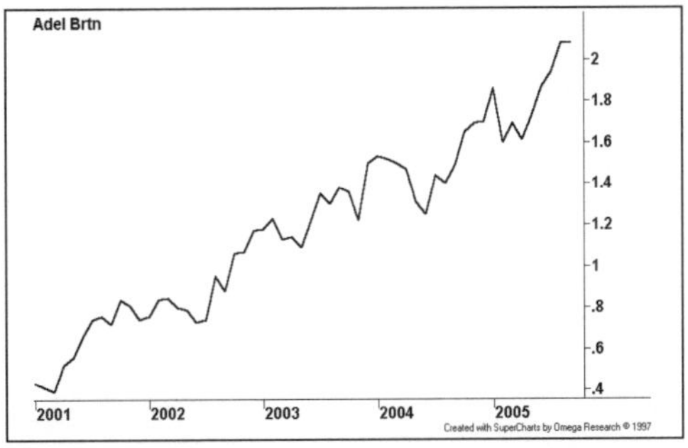

www.adbri.com.au

Adelaide Brighton Ltd

Share price ($)	2.13
12-month high ($)	2.16
12-month low ($)	1.36
Market capitalisation ($mn)	1076.2
Price-to-NTA-per-share ratio	2.6
5-year share price return (% pa)	41.9

Sector: Materials	Company	Sector
Price-earnings ratio (times)	14.2	17.0
Dividend yield (%)	3.5	2.2

Adelaide-based Adelaide Brighton, with roots that date back to 1882, is one of Australia's leaders in the production and supply of construction materials, notably cement, ready-mixed concrete and concrete masonry products. It also manufactures lime products for the alumina and steel industries.

Latest business results (June 2005, half year)

The company enjoyed a pleasing rise in sales and profits, though the profit rise would have been greater but for the restating of June 2004 results to accord with new Australian International Financial Reporting Standards. Demand for cement (59% of revenues) remained firm, with strength in Western Australia and the resources sector in South Australia and the Northern Territory offsetting weakness in the NSW residential sector. There was also a contribution from increases in bulk cement prices implemented late in 2004. Some short-term operational issues in the steel and alumina industries meant that lime sales (15% of revenues) fell short of expectations. Concrete (14%) saw weakness due to the NSW housing downturn.

Outlook

Adelaide Brighton is heavily dependent on the domestic construction industry, and the short-term outlook is that continuing strength in the resources, commercial, engineering and infrastructure sectors will offset regional downturns in the housing sector. In addition, the tightness of global cement supplies gives the company scope for further price rises. Lime demand is also steadily rising, particularly in the Western Australian mineral processing business, and Adelaide Brighton is the dominant supplier there, through its subsidiary Cockburn Cement. However, the market for the company's concrete remains weak, due to the continuing softness of the NSW market and competitive pressures in Victoria. Adelaide Brighton is working to boost capacity in key products and regions, to drive long-term growth. It sees great potential in its Austen Quarry in NSW, which marks its entry into aggregate production and supply. Aggregate supply is expected to tighten considerably in central NSW as the Penrith Lakes quarries move towards exhaustion by the end of the decade. Adelaide Brighton is investing $28 million to build a crushing and conveying plant and other facilities, and expects production to begin mid-2006.

ABC Year to 31 December	2003	2004
Revenues ($mn)	630.6	696.4
EBIT ($mn)	97.1	107.0
EBIT margin (%)	15.4	15.4
Gross margin (%)	31.7	35.6
Profit before tax ($mn)	84.4	94.9
Profit after tax ($mn)	57.7	81.5
Earnings per share (¢)	10.7	15.0
Cash flow per share (¢)	22.2	26.5
Dividend (¢)	6	7.5
Percentage franked	82	100
Interest cover (times)	7.7	8.8
Return on equity (%)	10.6	13.9
Half year to 30 June	**2004**	**2005**
Revenues ($mn)	321.1	347.2
Profit before tax ($mn)	42.9	52.5
Profit after tax ($mn)	33.7	38.5
Earnings per share (¢)	5.9	7.1
Dividend (¢)	3.5	4.25
Percentage franked	100	100
Net tangible assets per share ($)	0.71	0.82
Debt-to-equity ratio (%)	33.7	33.4
Current ratio	0.6	0.6

Alesco Corporation Ltd

Share price ($)	8.22	
12-month high ($)	9.00	
12-month low ($)	6.80	
Market capitalisation ($mn)	577.2	
Price-to-NTA-per-share ratio	20.7	
5-year share price return (% pa)	32.5	
Sector: Industrials	**Company**	**Sector**
Price-earnings ratio (times)	20.4	16.2
Dividend yield (%)	5.5	3.6

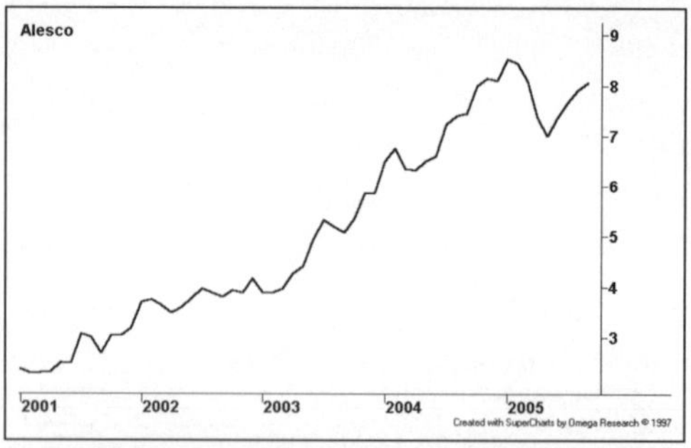

www.alesco.com.au

Alesco has its roots in a general merchant business established in Fremantle in 1896. Today, based in Sydney, it invests in and develops leading industrial brands that operate in niche markets. The mid-2004 acquisition of B&D Doors and Openers makes the company Australia's largest manufacturer of garage doors. The kitchen and laundry components division comprises Parbury-branded building products and the Robinhood kitchen rangehood business. The construction and mining division incorporates Marathon Tyres, which distributes heavy-duty tyres, and Parchem, which supplies chemical products to the construction industry. The scientific and medical division comprises Biolab, a major distributor of scientific and testing equipment in Australia and New Zealand. It has sold its Repco automotive business.

Latest business results (May 2005, full year)

The B&D acquisition was responsible for a big increase in Alesco's sales and profits. However, profitability ratios were substantially unchanged, and debt levels jumped. B&D performed in line with expectations, with demand remaining firm and the company able to pass on higher steel costs to customers. The Parbury and Robinhood businesses saw sales and profits essentially flat, with a slowing residential construction market impeding growth. Profits were down for the construction and mining division, hurt by sluggish first-half business for Marathon Tyres. Biolab realised strong expansion in sales and profits, thanks to organic growth and some acquisitions. A significant $13.5 million after-tax gain resulted from the profit on the sale of Alesco's Repco business, offset by restructuring costs and a goodwill writedown.

ALS Year to 31 May	2004	2005
Revenues ($mn)	481.5	632.6
Garage doors & openers (%)	0	28
Kitchen/laundry components (%)	32	25
Construction & mining (%)	30	22
Scientific & medical (%)	16	15
Automotive (%)	21	9
EBIT ($mn)	33.5	53.6
EBIT margin (%)	7.0	8.5
Gross margin (%)	33.1	33.8
Profit before tax ($mn)	29.8	43.4
Profit after tax ($mn)	19.8	27.6
Earnings per share (¢)	40.4	40.3
Cash flow per share (¢)	72.6	80.4
Dividend (¢)	33	45
Percentage franked	100	100
Net tangible assets per share ($)	1.96	0.40
Interest cover (times)	9.0	5.2
Return on equity (%)	11.0	10.6
Debt-to-equity ratio (%)	2.0	33.4
Current ratio	2.1	1.5

Outlook

The B&D acquisition means that more than two-thirds of Alesco's business is now geared to the housing construction and renovation markets, and it will suffer in the event of any substantial slowdown. However, the company has launched a major restructuring of B&D, and believes this will deliver considerable benefits from 2007. In February 2005 it acquired Dominator International, a leading garage-door manufacturer in New Zealand. It expects significant synergies with its existing NZ garage-door business. The company sees great potential in its scientific and medical business, and continues to seek new bolt-on acquisitions to expand this division. In January 2005 it acquired gas-detection company Sensor Technologies, increasing Biolab's strong presence in the environmental monitoring market.

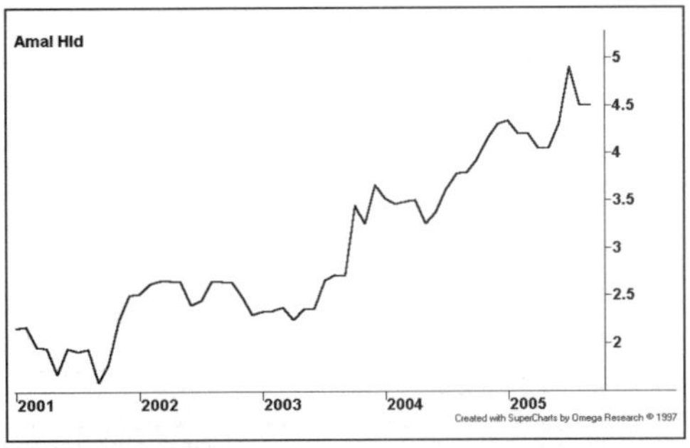

www.ahl.com.au

Amalgamated Holdings Ltd

Share price ($)	4.51
12-month high ($)	5.15
12-month low ($)	3.65
Market capitalisation ($mn)	551.6
Price-to-NTA-per-share ratio	1.5
5-year share price return (% pa)	22.3

Sector: Consumer discretionary	**Company**	**Sector**
Price-earnings ratio (times)	12.2	24.2
Dividend yield (%)	4.1	1.2

Sydney-based Amalgamated Holdings, founded in 1910, is one of Australia's leading entertainment, tourism and hotel companies. It divides its businesses into three broad groupings. The entertainment division comprises the Greater Union and the Birch Carroll & Coyle cinema chains, with 456 screens at 56 locations throughout Australia. It also operates 579 screens at 81 locations in Germany, and others in the Netherlands and the Middle East. The entertainment technology division is centred around the company's 50% stake in the Atlab film processing laboratory, the largest in the southern hemisphere. The hospitality and leisure division includes the Rydges hotel chain and the Thredbo Alpine Resort. The company also owns 50% of Roadshow Distributors, which handles theatrical distribution, TV sales, videos, video games and CD-ROMs.

Latest business results (June 2005, full year)

Revenues soared, largely reflecting the company's move from 50% to 100% ownership of a major German cinema chain, but profits just edged up. Domestic cinema profits were down, due principally to a lack of blockbuster movies, and the German business remained in the red. The best result came from the Atlab business, with profits more than doubling especially as a result of efficiency gains from the new Lane Cove laboratory. There was also a good result from the hotel business, with earnings up 15%. This was partly due to an increase in the number of hotels in the chain, from 33 to 36, but also reflected the strength of the domestic economy. Following a record 2004 season, Thredbo achieved a 5% increase in profits.

Outlook

Amalgamated Holdings occupies leading positions in its areas of activity, yet most of these are volatile, with a string of hit movies needed to generate good cinema business and other major operations quite dependent on levels of domestic and international tourism. During the June 2005 year, the company opened new 11-screen cinema complexes at Bondi Junction and Karingal, and in the current financial year it will open similar facilities at Campbelltown and Parramatta. It is also working to upgrade its German cinemas. The high-margin Atlab business is set to become more profitable following a $2.5 million upgrade to its digital post-production facilities and the relocation of its Artarmon laboratory to the new Lane Cove complex.

AHD Year to 30 June	2004	2005
Revenues ($mn)	440.3	580.2
Cinema exhibition—international (%)	32	49
Cinema exhibition—domestic (%)	25	17
Hotels (%)	20	16
Thredbo Alpine Resort (%)	11	8
Leisure & attractions (%)	7	6
EBIT ($mn)	71.9	71.9
EBIT margin (%)	16.3	12.4
Profit before tax ($mn)	59.3	61.2
Profit after tax ($mn)	43.0	46.2
Earnings per share (¢)	34.5	36.9
Cash flow per share (¢)	57.7	61.4
Dividend (¢)	13	18.5
Percentage franked	100	100
Net tangible assets per share ($)	2.86	3.03
Interest cover (times)	5.7	6.7
Return on equity (%)	10.9	12.1
Debt-to-equity ratio (%)	57.2	43.3
Current ratio	0.6	0.6

Angus & Coote (Holdings) Ltd

Share price ($)	7.55	
12-month high ($)	10.81	
12-month low ($)	7.51	
Market capitalisation ($mn)	90.1	
Price-to-NTA-per-share ratio	1.4	
5-year share price return (% pa)	26.3	
Sector: Consumer discretionary	**Company**	**Sector**
Price-earnings ratio (times)	11.1	24.2
Dividend yield (%)	5.3	1.2

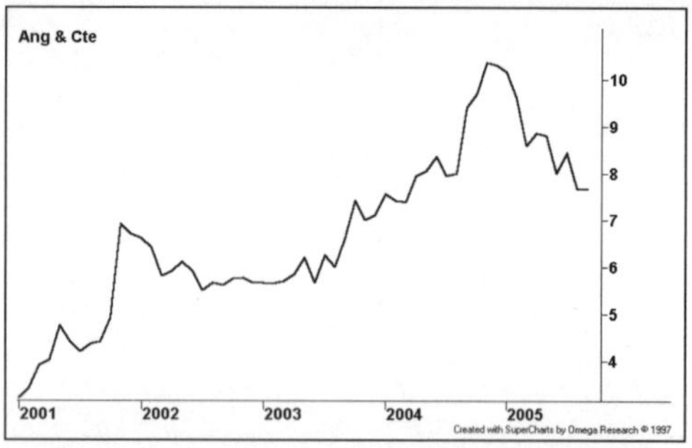

www.anguscoote.com.au

Sydney-based Angus & Coote, founded in 1895, is Australia's dominant specialist jewellery retailer, with a 15% market share. It operates through three divisions: the A&C division markets jewellery, watches, clocks, silverware, crystal and related products from 148 jewellery stores throughout Australia, under the names Angus & Coote, Dunklings the Jewellers, Amies the Family Jewellers and Edments. The division also operates tax-free stores at Sydney airport. The Goldmark division operates 124 jewellery stores throughout Australia, and is the country's largest national jewellery brand. The new J's Room division operates four stores in NSW. The founding Coote family owns 60% of the company's equity.

Latest business results (January 2005, half year)

Continuing strength in consumer spending boosted sales, and profits were also up in the company's core businesses. However, the results were hit by a loss at Angus & Coote's tax-free airport stores. These outlets have increasingly been suffering from growing competition elsewhere in the region and the strength of the Australian dollar, and they recorded a $1.3 million loss in the January half. For comparison purposes, note that the January 2005 half comprised 27 weeks, and the January 2004 half just 26 weeks.

ANC Year to 25 July*	2003	2004
Revenues ($mn)	217.9	239.0
EBIT ($mn)	10.4	12.9
EBIT margin (%)	4.8	5.4
Gross margin (%)	59.6	58.0
Profit before tax ($mn)	8.7	11.6
Profit after tax ($mn)	5.7	8.1
Earnings per share (¢)	47.5	68.2
Cash flow per share (¢)	110.7	135.2
Dividend (¢)	36	40
Percentage franked	100	100
Interest cover (times)	5.9	10.3
Return on equity (%)	11.0	14.8

* 27 July 2003

Half year to 30 January**	2004	2005
Revenues ($mn)	135.5	146.0
Profit before tax ($mn)	16.0	14.6
Profit after tax ($mn)	11.1	10.2
Earnings per share (¢)	93.3	85.4
Dividend (¢)	20	22
Percentage franked	100	100
Net tangible assets per share ($)	5.17	5.37
Debt-to-equity ratio (%)	14.0	1.1
Current ratio	1.8	1.7

** 25 January 2004

Outlook

Angus & Coote's business is quite dependent on trends in consumer discretionary spending. This has remained strong, although the company could be hurt by any economic slowdown, and especially by further rises in interest rates. It has now positioned its divisions to entice different age groups. The A&C Division is targeted at the 25- to 49-year-old market, with the company's sales strategies aimed particularly at appealing to women customers. The Goldmark business focuses on the fashion-conscious 14- to 29-year-old market. The J's Room division, specialising in fashion jewellery and accessories, was launched in December 2004. It targets women aged from 14 to 24, and the company plans a steady roll-out of new J's Room stores. Altogether, the company expects to open a further dozen new stores in 2005–06. It has closed its two Melbourne airport stores, though retains four in Sydney.

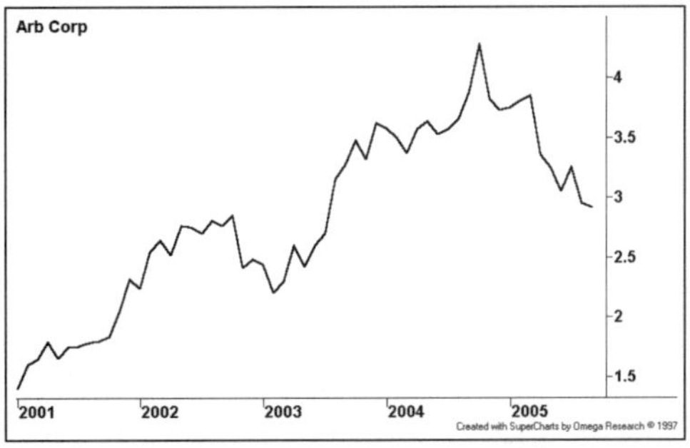

www.arb.com.au

ARB Corporation Ltd

Share price ($)	2.90	
12-month high ($)	4.40	
12-month low ($)	2.86	
Market capitalisation ($mn)	194.4	
Price-to-NTA-per-share ratio	4.1	
5-year share price return (% pa)	18.4	
Sector: Consumer discretionary	**Company**	**Sector**
Price-earnings ratio (times)	15.0	24.2
Dividend yield (%)	3.6	1.2

Melbourne-based ARB is a small manufacturer of specialty automotive accessories and an international leader in the design and production of equipment for four-wheel-drive (4WD) vehicles. Its products are divided into broad groupings: mechanical products, notably the 'air locker' air-operated locking differential system; fabricated metal products, such as bull bars, roof racks and tow bars; the Old Man Emu range of suspension products; ARB canopies; and imported and locally produced 4WD accessories, for which ARB acts as local distributor. ARB exports to some 80 countries.

Latest business results (June 2005, full year)

Sales achieved further double-digit growth, but profit expansion was more muted, in what was essentially a disappointing result for the once high-flying company. In particular, the second half of the financial year was difficult, with a softening in sales growth, a reduction in sales margins and declining profits, largely caused by steel price rises, skilled labour shortages and an adverse currency exchange rate. There was a good result from the company's Air Locker subsidiary in the US, with sales up 19% in American dollars, or 13% in local currency, and a nearly fourfold jump in profits. Nevertheless, US profitability remains low. A $1.6 million after-tax profit—treated as a significant item—came from the sale of the company's retail showroom in Abbotsford in Melbourne.

Outlook

ARB has conceded that the June 2006 year will be a challenging period of establishing a new platform for future growth. It remains a major beneficiary of the surging popularity of 4WD vehicles globally, though high petrol prices could stunt that trend. It has boosted profitability at its Kingsley Enterprises subsidiary by placing more emphasis on distribution and less on manufacture. In June 2005 it moved its US operations to a new warehouse and office building, significantly boosting operational efficiencies and providing scope for substantial future growth. A new showroom was opened in Brighton, Melbourne, in April 2005, and is already trading profitably. ARB is also building showrooms at Wentworthville, Sydney and Morphett Vale, Adelaide, both due to open during 2006, and views the establishment of ARB-brand retail outlets as a new growth opportunity. It is also building a new $4 million production facility in Thailand, to help overcome the problems of local labour shortages.

ARP Year to 30 June	2004	2005
Revenues ($mn)	100.7	114.7
EBIT ($mn)	17.3	18.4
EBIT margin (%)	17.2	16.1
Gross margin (%)	32.9	33.8
Profit before tax ($mn)	17.1	17.8
Profit after tax ($mn)	12.1	12.6
Earnings per share (¢)	19.2	19.3
Cash flow per share (¢)	24.9	25.5
Dividend (¢)	9.5	10.5
Percentage franked	100	100
Net tangible assets per share ($)	0.64	0.71
Interest cover (times)	87.9	28.2
Return on equity (%)	29.3	25.9
Debt-to-equity ratio (%)	7.9	29.4
Current ratio	1.6	1.1

AUSTRALAND PROPERTY GROUP

Share price ($)	1.72	
12-month high ($)	1.94	
12-month low ($)	1.36	
Market capitalisation ($mn)	1492.6	
Price-to-NTA-per-share ratio	1.3	
5-year share price return (% pa)	17.5	
Sector: Financials	**Company**	**Sector**
Price-earnings ratio (times)	9.2	14.3
Dividend yield (%)	9.6	4.5

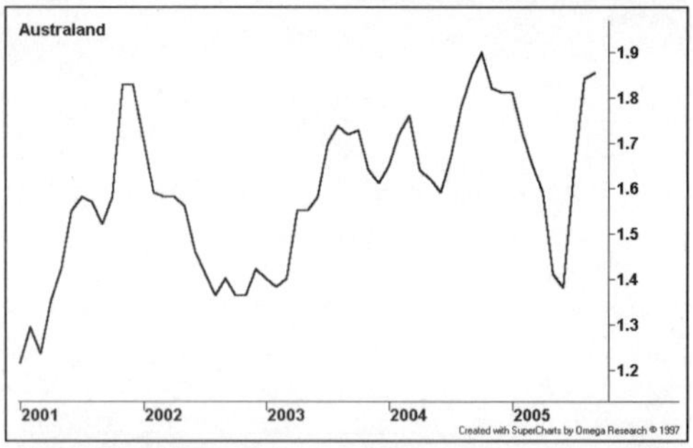

www.australand.com.au

Sydney-based Australand is one of Australia's largest property development companies, with operations covering: large-scale land development projects; medium density and detached housing projects in Sydney, Melbourne, Brisbane and Perth; apartment buildings; commercial office buildings; and purpose-built industrial facilities. It also manages property trusts. Australand is listed on the Singapore Stock Exchange.

Latest business results (June 2005, half year)

Despite a slowing property market, Australand's sales and profits soared. However, the main contributor was the company's property trust business. In addition, the results were skewed by the company's use of the new International Financial Reporting Standards, which necessitated a restatement of the June 2004 results. These new rules have quite significant implications for property development companies, as they change the timing of revenue and profit recognition, adding significant volatility to the results. (And according to the company's restatement of its June 2004 results, it would not even have qualified for *Top Stocks 2005*, due to an excessive debt-to-equity ratio.) In the June 2005 half, the Australand Property Trust generated a pre-tax profit of $67.7 million—up from $27.7 million in June 2004—which included a revaluation gain of $36.2 million. The company's residential business saw revenues up substantially, but profits fell due to the reduced profitability of its apartments business. The commercial and industrial division moved from loss to profit.

ALZ Year to 31 December	2003	2004
Revenue ($mn)	1405.4	1172.6
EBIT ($mn)	156.7	213.6
EBIT margin (%)	11.1	18.2
Gross margin (%)	20.9	22.5
Profit before tax ($mn)	146.4	186.6
Profit after tax ($mn)	95.2	145.1
Earnings per share (¢)	17.9	18.6
Cash flow per share (¢)	19.4	19.8
Dividend (¢)	13.36	16.5
Percentage franked	83	56
Interest cover (times)	15.2	7.9
Return on equity (%)	10.8	12.9
Half year to 30 June	**2004**	**2005**
Revenues ($mn)	388.6	913.0
Commercial & industrial (%)	16	51
Residential (%)	78	46
Profit before tax ($mn)	58.3	103.5
Profit after tax ($mn)	49.8	89.8
Earnings per share (¢)	6.9	10.6
Dividend (¢)	8	8
Percentage franked	100	58
Net tangible assets per share ($)	1.32	1.37
Debt-to-equity ratio (%)	109.2	61.5
Current ratio	1.8	3.4

Outlook

Australand is working to reduce its exposure to the volatile apartments business, and to boost recurrent property trust income. By 2006 it expects have to have only four apartment projects under construction. Nevertheless, the company has said that there has been a solid improvement in housing supply-demand fundamentals and, in the absence of further interest rate rises, it expects sales to start trending up. The company is also developing a significant pipeline of commercial and industrial properties, which will help sustain profits in coming years. The Australand Property Trust continues to acquire new assets, and has grown to a value of around $670 million.

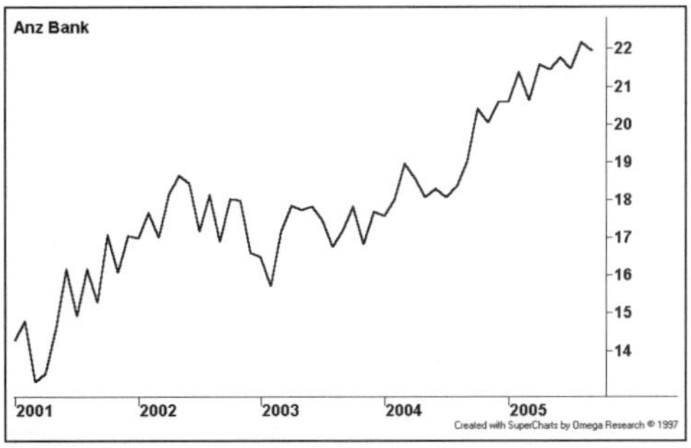

www.anz.com.au

Australia & New Zealand Banking Group Ltd

Share price ($)	22.14	
12-month high ($)	22.38	
12-month low ($)	17.68	
Market capitalisation ($mn)	40 369.2	
Price-to-NTA-per-share ratio	2.9	
5-year share price return (% pa)	24.9	
Sector: Financials	**Company**	**Sector**
Price-earnings ratio (times)	14.0	14.3
Dividend yield (%)	4.6	4.5

ANZ is one of Australia's four banking giants, with significant interests in numerous areas of finance and more than 740 branches nationwide. It has a stake in online stockbroker E*Trade Australia and operates a funds management joint venture with Dutch giant ING. Its ownership of the National Bank of New Zealand (NBNZ) makes it the market leader in NZ banking.

Latest business results (March 2005, half year)

Profits were up again, driven by ANZ's domestic strengths. Personal banking was especially strong, reflecting the benefits of new marketing initiatives, with a good performance also from the ING Australia wealth management joint venture. Lending activity grew 22%, though part of this was due to the December 2003 acquisition of NBNZ. A higher concentration of lower-yielding assets and intense institutional competition were among the factors forcing a contraction of the bank's interest margin. Staff numbers were up by nearly 7%, helping to push the cost to income ratio up. New Zealand business was essentially flat, as the company bedded down the NBNZ acquisition.

Outlook

ANZ continues to work to integrate its $4.9 billion NBNZ acquisition into its operations. It believes this will be completed by the end of 2005, with synergies from the acquisition annually delivering cost savings of $110 million by 2007. ANZ now has more than 90% of its assets in Australia and New Zealand, part of a deliberate policy to reduce risk by limiting exposure to offshore markets. Nevertheless, it is also making new moves into Asian markets, and has said it wishes to strengthen its large Pacific Islands banking network. It is working to use skills developed through its strong corporate banking businesses to revitalise its personal banking activities, where it lags its three large rivals. It has invested heavily in this business, including a series of new-concept banking outlets, with the aim of boosting market share. Like all the banks, it remains vulnerable to any sharp housing downturn. And because it is already highly efficient — it claims its productivity is among the top 5% of banks worldwide — there is limited scope for further efficiency gains.

ANZ Year to 30 September	2003	2004
Operating income ($mn)	7013.0	8500.0
Net interest income ($mn)	4311.0	5254.0
Operating expenses ($mn)	3228.0	4026.0
Profit before tax ($mn)	3277.0	3987.0
Profit after tax ($mn)	2348.0	2815.0
Earnings per share (¢)	155.1	158.7
Dividend (¢)	95	101
Percentage franked	100	100
Non-interest income to total income (%)	38.5	38.2
Cost to income ratio (%)	46.0	47.4
Return on equity (%)	18.6	17.8
Return on assets (%)	1.2	1.2
Half year to 31 March	**2004**	**2005**
Operating income ($mn)	4192.0	4557.0
Profit before tax ($mn)	1977.0	2098.0
Profit after tax ($mn)	1312.0	1492.0
Earnings per share (¢)	78.9	85.9
Dividend (¢)	47	51
Percentage franked	100	100
Net tangible assets per share ($)	7.48	7.69

THE AUSTRALIAN GAS LIGHT COMPANY

Share price ($)	14.26	
12-month high ($)	14.65	
12-month low ($)	12.06	
Market capitalisation ($mn)	6511.0	
Price-to-NTA-per-share ratio	3.6	
5-year share price return (% pa)	12.8	
Sector: Utilities	**Company**	**Sector**
Price-earnings ratio (times)	16.8	8.6
Dividend yield (%)	4.4	4.6

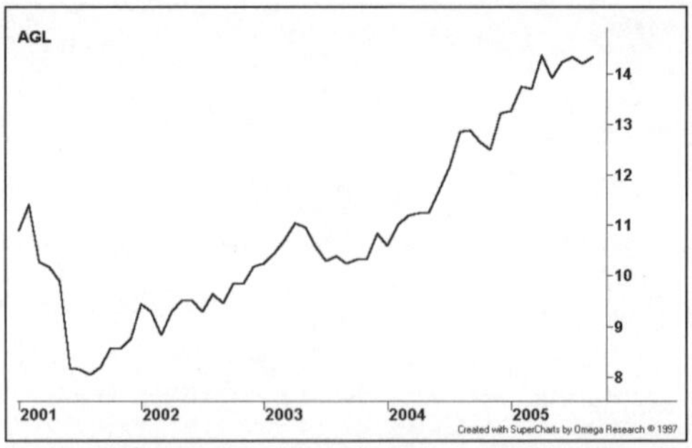

www.agl.com.au

AGL, established in 1837 to light the streets of Sydney, is one of the nation's oldest business enterprises. It now owns power generation facilities and operates a major supply network for gas and electricity, with more than three million customers nationwide. It owns 30% of the listed Australian Pipeline Trust and 50% of Elgas, Australia's largest liquefied petroleum gas distributor. It also operates a small gas distribution business in Chile.

Latest business results (June 2005, full year)

Profits just edged up in a difficult year marked by tight competition and mild weather conditions. This had an adverse impact on demand, and the company's core energy sales and marketing business saw EBIT down 6%. Nevertheless, AGL achieved a net increase of 56 200 energy accounts during the year, compared to a net loss of 46 400 in the previous year. The gas network business—which transports gas to customers across NSW—realised flat profits due to lower gas volumes. Electricity network activities—centred on the north-west suburbs of Melbourne—saw EBIT up 7.7%. AGL's flourishing Agility business, which operates and develops energy infrastructure assets, continued to grow, and saw EBIT up 14.2%. Power generation EBIT jumped 43.8%, thanks to a full year's contribution from the Loy Yang power plant. A $461.5 million after-tax gain, reported as a significant item, largely reflected profits from the sale of the company's New Zealand operations.

Outlook

AGL occupies a key position in Australia's energy infrastructure. It has built up an enviable collection of assets, and is now working to develop these and achieve further synergies. However, the short-term outlook is that there will be little growth for the company, with higher earnings from many of its businesses offset by a tighter regulatory environment for gas in NSW and for electricity in Victoria. In addition, competition in the retail market means the company must spend heavily on marketing to protect and build its customer base, and this is also having an impact on profit growth. Longer term, AGL sees great potential from its $400 million acquisition in July 2005 of 10% of the PNG Gas Project from Oil Search, and it is thought to be interested in acquiring further upstream gas assets.

AGL Year to 30 June	2004	2005
Revenues ($mn)	4153.8	4058.0
EBIT ($mn)	704.4	668.9
EBIT margin (%)	17.0	16.5
Gross margin (%)	31.3	27.0
Profit before tax ($mn)	579.8	585.0
Profit after tax ($mn)	361.8	386.8
Earnings per share (¢)	79.5	84.7
Cash flow per share (¢)	133.2	128.3
Dividend (¢)	60	63
Percentage franked	100	100
Net tangible assets per share ($)	3.13	3.92
Interest cover (times)	5.7	8.0
Return on equity (%)	12.2	12.2
Debt-to-equity ratio (%)	68.8	38.2
Current ratio	0.8	1.6

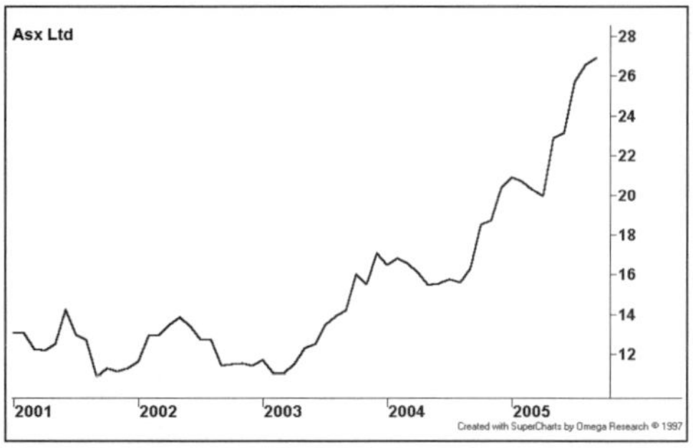

www.asx.com.au

Australian Stock Exchange Ltd

Share price ($)	26.10
12-month high ($)	26.32
12-month low ($)	14.68
Market capitalisation ($mn)	2681.3
Price-to-NTA-per-share ratio	9.5
5-year share price return (% pa)	24.8

Sector: Financials	Company	Sector
Price-earnings ratio (times)	24.7	14.3
Dividend yield (%)	3.6	4.5

The Australian Stock Exchange (ASX) was formed in 1987 through the amalgamation of six independent stock exchanges that formerly operated in the state capital cities. Each of those exchanges had a history of share trading dating back to the nineteenth century. Though originally a mutual organisation of stockbrokers, in 1998 the ASX become a listed company, with its shares traded on its own market. As well as operating Australia's primary national stock exchange for equities, derivatives and fixed-interest securities, it also provides a comprehensive market data service.

Latest business results (June 2005, full year)

Continuing stock market strength for much of the year delivered the ASX another great result. All four business areas showed strength. Equities trading revenues rose 11.7%, with an average daily trade of 89 178 equities, which was a 28% jump on the previous year. Revenues from listings surged 32.4%, with 222 new listings, compared to 180 in the June 2004 year. Derivatives trading revenues were 13.7%, with a 23% increase in daily average options contracts traded. There were 3595 new warrants listed, up from 2251 in the June 2004 year. Market data revenue rose 9.9%. Thanks to restructuring activities, total company expenses rose only 3.3%. A $71.5 million one-off payment from the National Guarantee Fund was treated as a significant item, offset by restructuring costs. The ASX Perpetual Registrars joint venture showed an 18% profit rise.

Outlook

The ASX's profits are highly geared to the levels of stock market activity. Much of its business is handled electronically, meaning that relatively small changes in the amount of business handled can deliver quite a substantial swing in profits. The company is working to reduce total costs by $15 to 20 million by 2007–08. It has initiated quite substantial levels of staff redundancies, and is looking to achieve reductions in its rental payments. It has also scaled down its under-used World Link service, which enabled Australians to trade on some overseas markets through the ASX, and it is trying to introduce new strategies that will boost its derivatives business. In response to demand from global investment banks, it is also expanding its Direct Market Access trading systems. In August 2005, the company announced the sale of ASX Perpetual Registrars, its joint venture with Perpetual Trustees Ausralia.

ASX Year to 30 June	2004	2005
Revenues ($mn)	241.2	279.7
Equities trading (%)	44	42
Listings (%)	22	26
Derivatives trading (%)	16	16
Market data (%)	12	12
EBIT ($mn)	109.4	144.1
EBIT margin (%)	45.3	51.5
Profit before tax ($mn)	116.6	153.3
Profit after tax ($mn)	82.7	108.5
Earnings per share (¢)	81.1	105.7
Cash flow per share (¢)	97.1	121.4
Dividend (¢)	56.6	95.1
Percentage franked	100	100
Net tangible assets per share ($)	2.11	2.75
Interest cover (times)	~	~
Return on equity (%)	38.3	42.8
Debt-to-equity ratio (%)	~	~
Current ratio	2.5	3.8

AV Jennings Homes Ltd

Share price ($)	1.35	
12-month high ($)	1.94	
12-month low ($)	1.22	
Market capitalisation ($mn)	287.3	
Price-to-NTA-per-share ratio	1.1	
5-year share price return (% pa)	34.0	
Sector: Financials	**Company**	**Sector**
Price-earnings ratio (times)	10.6	14.3
Dividend yield (%)	8.1	4.5

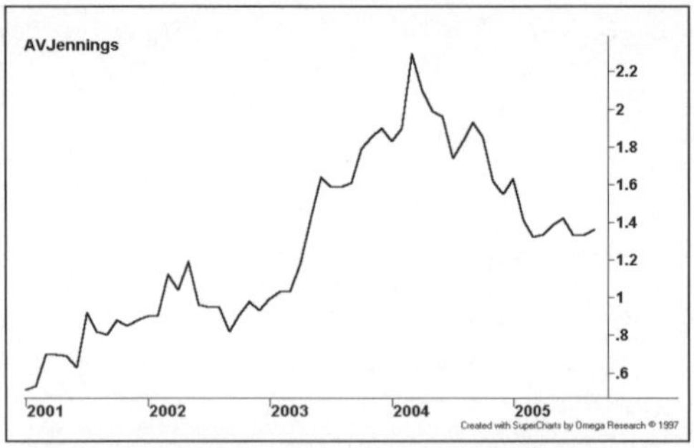

www.avjennings.com.au

Melbourne-based AV Jennings, one of Australia's best known names in housing developments, was founded in Victoria in 1932. Following an internal restructuring it operates in four core areas: land development, housing and townhouse development, apartment development and contract building. It has business in four states: New South Wales, Victoria, Queensland and South Australia. More than 40% of its equity is held by a Singapore public company, SG Global Developments.

Latest business results (March 2005, full year)

AV Jennings was hit hard by the housing downturn, with business sharply down. Higher margin projects were particularly weak, and profits slumped much more than sales revenues. Timing issues, especially for developments in northern Melbourne and the NSW central coast, dampened first-half business, while the second half was hurt badly by the introduction in NSW of a new vendor stamp duty for certain investment properties. Both land and housing development projects were weak. However, there was a slight increase in revenues for contract housing.

Outlook

AV Jennings has transformed itself from a builder of cheap contract housing into a developer of 'urban infill' projects, generally for existing homeowners who want to move into a bigger and/or newer dwelling in their own suburb. It is also boosting its land development business with sales to other home builders, who then develop their own house and land packages. In line with its strategy of long-term growth, the company is working to acquire quality sites suitable for residential subdivision, particularly in the Brisbane and Melbourne metropolitan regions. Its target is to double within four years its inventory of housing lots, from 8000 in March 2004. By March 2005 it had boosted its holdings to 10 000 lots. Its projects are also larger and more concentrated than previously — and thus more cost-effective — with 45 projects in mid-2005, compared to 50 a year earlier and 70 two years earlier. The company sees good potential from its moves into apartment developments, particularly with urban infill projects in the Sydney metropolitan region. It currently has four such low-rise projects under development, each comprising around 40 apartments. The company has reported that by mid-2005 it was seeing an upturn in its businesses, in comparison to the previous year.

AVJ Year to 31 March	2004	2005
Revenues ($mn)	550.0	436.7
Developments (%)	69	56
Project housing (%)	31	44
EBIT ($mn)	98.1	39.3
EBIT margin (%)	17.8	9.0
Profit before tax ($mn)	97.7	39.2
Profit after tax ($mn)	68.5	27.5
Earnings per share (¢)	31.8	12.8
Cash flow per share (¢)	34.2	15.1
Dividend (¢)	11	11
Percentage franked	100	100
Net tangible assets per share ($)	1.22	1.24
Interest cover (times)	228.7	277.1
Return on equity (%)	27.9	10.2
Debt-to-equity ratio (%)	40.4	65.9
Current ratio	2.6	2.8

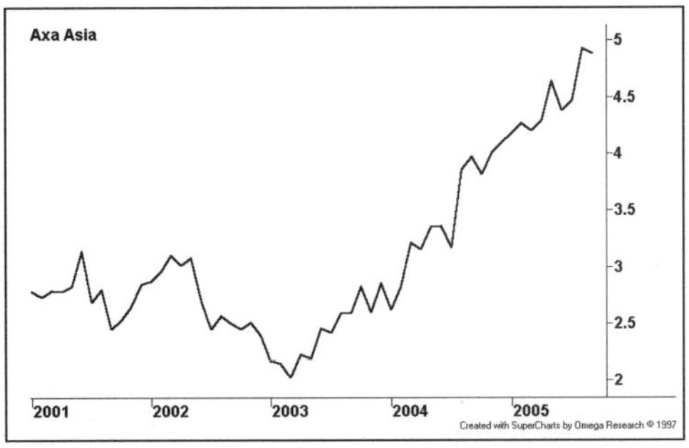

www.axaasiapacific.com.au

AXA Asia Pacific Holdings Ltd

Share price ($)	4.58	
12-month high ($)	4.72	
12-month low ($)	3.66	
Market capitalisation ($mn)	7979.1	
Price-to-NTA-per-share ratio	4.5	
5-year share price return (% pa)	16.6	
Sector: Financials	**Company**	**Sector**
Price-earnings ratio (times)	14.8	14.3
Dividend yield (%)	2.6	4.5

AXA Asia Pacific is one of Australia's insurance giants. Established in 1869 as the National Mutual Life Association of Australasia, it is now a 52%-owned subsidiary of the French insurance and financial services giant AXA SA. It is a leading supplier of life insurance and superannuation products in Australia and New Zealand, with a big funds management operation and a growing financial planning business. It has a major business in Hong Kong that is responsible for nearly half the company's profit, and operations in China, Indonesia, the Philippines, Singapore and Thailand.

Latest business results (June 2005, half year)

Profits rose firmly, with strength across all the company's major areas of activity. Operating earnings, which exclude investment earnings, rose 18%. There was particular strength in Australia and New Zealand, where operating earnings increased 32%, with a notable performance from wealth management products, which surged 48%. Funds under management, administration and advice in the two countries rose 9% to $57 billion. Operating earnings in Hong Kong rose nearly 10% in local currency, but just 4% in Australian dollars. However, a big jump in Hong Kong investment earnings—compared to a decline in Australia and New Zealand—meant that Hong Kong after-tax profit actually rose considerably. There was substantial new business from China and South-East Asia. The results were the first reported under the new Australian International Financial Reporting Standards, and the company said this had the effect of reducing after-tax profit by $16.3 million.

Outlook

In Australia and New Zealand, AXA has become a prominent beneficiary of the boom in wealth management and superannuation markets. It has also achieved success with its portfolio of financial protection products. In Hong Kong the company is forecasting that the retirement savings market will more than double over the coming five years, and it is working to position itself with a range of appropriate products and strategies. Elsewhere in Asia, the company intends to spend up to $300 million over the coming three or four years to boost its presence. In August 2005, it announced plans for a life insurance joint venture in Malaysia, and it also plans an entry into India.

AXA Year to 31 December	2003	2004
Revenues ($mn)	4761.0	4945.0
Profit before tax ($mn)	898.0	594.0
Profit after tax ($mn)	547.0	540.0
Earnings per share (¢)	31.4	31.0
Dividend (¢)	10.25	11.75
Percentage franked	39	23
Return on equity (%)	16.2	14.0
Half year to 30 June	**2004**	**2005**
Revenues ($mn)	1741.0	2139.0
Profit before tax ($mn)	155.1	282.0
Profit after tax ($mn)	181.5	246.0
Earnings per share (¢)	10.4	14.2
Dividend (¢)	5.25	6.25
Percentage franked	15	30
Net tangible assets per share ($)	1.01	1.15
Debt-to-equity ratio (%)	~	~

BANK OF QUEENSLAND LTD

Share price ($)	11.88	
12-month high ($)	12.00	
12-month low ($)	9.35	
Market capitalisation ($mn)	1169.4	
Price-to-NTA-per-share ratio	1.8	
5-year share price return (% pa)	22.1	
Sector: Financials	**Company**	**Sector**
Price-earnings ratio (times)	16.5	14.3
Dividend yield (%)	3.6	4.5

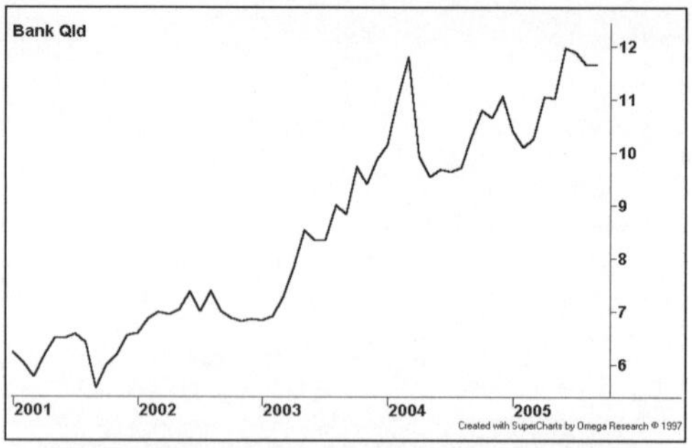

www.boq.com.au

The Bank of Queensland was established in 1874 as the Brisbane Permanent Benefit Building and Investment Society, later gaining a banking licence. It has an estimated 6% share of the banking market in Queensland, with some 138 branches, as well as an additional 22 interstate branches.

Latest business results (February 2005, half year)

In an excellent performance, profits rocketed ahead again, thanks especially to the bank's expanding branch network and its drive into business banking. The withdrawal from the mortgage broker market meant that loan approvals fell 17% to $3.5 billion. However, retail deposits were up 17% to $5.4 billion, and total assets under management rose 18% to $13.3 billion. During the half, the bank opened 15 new interstate branches, and one in Queensland, along with two new business banking centres.

Outlook

The Bank of Queensland has embarked upon an ambitious restructuring and growth program that includes interstate expansion and a new concept of franchised bank branches that are owned and operated by individual managers. Thanks to this model, it has been able to open 26 new branches in NSW, Victoria and ACT in a relatively short period of time, and its target is for 100 interstate branches by August 2006. It has also sold one of its Queensland branches to an owner-operator. Its withdrawal from the mortgage broker market has had a short-term negative impact on lending growth, but has also enabled the bank to boost its lending margin, enhancing profitability. The bank now operates 13 business banking centres, and some 40% of total loans under management derive from business banking. The bank is also striving to diversify its activities, including the acquisition of the equipment finance company UFJ Finance Australia, although in July 2005 it announced the sale of its ATM Solutions Australasia subsidiary—acquired only in September 2003—to Macquarie Bank for $64 million, resulting in an after-tax profit of $15.5 million. Takeover speculation has sometimes fuelled the Bank of Queensland share price, although in May 2004 the Commonwealth Bank sold its 12% stake.

BOQ Year to 31 August	2003	2004
Operating income ($mn)	214.3	291.9
Net interest income ($mn)	132.7	183.3
Operating expenses ($mn)	139.0	185.0
Profit before tax ($mn)	63.6	93.3
Profit after tax ($mn)	44.7	64.5
Earnings per share (¢)	64.1	72.1
Dividend (¢)	37	43
Percentage franked	100	100
Non-interest income to total income (%)	38.1	37.2
Cost to income ratio (%)	64.9	63.4
Return on equity (%)	14.0	13.1
Return on assets (%)	0.7	0.8
Half year to 28 February*	**2004**	**2005**
Operating income ($mn)	136.1	155.5
Profit before tax ($mn)	40.5	49.0
Profit after tax ($mn)	28.1	35.9
Earnings per share (¢)	29.8	33.3
Dividend (¢)	21	23
Percentage franked	100	100
Net tangible assets per share ($)	5.88	6.46

* 29 February 2004

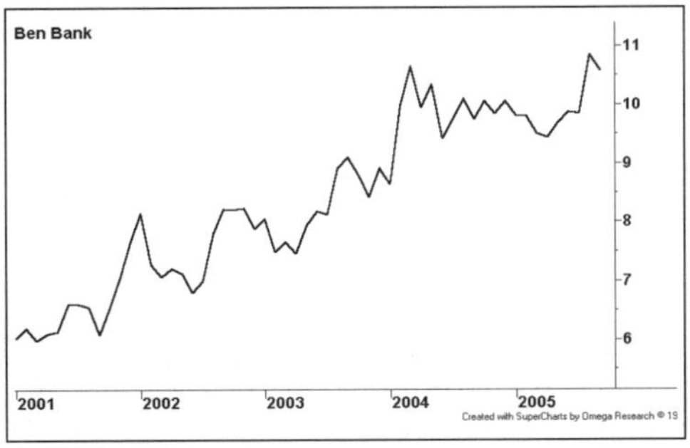

www.benbank.com.au

Bendigo Bank Ltd

Share price ($)	10.43	
12-month high ($)	10.52	
12-month low ($)	9.01	
Market capitalisation ($mn)	1432.7	
Price-to-NTA-per-share ratio	2.2	
5-year share price return (% pa)	22.6	
Sector: Financials	**Company**	**Sector**
Price-earnings ratio (times)	16.8	14.3
Dividend yield (%)	4.3	4.5

Established as a building society in 1858, Victoria's Bendigo Bank is today Australia's only remaining regionally based bank, and is also one of the smallest of all the listed banks. It has a growing network of branches—including over 150 that are company-owned and more than 155 community banks—concentrated in Victoria, Queensland, Western Australia and southern NSW. Its businesses also include the trustee company and funds manager Sandhurst Trustees, the financial planners Bendigo Investment Services and Worley Securities, the debenture company Victorian Securities and the mortgage originator National Mortgage Market Corporation. It has established Elders Rural Bank with Futuris Corporation to provide banking services to rural Australia, and Tasmanian Banking Services with Tasmanian Perpetual Trustees.

Latest business results (June 2005, full year)

Bendigo Bank overcame the housing slowdown to report its fifth consecutive year of strong profit growth, as it continued to expand. Total loans under management grew 14% to $12.9 billion, despite a slight dip in lending approvals to $5.9 billion. Total deposits and funds under management rose 19% to $14.7 billion, thanks to a 26% jump in Sandhurst Trustees managed funds to $2.7 billion and an 18% increase in deposits to $12 billion. All businesses were strong, with community banking profits more than doubling, wealth solutions—principally funds management and financial planning—up 33%, and solid increases in profit for Elders Rural Bank and Tasmanian Banking Services. An after-tax profit of $3 million—reflecting property and share sales—was treated as a significant item.

Outlook

Bendigo Bank continues its impressive expansion, and is now represented in all states. It plans to open a further 35 branches in the June 2006 year, the majority of them outside Victoria. It is steadily reducing its dependence on housing, though it remains high, as do the bank's costs. It is working to expand its relationships with its nearly one million customers, of whom 400 000 have joined the bank within the past four years, and it is also planning a new advertising campaign to attract new customers. It sees continuing strong contributions from funds management, community banking and its partnerships with Elders Rural Bank and Tasmanian Banking Services, and it forecasts a further double-digit rise in profits in the June 2006 year.

BEN Year to 30 June	2004	2005
Operating income ($mn)	394.1	452.1
Net interest income ($mn)	253.6	280.8
Operating expenses ($mn)	287.5	324.2
Profit before tax ($mn)	106.6	127.9
Profit after tax ($mn)	73.2	87.4
Earnings per share (¢)	55.2	62.3
Dividend (¢)	40	45
Percentage franked	100	100
Non-interest income to total income (%)	35.7	37.9
Net tangible assets per share ($)	4.40	4.82
Cost to income ratio (%)	73.0	71.7
Return on equity (%)	11.9	12.3
Return on assets (%)	0.7	0.7

BHP Billiton Ltd

Share price ($)	20.90	
12-month high ($)	21.27	
12-month low ($)	12.98	
Market capitalisation ($mn)	72 750.7	
Price-to-NTA-per-share ratio	5.5	
5-year share price return (% pa)	21.1	
Sector: Materials	**Company**	**Sector**
Price-earnings ratio (times)	16.1	17.0
Dividend yield (%)	1.8	2.2

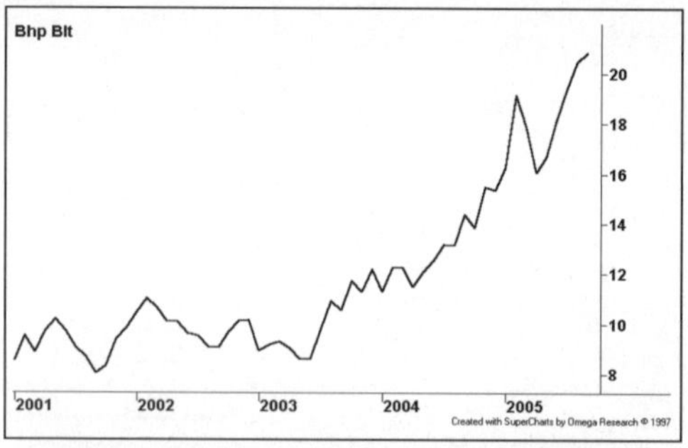

www.bhpbilliton.com.au

Formed from the merger in 2001 of Australian resources giant BHP and British-based mining major Billiton, BHP Billiton is the world's largest diversified resources company. It has more than 100 operations in approximately 20 countries, and occupies industry leader or near industry leader positions in major commodity businesses, including aluminium, energy coal and metallurgical coal, copper, ferro-alloys, iron ore and titanium minerals, along with substantial interests in oil, gas, liquefied natural gas, nickel, diamonds and silver. In mid-2005, it acquired WMC Resources.

Latest business results (June 2005, full year)

Rising commodities prices and the continuing boom in China powered BHP to a massive profit, the largest ever reported by an Australian company. The result included a one-month contribution from WMC. All divisions reported increased earnings, with the best performance coming from the carbon steel materials division, with revenues up 57% and profits up nearly two-and-a-half times, thanks to stronger prices for all products and record sales volumes from Western Australian iron ore and Queensland coal. Base metals were also strong, with revenues up 48% and profits soaring 88%, due mainly to higher copper prices and volumes. Petroleum sales rose just 7% but, thanks to higher prices, profits rose 32%. Energy coal sales rose 32%, with profit up 163%; aluminium sales were up 19%, with profit ahead 26%; and stainless steel material sales jumped 30%, with profits rising 33%. Diamond and specialty product sales fell 10%, due to lower output, but profits edged up 2%. (Note that BHP Billiton reports its financial results in US dollars. For the purposes of this book, these have been converted into Australian dollars at the rates of A$1 = US$0.718 for the June 2004 results and A$1 = US$0.755 for the June 2005 results. Thus, figures in this book should be used for general guidance only.)

BHP Year to 30 June*	2004	2005
Revenues ($mn)	31 876.0	39 270.2
Carbon steel materials (%)	19	24
Petroleum (%)	22	19
Aluminium (%)	18	17
Base metals (%)	14	16
Energy coal (%)	10	11
Stainless steel materials (%)	7	7
Diamonds & specialty products (%)	7	5
EBIT ($mn)	7310.6	11 762.9
EBIT margin (%)	31.9	30.0
Profit before tax ($mn)	6736.8	11 233.1
Profit after tax ($mn)	4682.5	7958.9
Earnings per share (¢)	75.3	130.0
Cash flow per share (¢)	115.5	173.1
Dividend (¢)	36.21	37.1
Percentage franked	100	100
Net tangible assets per share ($)	3.07	3.79
Interest cover (times)	17.7	22.2
Return on equity (%)	26.4	37.7
Debt-to-equity ratio (%)	33.0	56.6
Current ratio	1.7	1.1

* BHP Billiton reports its financial results in US dollars. For this book they have been converted to Australian dollars.

Outlook

BHP Billiton is one of the great beneficiaries of the global boom in resources that has in large part been ignited by the spectacular growth of the Chinese economy. The company itself believes that China will remain a large and sustainable consumer of raw materials in the coming decades, and it expects prices to remain high.

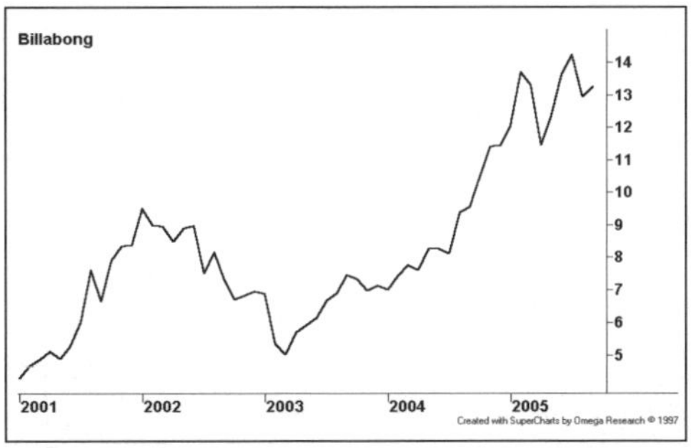

www.billabongcorporate.com

Billabong International Ltd

Share price ($)	13.65	
12-month high ($)	14.61	
12-month low ($)	7.98	
Market capitalisation ($mn)	2874.6	
Price-to-NTA-per-share ratio	26.4	
5-year share price return (% pa)	34.9	
Sector: Consumer discretionary	**Company**	**Sector**
Price-earnings ratio (times)	22.4	24.2
Dividend yield (%)	2.8	1.2

Surfwear company Billabong International, based on the Gold Coast, was established in 1973. It is today the leading surfwear apparel brand in Australia, with production facilities in a dozen countries as well as sales in more than 60 countries. Its products include board shorts, t-shirts, swimwear, fleece tops, jumpers, walk shorts, pants, jeans, bags and accessories. It also operates its own retail chain of 64 company-owned stores and 22 licensed stores.

Latest business results (June 2005, full year)

Billabong enjoyed another outstanding year, with profits surging ahead in the first half, though with the momentum more subdued in the second half. The Australia/New Zealand/Japan region enjoyed an exceptional year, with sales up 43% and pre-tax profit ahead 32%. This region is responsible for a third of company sales but accounts for nearly two-thirds of total profit. America/Brazil (47% of total turnover) saw sales up 22% and profit soar 98%. Europe achieved 9% sales growth, with profit up 16%. All brands performed strongly, with particular demand for the skateboard-inspired Element brand and the Von Zipper brand.

Outlook

Billabong has become a global Australian success story, as well as a stock market superstar, thanks to its ability to take advantage of fashion trends in its target markets of affluent youth in many countries. This makes it vulnerable to trends in discretionary consumer spending; however, thanks to its global reach it is now often able to absorb slowdowns in particular markets, such as in Australia in early 2005. The company's own medium-term forecast is for the consistent delivery of 15% annual EPS growth, and it has reiterated that it expects to reach this target in the June 2006 year. Its core brand of Billabong remains the biggest contributor to revenues, and the company continues to open flagship Billabong outlets, including one in New York's Times Square. The skateboard brand Element has also become a major success. The company is seeing good demand for new brands such as Honolua Surf Company—which has its own network of 22 retail stores in the US—Palmers Surf and Kustom. It has achieved notable success in Brazil, where sales rose 85% in local currency in the June 2005 year, and it is looking to enter more markets.

BBG Year to 30 June	2004	2005
Revenues ($mn)	677.3	843.6
EBIT ($mn)	133.1	188.3
EBIT margin (%)	19.6	22.3
Gross margin (%)	49.0	51.8
Profit before tax ($mn)	127.9	183.5
Profit after tax ($mn)	87.0	125.4
Earnings per share (¢)	43.0	61.0
Cash flow per share (¢)	48.5	67.0
Dividend (¢)	26.5	38
Percentage franked	100	100
Net tangible assets per share ($)	0.30	0.52
Interest cover (times)	25.5	38.7
Return on equity (%)	15.6	20.5
Debt-to-equity ratio (%)	16.4	10.1
Current ratio	2.8	2.6

BLACKMORES LTD

Share price ($)	13.79	
12-month high ($)	14.98	
12-month low ($)	10.50	
Market capitalisation ($mn)	221.5	
Price-to-NTA-per-share ratio	7.7	
5-year share price return (% pa)	21.9	
Sector: Health care	**Company**	**Sector**
Price-earnings ratio (times)	18.6	28.0
Dividend yield (%)	4.2	1.7

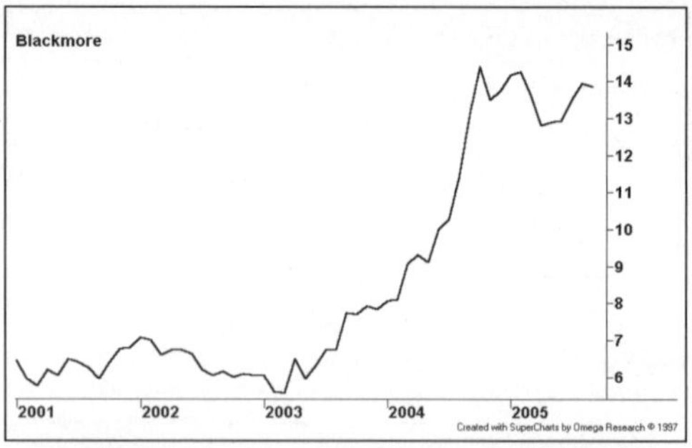

www.blackmores.com.au

Founded in the 1930s, Sydney-based Blackmores is a leading manufacturer and distributor of a wide range of natural health care products, nutritional supplements and cosmetics. Its brands include Vitaglow and BioACE. It exports to South-East Asia and New Zealand.

Latest business results (June 2005, full year)

Blackmores enjoyed another year of excellent growth, thanks to strong domestic demand for its products. Australian sales (86% of the total) rose 18%, with the company reporting success in retaining a significant proportion of the market-share gains it made following the mass recall of the products of Pan Pharmaceuticals in April 2003. Another factor was also a significant increase in the company's investment in marketing and brand-support activity. Asia represents 11% of total company revenues, and sales there were up 13%. However, all the growth came from Thailand, where revenues were up 30% in local currency as a result of a series of successful marketing initiatives and growing acceptance of the Blackmores brand. The other key Asian market, Malaysia, recorded a slight sales decline, and Asian pre-tax profit plunged 34%. New Zealand represents just 2% of company business, and sales there rose nearly 5%. However, New Zealand operations are extremely profitable, and account for around 5% of total company pre-tax profit.

Outlook

Blackmores has become a stellar corporate and stock market performer in the wake of the Pan Pharmaceuticals mass recall, which resulted in consumers moving to brands that enjoyed a reputation for quality. Blackmores continues to expand, and is achieving notable success in gaining more retail shelf space for its products, particularly in supermarkets and pharmacies. It also maintains a steady stream of new product launches, the latest including Blackmores 10-Day Detox Program, Women's Vitality Multi, Women's D-Stress, and MSM Glucosamine Chondrotin Joint Support Powder and Joint Formula. It is planning to build major new production facilities, and is purchasing a $10 million plot of land in Warriewood, Sydney. Construction of new facilities is expected to be completed late in 2007. Building on its success in Asia, Blackmores plans further expansion there. It will enter the Taiwan market during the June 2006 year, and is investigating other countries. Blackmores provides a shareholders' card that gives a 25% discount on its products.

BKL Year to 30 June	2004	2005
Revenues ($mn)	115.7	134.4
EBIT ($mn)	14.1	17.4
EBIT margin (%)	12.2	12.9
Gross margin (%)	60.0	60.7
Profit before tax ($mn)	13.2	16.9
Profit after tax ($mn)	9.3	11.7
Earnings per share (¢)	59.5	74.0
Cash flow per share (¢)	73.5	85.8
Dividend (¢)	46	58
Percentage franked	100	100
Net tangible assets per share ($)	1.72	1.80
Interest cover (times)	16.7	39.7
Return on equity (%)	37.0	40.4
Debt-to-equity ratio (%)	21.8	16.8
Current ratio	1.6	1.5

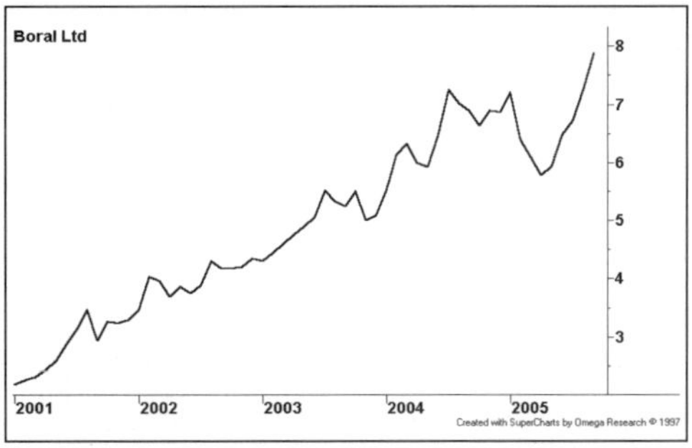

www.boral.com.au

Boral Ltd

Share price ($)	7.18	
12-month high ($)	7.46	
12-month low ($)	5.57	
Market capitalisation ($mn)	4074.4	
Price-to-NTA-per-share ratio	1.9	
5-year share price return (% pa)	38.8	
Sector: Materials	**Company**	**Sector**
Price-earnings ratio (times)	11.1	17.0
Dividend yield (%)	4.7	2.2

Sydney-based Boral—incorporated in 1946 as Bitumen and Oil Refineries (Australia) Limited—is one of Australia's largest producers of building and construction materials, and it has operations in several countries. Domestically, it is a major brick, clay paver and concrete masonry producer, and it is also one of the largest in America. It owns half of a large plasterboard joint venture in Asia. A quarter of total sales revenues—including exports and overseas production—comes from abroad.

Latest business results (June 2005, full year)

Boral's sales revenues and after-tax profit edged up, with weakness in the Australian housing market offset by improved earnings in other businesses. Around 40% of Boral's domestic revenues are derived from the NSW housing market, where new dwelling approvals have declined sharply, and Australian EBIT—75% of the total—edged down. However, a booming US housing market saw earnings there jump 22%. Asian business—about 3% of total profits—slumped, with difficult trading conditions for plasterboard in both Thailand and Korea.

Outlook

With the domestic housing business responsible for more than a third of company turnover and with a particularly high exposure to NSW, the worst-performing housing market, Boral faces a period of uncertainty, and it has raised the prospect of temporarily closing some of its eastern seaboard plants. However, domestic non-dwelling and infrastructure construction markets remain firm—including some major new highway projects, such as the Mitcham-Frankston freeway—and the company expects this to balance the housing downturn. It also believes it will be able to raise construction material prices by 3% to 4%. Housing activity in the United States remains buoyant, with demand growing for the company's products. Non-dwelling construction activity there is also expected to increase, and the company is confident of increased earnings. It has upgraded some of its US plants, which will boost efficiencies. The small Asian business also looks set to deliver increased earnings, with Boral achieving success in raising plasterboard and building material prices in Thailand. Through its Asian joint venture, Lafarge Boral Gypsum Asia, the company is planning a major push into China, with new plasterboard plants in Shanghai and Chongging that will double its annual production capacity to more than 70 million square metres.

BLD Year to 30 June	2004	2005
Revenues ($mn)	4149.8	4296.7
EBIT ($mn)	599.6	587.9
EBIT margin (%)	14.4	13.7
Gross margin (%)	38.4	36.9
Profit before tax ($mn)	534.0	516.8
Profit after tax ($mn)	369.8	376.8
Earnings per share (¢)	63.8	64.7
Cash flow per share (¢)	97.4	101.6
Dividend (¢)	30	34
Percentage franked	100	100
Net tangible assets per share ($)	3.65	3.76
Interest cover (times)	9.1	8.3
Return on equity (%)	16.5	15.6
Debt-to-equity ratio (%)	39.8	56.4
Current ratio	1.3	1.4

Brickworks Ltd

Share price ($)	11.21	
12-month high ($)	12.21	
12-month low ($)	8.96	
Market capitalisation ($mn)	1490.1	
Price-to-NTA-per-share ratio	2.1	
5-year share price return (% pa)	25.5	
Sector: Materials	**Company**	**Sector**
Price-earnings ratio (times)	9.4	17.0
Dividend yield (%)	2.1	2.2

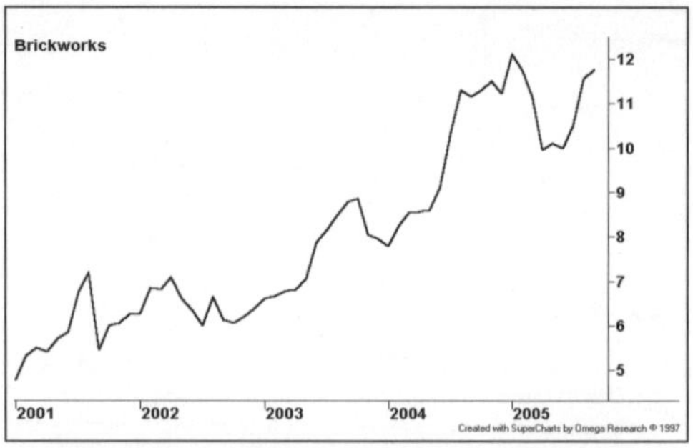

www.brickworks.com.au

Sydney-based Brickworks, founded in 1934, is one of Australia's largest producers of bricks, and roof and floor tiles. Its brands include Austral Bricks, Bristile Roofing and Eureka Tiles. It also manages an extensive land portfolio. It has spun off its equity portfolio into a new listed entity, Brickworks Investment Company, in which it retains a 23% share. In a cross-shareholding arrangement designed to prevent takeovers, it owns 43% of the equity of Washington H. Soul Pattinson, while Soul Pattinson owns nearly 50% of the equity in Brickworks.

Latest business results (December 2004, half year)

Brickworks has announced that it will change its financial year end from June to July. The July 2005 results will be for 13 months, and will also include a 12-month report for June 2005. The latest available figures for this book are the December 2004 half-year results. The comparative results were skewed by a big $70 million profit in the December 2003 half from the company's divestment of its investment portfolio. On a normalised basis, profits showed a modest increase, due mainly to equity-accounted earnings from the Soul Pattinson holding, up from $13.1 million to $18.4 million. In a generally softening housing market, building products profits were flat, with price rises and a strong performance in Western Australia offsetting weakness in the eastern states.

BKW Year to 30 June	2003	2004
Revenues ($mn)	179.6	485.7
EBIT ($mn)	78.7	126.2
EBIT margin (%)	43.8	26.0
Gross margin (%)	40.2	38.6
Profit before tax ($mn)	75.3	102.1
Profit after tax ($mn)	72.7	76.0
Earnings per share (¢)	55.2	57.7
Cash flow per share (¢)	63.8	86.1
Dividend (¢)	20	24
Percentage franked	100	100
Interest cover (times)	23.0	5.2
Return on equity (%)	12.6	10.1
Half year to 31 December	**2003**	**2004**
Revenues ($mn)	250.2	251.3
Profit before tax ($mn)	43.7	49.9
Profit after tax ($mn)	36.1	38.3
Earnings per share (¢)	27.4	24.9
Dividend (¢)	9	10
Percentage franked	100	100
Net tangible assets per share ($)	4.62	5.34
Debt-to-equity ratio (%)	30.8	26.7
Current ratio	0.4	1.2

Outlook

Brickworks is greatly influenced by trends in the housing market, although such has been the strength of demand for its products that the recent slowdown has allowed it to catch up with order backlogs and undertake necessary maintenance of its plants, with little decline in sales. It is developing a fast-growing export business for many of its products. It will also benefit from continuing plans to develop its large surplus land holdings, with active developments in NSW, Victoria, South Australia and Western Australia. It expects its development at Horsley Park, west of Sydney, to deliver $150 million in revenues over ten to twelve years. In mid-2005, Brickworks announced the acquisition of Auswest Timbers, taking the company into the timber products business for the housing market, which it believes will complement its brick and tile activities.

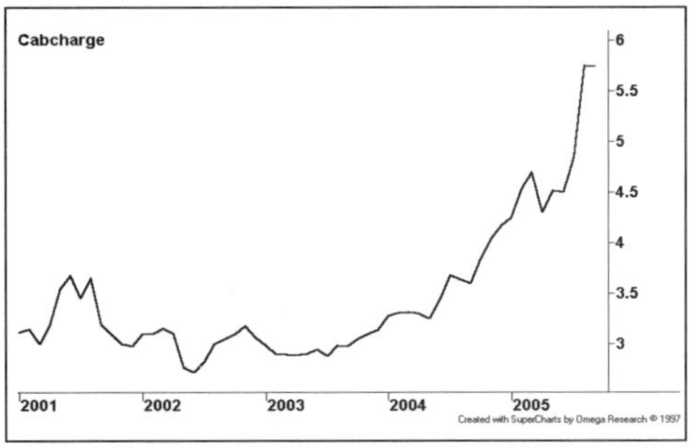

www.cabcharge.com.au

Cabcharge Australia Ltd

Share price ($)	5.02	
12-month high ($)	5.24	
12-month low ($)	3.43	
Market capitalisation ($mn)	564.5	
Price-to-NTA-per-share ratio	4.4	
5-year share price return (% pa)	20.3	
Sector: Industrials	**Company**	**Sector**
Price-earnings ratio (times)	20.7	16.2
Dividend yield (%)	3.4	3.6

Sydney-based Cabcharge, founded in 1976, manages a charge-card system that allows taxi users to pay fares without requiring cash. The system, which is now online, is used by more than 95% of Australian taxis, and also by other companies, such as limousine services. Cabcharge has more than 44 000 account customers, ranging from large corporations and government departments to small businesses and individuals. Cabcharge also owns Australia's largest taxi company, Sydney-based Combined Communications Network, as well as Melbourne-based Black Cabs Combined and ABC Radio Taxi Cooperative in Sydney. It has established a small presence in the UK, with a joint venture operation in several cities, and is working to expand globally.

Latest business results (June 2005, full year)

Cabcharge recorded another strong result. The company's revenues rose on the back of a 12.5% increase in both its taxi charge business and its own much smaller taxi service operation. Profits increased at a faster rate, thanks especially to more efficient processing of transactions via the new GPRS (General Packet Radio Service) wireless technology service, which uses existing mobile phone networks to allow laptops and handheld phones to maintain connectivity. The number of electronic transactions continued to rise, to represent 57% of all transactions during the year, up from 52% in the previous year.

Outlook

Cabcharge continues to enhance its technology, with new systems that are aimed at reducing costs, and it is seeing a steady move to its online systems. The acquisition of taxi companies hands Cabcharge a new stream of earnings, and the company also reaps higher profits when its charge cards are used on its own taxis. In July 2005, it completed the installation of 17 000 GPRS taxi terminals, and this should further drive down costs. It is now working to introduce electronic ticketing across its system, to replace Cabcharge blue dockets, with further long-term cost benefits. It continues to expand in the UK, and has established a new Communication Network Centre in Birmingham, which it expects to become profitable during the June 2006 year. In August 2005, Cabcharge and Singapore's ComfortDelGro entered into a $107 million agreement to buy the leading Western Sydney bus company Westbus, providing Cabcharge with a new base for growth.

CAB Year to 30 June	2004	2005
Revenues ($mn)	681.1	766.5
EBIT ($mn)	30.6	36.3
EBIT margin (%)	4.5	4.7
Profit before tax ($mn)	32.5	38.3
Profit after tax ($mn)	23.1	27.2
Earnings per share (¢)	20.6	24.3
Cash flow per share (¢)	28.5	34.9
Dividend (¢)	13.75	17
Percentage franked	100	100
Net tangible assets per share ($)	1.05	1.15
Interest cover (times)	~	~
Return on equity (%)	18.7	20.6
Debt-to-equity ratio (%)	~	~
Current ratio	3.3	3.5

Campbell Brothers Ltd

Share price ($)	9.71	
12-month high ($)	11.49	
12-month low ($)	7.00	
Market capitalisation ($mn)	410.1	
Price-to-NTA-per-share ratio	4.7	
5-year share price return (% pa)	23.9	
Sector: Materials	**Company**	**Sector**
Price-earnings ratio (times)	18.1	17.0
Dividend yield (%)	4.3	2.2

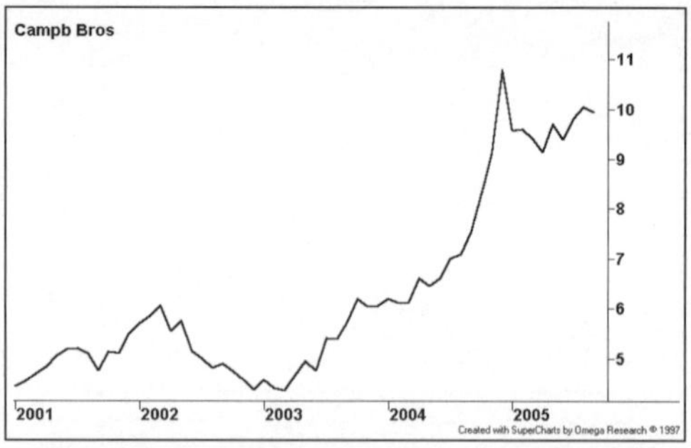

www.campbell.com.au

Established in 1863, Brisbane-based Campbell Brothers is one of the world's largest providers of laboratory analysis services to the minerals industry, with 44 laboratories in 19 countries. Its industrial division comprises three business units—hospitality distribution, chemical manufacturing and chemical importing—with operations in Australia and New Zealand. Its consumer operation concentrates on service-based businesses after the sale in 2004 of its branded consumer products business to Colgate Palmolive.

Latest business results (March 2005, full year)

Campbell's buoyant laboratory services division powered the company to another big jump in profits. The division's ALS Chemex mineral-assaying business made a particularly strong contribution, thanks to the resources boom. Though it constitutes less than 40% of company revenues, laboratory services contributed more than 70% of profit. The industrial division saw revenues up, thanks especially to strategic acquisitions by the Reward Distribution business unit, though profits were down. The consumer division recorded a 27% rise in profits, despite a slight dip in sales revenues, following the disposal of its branded consumer products business.

Outlook

Campbell continues to boost its high-flying laboratory business at a time when rapidly expanding global minerals exploration activity is handing it increasing amounts of business. New laboratories in China and South Africa give it access to the sizeable minerals market in Africa and to the emerging environmental and chemical testing markets in China. It is also pursuing a number of opportunities in the emerging 'green testing'—or product certification—for environmental contaminants in the electrical and electronic equipment markets. It views this business as offering great potential. With the sale of parts of its underperforming consumer operation, it now sees good prospects for the division from moves to create a national network of pest control and washroom-hygiene operations. Thanks to recent acquisitions, it expects significant increases in revenue and profit for this division. The industrial division is benefiting from a series of acquisitions and expanded market share for its distribution business.

CPB Year to 31 March	2004	2005
Revenues ($mn)	390.3	435.6
Laboratory services (%)	31	36
Industrial (%)	36	35
Consumer (%)	33	28
EBIT ($mn)	30.2	39.0
EBIT margin (%)	7.7	8.9
Gross margin (%)	30.1	28.3
Profit before tax ($mn)	24.4	33.5
Profit after tax ($mn)	14.6	21.9
Earnings per share (¢)	36.8	53.7
Cash flow per share (¢)	76.5	96.9
Dividend (¢)	33	42
Percentage franked	100	100
Net tangible assets per share ($)	1.53	2.08
Interest cover (times)	5.2	7.1
Return on equity (%)	11.2	15.5
Debt-to-equity ratio (%)	69.3	48.4
Current ratio	2.3	2.1

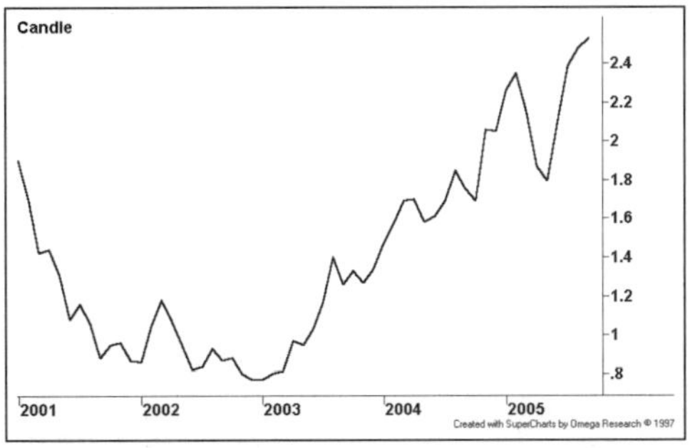

www.candle.com.au

Candle Australia Ltd

Share price ($)	2.50	
12-month high ($)	2.52	
12-month low ($)	1.62	
Market capitalisation ($mn)	113.9	
Price-to-NTA-per-share ratio	5.6	
5-year share price return (% pa)	7.1	
Sector: Industrials	**Company**	**Sector**
Price-earnings ratio (times)	15.0	16.2
Dividend yield (%)	4.6	3.6

Sydney-based Candle Australia, founded in 1984, has grown through a series of mergers and acquisitions to become a leading nationwide specialist provider of recruitment services to the information communications technology (ICT), banking, finance, insurance and government sectors. Its divisions include Candle Information and Communications Technology (Candle ICT), Alliance Recruitment, Freeman Adams, Technology Co-Sourcing Solutions, Workskills Professionals, Premier Personnel and The One Umbrella. It also provides payroll services, and it operates in New Zealand. In July 2005 it acquired Sydney accounting profession recruiter Parker Bridge Australia and Adelaide IT recruiter Choice IT.

Latest business results (June 2005, full year)

Candle achieved another superb result, thanks again to the strong Australian economy and a tight labour market. There was strong growth from the company's core ICT recruitment business, as well as from most other areas. With some 70% of its income dependent on the contractor and temporary personnel market, the company reaped the benefits of looming skill shortages in some professions. However, it also achieved strong growth in the permanent-placement market, with an excellent contribution from its new permanent executive division, Executive Search and Selection. There was a good performance from the company's new The One Umbrella acquisition, which provides specialist personnel in records management, library and knowledge management.

Outlook

Candle is a market leader in the technology recruitment field, at a time when concerns of a skills shortage in Australia are mounting, and it is realising growing demand for its businesses. However, it is also working to diversify, in order that it not become too dependent on this single area of the market. It is striving to broaden its client base, is seeking new cross-selling opportunities and it also plans new lines of business, both in recruitment and in the broader area of employment services. Already, non-ICT businesses provide around 40% of company income. It sees particular promise from The One Umbrella, which now has new managers and has established plans for future expansion. The Choice IT acquisition will boost Candle's position in South Australia, and the Parker Bridge Australia acquisition will provide Candle with the platform for a national business in commercial accounting recruitment. With no debt and more than $7 million in cash holdings, Candle plans further acquisitions.

CND Year to 30 June	2004	2005
Revenues ($mn)	179.2	231.8
EBIT ($mn)	7.0	10.7
EBIT margin (%)	3.9	4.6
Profit before tax ($mn)	6.8	10.6
Profit after tax ($mn)	4.6	7.2
Earnings per share (¢)	11.8	16.6
Cash flow per share (¢)	16.2	21.0
Dividend (¢)	9	11.5
Percentage franked	100	100
Net tangible assets per share ($)	0.31	0.45
Interest cover (times)	38.7	79.2
Return on equity (%)	10.2	13.7
Debt-to-equity ratio (%)	0.5	~
Current ratio	1.4	1.7

Cellnet Group Ltd

Share price ($)	1.35
12-month high ($)	1.82
12-month low ($)	1.07
Market capitalisation ($mn)	68.9
Price-to-NTA-per-share ratio	1.7
5-year share price return (% pa)	–4.2

Sector: Information technology	Company	Sector
Price-earnings ratio (times)	11.2	34.4
Dividend yield (%)	5.2	1.7

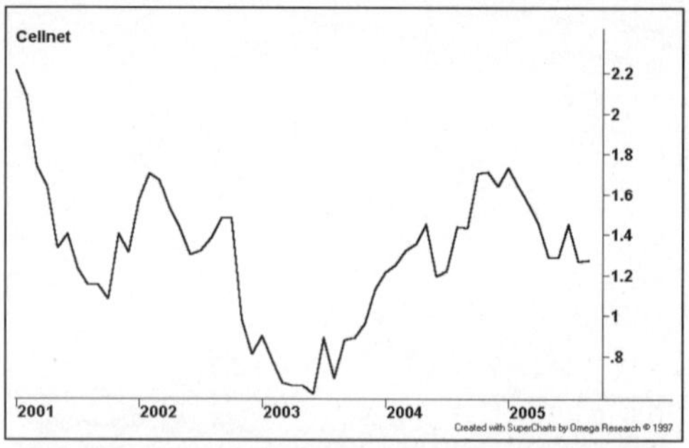

www.cellnetgroup.com.au

Brisbane-based Cellnet, established in 1992, is a prominent wholesale distributor in Australia and New Zealand of mobile phones and accessories and of IT products and related consumables. With warehouse facilities and offices in Brisbane, Sydney, Melbourne, Perth, Adelaide and Auckland, the company distributes a wide range of products. It is a leading distributor of IBM products, but is involved in numerous other prominent brands. Its Mercury Mobility venture provides innovative content for mobile phones, and its Comms+ business is engaged in marketing and advertising, and has evolved into a specialised agency for some of the major mobile phone manufacturers and retail outlets. Cellnet has also moved into the distribution of a variety of consumer electronics products.

Latest business results (June 2005, full year)

Sales continued to rise strongly, but profits slumped. Much of the damage was done in the final months of the financial year, with a lower-than-expected performance in the markets for the company's higher margin products, along with a decline in the average margin. In addition, the result was hurt by decisions to increase inventory write-offs. Mobile phone revenues rose 19%, but profits tumbled 43%. By contrast, IT products saw sales up 52%, and profits jumped 150%. However, profits for the latter business represent just 25% of Cellnet's total.

Outlook

Cellnet occupies strong positions in the fast-growing mobile phone and IT markets. However, competition is fierce, and it must be innovative and nimble to maintain profit growth. In June 2005, it appointed a new managing director, charged with the immediate priority of undertaking a detailed review of the company's structures and operations, with recommendations of the changes needed to restore profitability. The company has already initiated a comprehensive restructuring of its business units and management. It is making substantial reductions in the number of individual stock items held, and in inventory levels, with a focus on holding mainly high-margin inventory that attracts high demand. In mid-2005, Cellnet announced that it had won a major new contract with Toshiba for the nationwide distribution of Toshiba's mobile computing products, data projectors, portable storage and associated accessories. Cellnet expects Toshiba business to grow to $4 million in monthly revenues.

CLT Year to 30 June	2004	2005
Revenues ($mn)	446.6	585.9
Mobile phones & accessories (%)	62	56
IT products (%)	38	44
EBIT ($mn)	14.6	11.5
EBIT margin (%)	3.3	2.0
Gross margin (%)	8.8	8.6
Profit before tax ($mn)	13.5	8.9
Profit after tax ($mn)	9.1	6.1
Earnings per share (¢)	18.3	12.0
Cash flow per share (¢)	22.8	16.9
Dividend (¢)	11.5	7
Percentage franked	100	100
Net tangible assets per share ($)	0.97	0.78
Interest cover (times)	13.2	4.4
Return on equity (%)	16.7	10.6
Debt-to-equity ratio (%)	38.0	69.8
Current ratio	1.7	1.4

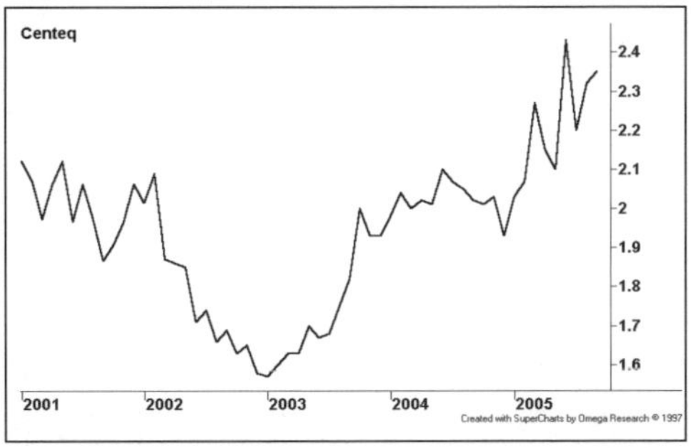

www.centralequity.com.au

Central Equity Ltd

Share price ($)	2.27	
12-month high ($)	2.43	
12-month low ($)	1.90	
Market capitalisation ($mn)	180.3	
Price-to-NTA-per-share ratio	1.0	
5-year share price return (% pa)	9.6	
Sector: Financials	**Company**	**Sector**
Price-earnings ratio (times)	8.1	14.3
Dividend yield (%)	5.3	4.5

Melbourne-based property developer Central Equity was founded in 1987, and has been responsible for more than $2.3 billion worth of residential property developments in the city. It has achieved renown for its pioneering inner-city apartment projects, including the conversion of older buildings into residential properties. It has achieved notable success in the riverside Southbank precinct, where the company has been responsible for some 70% of all residential development. It has also moved into medium-density housing in Melbourne's inner suburbs. Altogether, it has sold more than 7000 homes and apartments in the city, in more than 50 apartment towers and housing estates. Its real estate subsidiary Melbourne Inner City Management has an extensive business managing many of the properties the company has sold.

Latest business results (June 2005, full year)

Sales and profits fell sharply, as the housing downturn took its toll. The company was also hit by rising construction costs. Two major new developments were completed during the period, Melbourne Tower and City Tower, both in Southbank, worth $300 million and offering a total of 630 apartments. Also completed was the Pinnacle Gardens development of 21 townhouses in suburban Melbourne.

Outlook

Central Equity has warned of falling sales and profits, with Melbourne having an oversupply of inner-city apartments, forcing the company to cut back on new projects. It expects the major impact of this to be felt in the June 2006 and 2007 years. The $40 million Market Square Condos development in West Melbourne was completed in August 2005. It was virtually sold out prior to completion, with settlement due in September and October 2005. Central Equity has more than $85 million in net cash, and is well-placed to take advantage of any decline in land prices. It owns two major sites at Southbank that are suitable for development once the market cycle turns favourable again. During 2005 it conducted two share buybacks, to take advantage of its cash holdings and to support the share price. The company has also established a new entity, Central Equity Land Corporation, which is engaged in land subdivision work. Current holdings are expected to yield a total of around 2000 blocks, some of which the company will develop itself, with the remainder sold.

CEQ Year to 30 June	2004	2005
Revenues ($mn)	281.7	171.0
EBIT ($mn)	41.2	24.7
EBIT margin (%)	14.6	14.4
Gross margin (%)	22.0	24.7
Profit before tax ($mn)	48.0	34.4
Profit after tax ($mn)	33.6	24.1
Earnings per share (¢)	39.0	27.9
Cash flow per share (¢)	41.1	29.7
Dividend (¢)	13	12
Percentage franked	100	100
Net tangible assets per share ($)	2.39	2.36
Interest cover (times)	~	~
Return on equity (%)	17.2	11.7
Debt-to-equity ratio (%)	21.3	~
Current ratio	1.9	2.9

CMI Ltd

Share price ($)	1.57	
12-month high ($)	2.33	
12-month low ($)	1.23	
Market capitalisation ($mn)	54.2	
Price-to-NTA-per-share ratio	0.9	
5-year share price return (% pa)	11.4	
Sector: Industrials	**Company**	**Sector**
Price-earnings ratio (times)	4.6	16.2
Dividend yield (%)	7.6	3.6

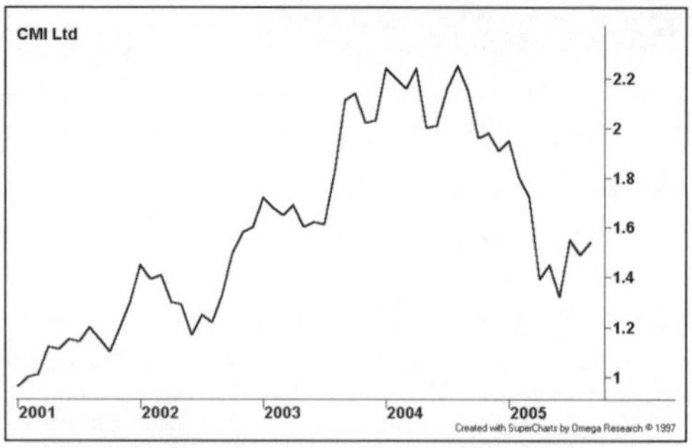

www.cmilimited.com.au

Brisbane-based CMI, established in 1991, is a manufacturer and distributor of a range of specialist industrial components, with most sales to Australian and international automotive companies. It also supplies the white goods, mining, construction and IT industries. It has 14 manufacturing and/or distribution centres in Australia, New Zealand and the US, and its customers include Ford, Holden, Mitsubishi, Nissan, Bosch and BHP Billiton. It also operates a financial services subsidiary, Capitalcorp Finance & Leasing, with more than 30 offices throughout Australia.

Latest business results (June 2005, full year)

Revenues and profits rose modestly, restrained by increasing raw materials prices and competition from cheaper imports. The core engineered components business—more than 80% of total company turnover—saw sales edge up less than 1%, with profits also up just slightly. Sales from the company's American units fell sharply, from $9 million to $5.9 million, and this business remained in the red. By contrast, the electrical components business, which makes specialist cabling and electrical products for a variety of industries, achieved excellent 50% sales growth and 44% profit growth. The financial services division—the provision of consumer finance from Capitalcorp—saw revenues up 10%, though profits fell.

Outlook

CMI continues to benefit from strong components demand from the auto industry. Its engineered components division has won a series of new contracts, including for the 2006 Holden Commodore and the new Mitsubishi Magna. Its TJM four-wheel-drive components business has built a major new production facility and is launching a range of smooth-shell canopies and stainless steel products. Overseas, CMI Springs New Zealand has boosted capacity and CMI USA has extended its supply arrangement with Pacifica's PBR brake business until 2008. However, CMI's high gearing in the US to the activities of Pacifica means that it is being hurt by the short-term downturn in Pacifica's business. The company is concerned about sharply rising prices for steel and other raw materials. In addition, the appreciating Australian dollar has made Asia more competitive. In response, CMI is sourcing more from China and Thailand, and plans to buy wheel products from India. The company sees a great future in financial services, following the acquisition in November 2003 of Capitalcorp.

CMI Year to 30 June	2004	2005
Revenues ($mn)	269.6	280.7
EBIT ($mn)	19.5	20.4
EBIT margin (%)	7.2	7.3
Gross margin (%)	23.2	25.4
Profit before tax ($mn)	16.0	17.0
Profit after tax ($mn)	10.6	11.5
Earnings per share (¢)	38.9	34.3
Cash flow per share (¢)	65.8	58.8
Dividend (¢)	12	12
Percentage franked	100	100
Net tangible assets per share ($)	1.61	1.71
Interest cover (times)	5.6	6.0
Return on equity (%)	15.6	14.5
Debt-to-equity ratio (%)	83.5	63.5
Current ratio	1.7	1.9

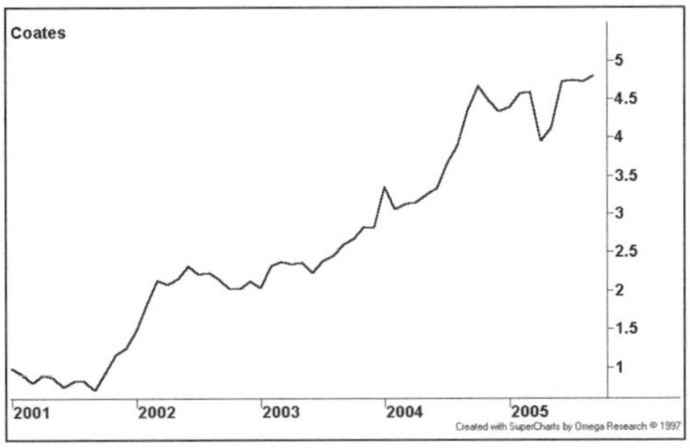

www.coates.com.au

Coates Hire Ltd

Share price ($)	5.15	
12-month high ($)	5.27	
12-month low ($)	3.61	
Market capitalisation ($mn)	1113.0	
Price-to-NTA-per-share ratio	3.0	
5-year share price return (% pa)	32.5	
Sector: Industrials	**Company**	**Sector**
Price-earnings ratio (times)	16.8	16.2
Dividend yield (%)	2.9	3.6

Sydney-based Coates Hire Limited is Australia's largest hire equipment company, with more than 180 branches and locations nationwide. Following the acquisition of its largest rival, Wreckair, it now has around a third of the market. Domestically, it divides its operations into four businesses: Coates Hire provides a large range of general equipment; Coates Shorco Sykes supplies specialist pumps and excavation support equipment; Coates Prestige provides portable buildings and toilets; and Coates Conrent is a leading supplier of construction hoists. It has a small operation, Coates Offshore, in Aberdeen in the UK, providing specialised equipment to the offshore oil and gas industry, and seven offices in Indonesia supporting the mining, resources and offshore sectors.

Latest business results (June 2005, full year)

A strong domestic construction environment handed Coates another excellent result. The company's strong focus on operational efficiencies led to higher margins. Domestically, the company's core hiring business saw continuing strength in booming Western Australia, and a big surge in activity in Melbourne, thanks to the acquisition of Western Access, Hi Tower and Lilydale Hiring. NSW and Queensland remained firm, but northern regions faced patchy market conditions. All the company's specialist businesses also delivered excellent results. In the UK, the Coates Offshore business has moved out of the red and into profit, following its exit from its onshore activities. After a big loss in the previous year, Indonesian operations recorded a tiny profit.

Outlook

Coates remains a major beneficiary of the strong domestic construction and resources markets, and the near-term outlook is for continuing strength. In July 2005, it completed the $136 million acquisition of Allied Equipment (an independent provider of large earthmoving equipment), giving Coates a step-up in equipment size and penetration into the mining sector. The company is realising extremely attractive growth in Melbourne — thanks in part to its recent acquisitions there — and it expects more gains from the March 2006 Commonwealth Games in the city, for which Coates is an official sponsor. In Western Australia, the company is benefiting from not just resources and minerals-related business, but also shut-down projects and general non-residential and engineering construction projects. The British operation is starting to become very profitable, and the company is considering an expansion into the Asia-Pacific region.

COA Year to 30 June	2004	2005
Revenues ($mn)	456.9	527.6
EBIT ($mn)	78.6	104.0
EBIT margin (%)	17.2	19.7
Profit before tax ($mn)	68.3	92.4
Profit after tax ($mn)	52.1	63.5
Earnings per share (¢)	25.6	30.7
Cash flow per share (¢)	59.8	66.7
Dividend (¢)	13	15
Percentage franked	100	100
Net tangible assets per share ($)	1.64	1.73
Interest cover (times)	7.6	8.9
Return on equity (%)	15.9	17.3
Debt-to-equity ratio (%)	40.0	61.3
Current ratio	1.1	1.3

Cochlear Ltd

Share price ($)	39.51	
12-month high ($)	41.25	
12-month low ($)	18.69	
Market capitalisation ($mn)	2155.3	
Price-to-NTA-per-share ratio	na	
5-year share price return (% pa)	11.0	
Sector: Health care	**Company**	**Sector**
Price-earnings ratio (times)	39.3	28.0
Dividend yield (%)	2.0	1.7

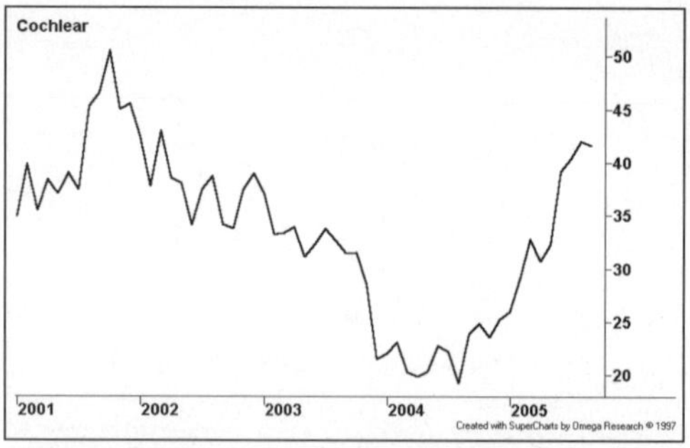

www.cochlear.com.au

Sydney-based Cochlear, founded in 1981, has more than two-thirds of the world market for cochlear bionic-ear implants, which are intended to assist the communication ability of people suffering from severe hearing impediments. It has sold more than 60 000 of its Nucleus 22 and Nucleus 24 implant systems in around 80 countries. Overseas business accounts for over 95% of sales and profits.

Latest business results (June 2005, full year)

Cochlear enjoyed a resounding recovery after the slump of the previous year, buoyed by the launch of the new-generation Nucleus Freedom implant in the fourth quarter. There was an excellent comeback in the Americas region, with sales up 21% and EBIT soaring more than three times. The company reported that it regained market share lost there in the previous year. European sales jumped 40%, in part because of the acquisition of Entific Medical Systems in March 2005. Excluding this, sales rose 27%, with growth in all countries. European profits were up 75%. The Asia Pacific region saw sales growth of 12%, with profits ahead 36%. Altogether, the company sold 10 802 implant units, up from 9306 in the previous year. The Entific acquisition was behind a sharp increase in the company's debt.

Outlook

Cochlear has reclaimed much of its lost vigour, and reports that its global market share appears to have risen to the 70% level. It believes that it is now set on a path of sustainable long-term expansion, with earnings growth of at least 20% in the June 2006 year. It sees particularly bright prospects for the new Nucleus Freedom product, which takes the company's technology to a new level, with impressive benefits for implant recipients. The company also sees great potential for its $195 million Entific Medical Systems acquisition. Entific, based in Sweden, has developed its own implant product that does not compete with Cochlear's, and Cochlear sees great synergies arising from the acquisition. It has strengthened its position in the important Japanese market with the acquisition of its distributor's business there. It has developed a low-price speech processor for the Chinese market, and this has been well received. The company has also acquired distributors in several key European countries, and over 75% of European sales are now through direct sales operations.

COH Year to 30 June	2004	2005
Revenues ($mn)	252.5	318.1
EBIT ($mn)	45.5	75.1
EBIT margin (%)	18.0	23.6
Gross margin (%)	69.6	71.2
Profit before tax ($mn)	47.3	74.9
Profit after tax ($mn)	36.8	54.5
Earnings per share (¢)	68.2	100.5
Cash flow per share (¢)	85.7	125.2
Dividend (¢)	79	80
Percentage franked	100	100
Net tangible assets per share ($)	2.43	~
Interest cover (times)	~	329.4
Return on equity (%)	28.4	36.3
Debt-to-equity ratio (%)	~	58.7
Current ratio	1.9	1.3

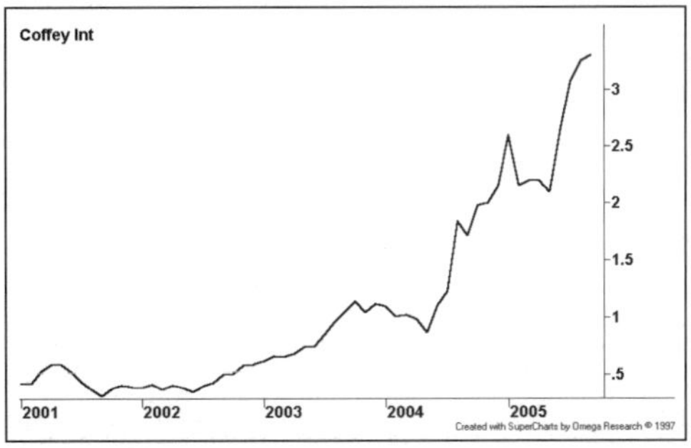

www.coffey.com.au

Coffey International Ltd

Share price ($)	3.12	
12-month high ($)	3.19	
12-month low ($)	1.20	
Market capitalisation ($mn)	203.8	
Price-to-NTA-per-share ratio	9.5	
5-year share price return (% pa)	59.5	
Sector: Industrials	**Company**	**Sector**
Price-earnings ratio (times)	19.7	16.2
Dividend yield (%)	3.4	3.6

Sydney-based Coffey, established in 1959, has grown through acquisition from its roots as a specialist scientific and engineering consulting partnership into a diverse group of consulting and project management businesses. Its consulting group operates through a string of offices in Australia and South-East Asia, and offers particular expertise in geotechnical engineering, environmental engineering, hydrogeology, hydrology, natural resources, geophysics, mining and civil engineering. Its international development business group offers project management and administration expertise in the areas of water supply and sanitation, governance, health, community development, land services, tourism, agriculture and the environment.

Latest business results (June 2005, full year)

Coffey realised another excellent result, ahead even of the most buoyant forecasts. In part this was a consequence of the company's strategy of growth through acquisition, though there was also considerable organic growth from existing businesses. The company's consulting business was the star, with revenues up 46% and pre-tax profit up 47%, with good contributions in the second half from the IT Environmental and Enesar acquisitions. International development revenues rose 12% but, due to a growing amount of lower-margin work, profits fell 13%.

Outlook

Coffey continues to expand through acquisition. It bought Specialist Training Australia in March 2005 and BFP Consultants in July 2005, and has made a $43.5 million takeover bid for project management company Farsands Solutions. It has already said that it expects profit growth of 15% to 20% in the June 2006 year, and even more if the Farsands acquisition is successful. Domestically, Coffey is a major beneficiary of strong infrastructure and resource engineering markets. Recent major contract wins include the Windsor Road Alliance in Sydney, the Inner Northern Busway in Brisbane and the Karratha to Top Price Alliance in Western Australia. The new Enesar acquisition has won several important new contracts, notably a major PNG Gas pipeline project. The international development division has a record amount of contracts under management, though the trend towards tighter margins may limit profit growth. Coffey believes its strengths in Indonesia and Sri Lanka make it well-placed to win some of the tsunami-related tenders now coming to market.

COF Year to 30 June	2004	2005
Revenues ($mn)	131.0	168.5
Consulting (%)	47	54
International development (%)	53	45
EBIT ($mn)	10.8	15.3
EBIT margin (%)	8.2	9.1
Profit before tax ($mn)	10.4	14.5
Profit after tax ($mn)	7.0	10.2
Earnings per share (¢)	11.9*	15.8
Cash flow per share (¢)	14.4*	19.1
Dividend (¢)	8.8*	10.5
Percentage franked	100	100
Net tangible assets per share ($)	0.23*	0.33
Interest cover (times)	32.6	17.7
Return on equity (%)	32.5	34.2
Debt-to-equity ratio (%)	18.7	9.2
Current ratio	1.3	1.5

* adjusted for a five-for-one share split

Coles Myer Ltd

Share price ($)	9.75	
12-month high ($)	10.11	
12-month low ($)	8.20	
Market capitalisation ($mn)	11 753.0	
Price-to-NTA-per-share ratio	3.8	
5-year share price return (% pa)	11.0	
Sector: Consumer staples	**Company**	**Sector**
Price-earnings ratio (times)	19.2	15.6
Dividend yield (%)	3.0	3.3

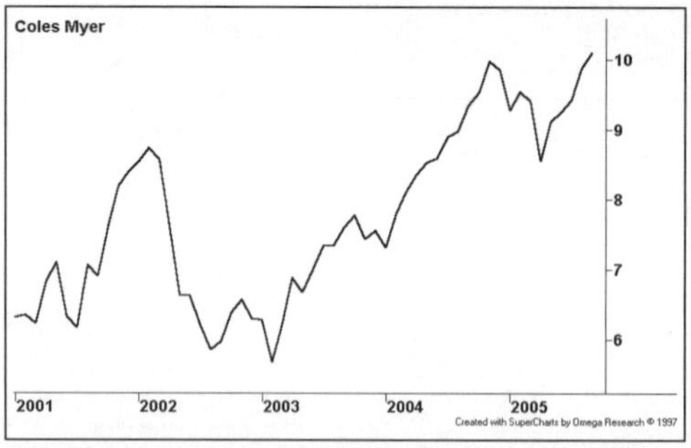

www.colesmyer.com.au

Melbourne-based Coles Myer is Australia's largest retailer and one of the biggest in the world. It operates more than 2650 stores, including Coles, Myer, Kmart, Target, Bi-Lo, Megamart, Coles Express, Liquorland, Vintage Cellars, Theo's Liquor, Harris Technology and Officeworks.

Latest business results (January 2005, half year)

Coles Myer had not officially announced its July 2005 results as this book was going to press, and the figures in the tables on this page are for January 2005. However, the company had announced that, in the year to 30 July 2005, it had achieved sales of $36.6 billion, up 13% on the previous year (note, though, that the July 2005 year comprised 53 weeks, compared to 52 weeks for July 2004). The company was expecting a July 2005 after-tax profit of around $675 million. Food and liquor comprised 53% of total sales, with turnover up 7%. Coles Express—incorporating the company's petrol business—saw a big 75% jump in sales, reflecting higher petrol prices and the continued roll-out of new outlets. Officeworks continued its expansion, with double-digit growth in sales, and there was single-digit sales growth for Myer, Kmart and Target. The Megamart business saw sales down.

CML Year to 25 July*	2003	2004
Revenues ($mn)	27 016.6	32 266.8
EBIT ($mn)	680.4	888.1
EBIT margin (%)	2.5	2.8
Gross margin (%)	27.4	25.4
Profit before tax ($mn)	617.2	874.6
Profit after tax ($mn)	429.5	616.5
Earnings per share (¢)	36.0	50.7
Cash flow per share (¢)	78.3	94.1
Dividend (¢)	26	29
Percentage franked	100	100
Interest cover (times)	10.8	65.8
Return on equity (%)	12.1	15.7

* 27 July 2003

Half year to 23 January**	2004	2005
Revenues ($mn)	15 871.1	18 426.9
Food, liquor & fuel (%)	62	66
Kmart (%)	13	12
Myer & Megamart (%)	11	9
Target (%)	10	9
Officeworks (%)	3	3
Profit before tax ($mn)	501.3	577.7
Profit after tax ($mn)	349.5	403.8
Earnings per share (¢)	26.9	31.0
Dividend (¢)	14	16.25
Percentage franked	100	100
Net tangible assets per share ($)	2.24	2.54
Debt-to-equity ratio (%)	4.5	2.0
Current ratio	1.3	1.1

**25 January 2004

Outlook

Coles Myer believes it is still on track to deliver an $800 million after-tax profit in July 2006, and has begun the development of Coles Myer's next five-year development plan. It has launched the 1st Choice liquor superstore chain with the initial two stores in Melbourne. It has also announced a major move into own-brand supermarket products, which carry the potential of higher margins than regular branded goods. Kmart and Target store sales remain firm, though could be hurt by any slowdown in consumer spending. Myer department stores and Megamart electrical goods stores have been adversely affected by the removal of the Coles Myer shareholders' discount card. The company has announced that it is considering the sale of the Myer chain, and it also plans to sell its nine Megamart stores.

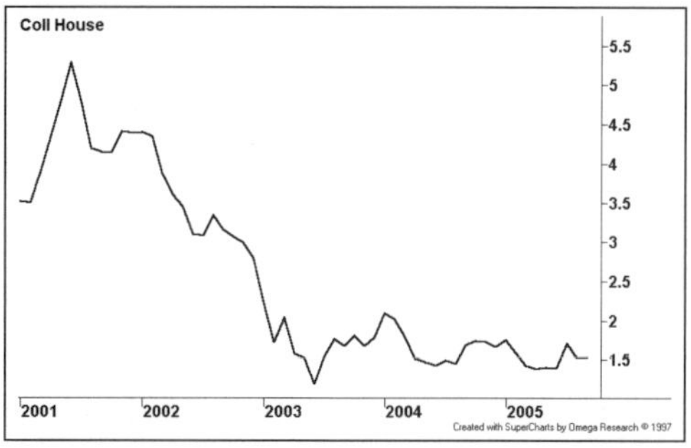

www.collectionhouse.com.au

Collection House Ltd

Share price ($)	1.66	
12-month high ($)	1.87	
12-month low ($)	1.28	
Market capitalisation ($mn)	163.3	
Price-to-NTA-per-share ratio	2.3	
4-year share price return (% pa)	–15.5	
Sector: Industrials	**Company**	**Sector**
Price-earnings ratio (times)	13.2	16.2
Dividend yield (%)	4.8	3.6

Brisbane-based Collection House, founded in 1992, is a leading receivables management company, with operations in Australia and New Zealand. It divides its activities into four main groupings: account asset management handles the collection of debts from client ledgers acquired by the company; contingent collection services involves the earning of commission on the collection of debts for clients; credit reporting is the provision of consumer credit enquiry information on a fee-for-service basis; and other operations include insurance claims services and corporate risk rating.

Latest business results (June 2005, full year)

The company reported a solid increase in revenues and profits. Its debt purchasing business—the account asset management division—was the driving force, with revenues up 27% to $54.3 million and profits ahead by 43%. The other two main divisions, credit reporting and contingent collection services, both saw revenues and profits down. There was good growth among the company's diverse other operations, with revenues up 63% to $6 million, though this group of businesses remained in the red.

Outlook

Collection House has had a volatile profit and share price performance since its 2000 listing. Its debt recovery business stands to do well if interest rates rise, and could also benefit from the prevailing record high levels of consumer credit. The company is striving to purchase debt ledgers at more attractive multiples, and this is one of the factors behind the strong profit growth—ahead of sales growth—in the latest results. It is also benefiting from a new focus on cost containment, including a 5% reduction in employee costs during the June 2005 year. Based on trends in Europe and the United States, Collection House has made the claim that the purchased-debt business is one of the most significant emerging segments of the Australian financial services industry, and it is forecasting strong continued growth for its account asset management division. Looking ahead, it also expects to reap further benefits in the June 2006 year from its cost containment programme. It also forecasts an improvement in margins for its credit reporting division. The company is investigating the possibility of separate stock market listings for two of its subsidiaries Australian Business Research and risk report specialist Rapid Ratings.

CLH Year to 30 June	2004	2005
Revenues ($mn)	116.5	125.1
Account asset management (%)	37	43
Contingent collection services (%)	40	34
Credit reporting (%)	20	17
EBIT ($mn)	18.2	21.1
EBIT margin (%)	15.7	16.8
Profit before tax ($mn)	15.3	17.6
Profit after tax ($mn)	10.6	12.2
Earnings per share (¢)	11.0	12.6
Cash flow per share (¢)	29.2	37.5
Dividend (¢)	7	8
Percentage franked	0	0
Net tangible assets per share ($)	0.65	0.72
Interest cover (times)	6.2	6.2
Return on equity (%)	12.3	13.1
Debt-to-equity ratio (%)	46.8	55.0
Current ratio	2.0	1.7

Colorado Group Ltd

Share price ($)	4.73	
12-month high ($)	6.58	
12-month low ($)	4.30	
Market capitalisation ($mn)	435.5	
Price-to-NTA-per-share ratio	3.5	
5-year share price return (% pa)	33.0	
Sector: Consumer discretionary	**Company**	**Sector**
Price-earnings ratio (times)	9.7	24.2
Dividend yield (%)	5.1	1.2

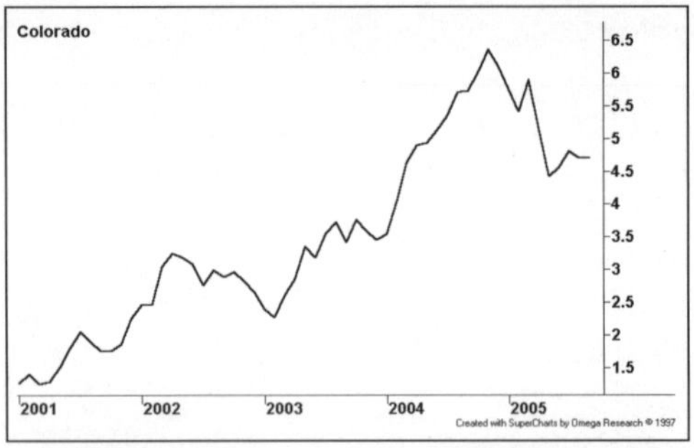

www.coloradogroup.com.au

Brisbane-based Colorado, with roots dating back to the establishment of the first Williams shoe store in Ballarat in 1864, is a prominent footwear and apparel retailer and wholesaler. It comprises 400 stores in Australia and New Zealand, across five divisions—Colorado Adventurewear, Mathers Shoes, Williams the Shoemen, Diana Ferrari and Jag.

Latest business results (January 2005, full year)

Continuing strong consumer spending and the impact of the stronger dollar propelled Colorado to a stunning rise in profits, despite only a modest gain in sales revenues. Each of the company's five divisions contributed to the result. The Colorado stores were especially strong, thanks to greater penetration into the lucrative women's wear market, offsetting weaker demand for men's wear. The Williams stores also posted a further strong result. The Mathers shoe business saw sales flat for the year, but profits were up. Jag and Diana Ferrari were also strong. The after-tax profit also received a $1.6 million boost from a change in the company's inventory accounting procedures.

Outlook

Colorado has been a prominent beneficiary of surging consumer spending in Australia, but is now being affected by a slowdown in this spending. It has already announced that first-quarter business was below expectations, and that first-half profits would likely be weak. Consequently, the level of full-year profit will depend heavily on the crucial Christmas 2005 trading period, but the latest company forecast (issued in August 2005) is that profits will drop by about 5% in the January 2006 year. During 2004, the company implemented a new $10 million retail stock management system, and this is expected to reduce costs and boost efficiencies across all businesses. It is also doubling capital spending for stores, and during 2005 it expects to open around 30 new stores and refurbish a further 100. Its new 'Project LINK' supply chain initiative is intended to streamline inventory management processes, delivering significant cost benefits in coming years. With no net debt, it is also eager to grow by acquisition, and management has already indicated that Colorado might expand into the accessories business. If suitable acquisition opportunities fail to present themselves, the company may arrange some kind of capital return to shareholders.

CDO Year to 29 January*	2004	2005
Revenues ($mn)	440.8	466.5
EBIT ($mn)	42.5	62.3
EBIT margin (%)	9.6	13.4
Gross margin (%)	50.9	55.7
Profit before tax ($mn)	41.5	62.8
Profit after tax ($mn)	28.8	44.2
Earnings per share (¢)	32.6	48.9
Cash flow per share (¢)	46.3	61.2
Dividend (¢)	16	24
Percentage franked	100	100
Net tangible assets per share ($)	1.02	1.36
Interest cover (times)	40.3	~
Return on equity (%)	29.3	34.3
Debt-to-equity ratio (%)	~	~
Current ratio	2.3	2.4

* 31 January 2004

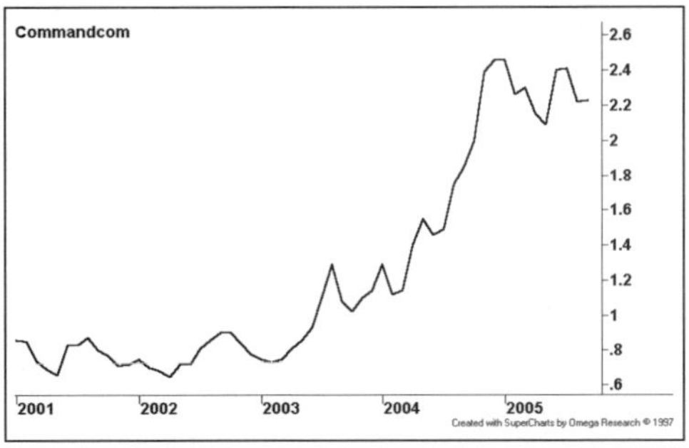

www.commander.com.au

Commander Communications Ltd

Share price ($)	2.51
12-month high ($)	2.60
12-month low ($)	1.51
Market capitalisation ($mn)	434.2
Price-to-NTA-per-share ratio	8.0
4-year share price return (% pa)	37.1

Sector: Information technology	Company	Sector
Price-earnings ratio (times)	17.3	34.4
Dividend yield (%)	2.4	1.7

Melbourne telecommunications company Commander Communications was founded in 1998 as a joint venture between Plessey and Telstra, and was originally called PlesTel. It has grown from its origins as a simple seller of business telephone systems due to some major acquisitions, notably Centari Systems (a systems integration and IT business) and RSL COM (a national fixed-line service provider). Now it is a specialist in the provision of a wide range of telecommunications services, including telephone systems, computer systems, broadband internet and website hosting, to small and medium-sized enterprises. Its customer base includes more than 60 000 businesses, with an estimated one million individual users of its business telephone systems.

Latest business results (June 2005, full year)

Commander achieved an excellent result, experiencing growth across all its business segments. Network services sales were up more than 10%, with profits ahead 34%. The key to this growth was the bundling of network services with 40% of the voice systems that the company sold. Also driving growth was the successful introduction of mobile phone products. The data services business saw sales up 63% with profits soaring 87%, thanks to the August 2004 acquisition of Axon (an IT products and services company), which increased volume with key suppliers, leading to increased supplier support and improved economies of scale. The voice services business achieved revenues growth of 11%, but profits were only up 2%, due to a decline in high-margin maintenance business and moves into lower-margin wholesale activities.

Outlook

Commander was one of the noteworthy survivors of the tech wreck of 2000, and it has continued to thrive. It works with some of the world's leading technology companies—including NEC, Nortel Networks, Siemens, Lake Communications, Hewlett-Packard, Microsoft, Cisco Systems and Toshiba—in providing communications products to Australian businesses under the Commander brand. A series of strategic acquisitions has prompted it to grow rapidly. The Axon acquisition has achieved immediate synergies, and has reinforced the company's strength in the education sector. In June 2005, it acquired Personal Broadband Australia, considerably enhancing its data network services. It is investing heavily in reducing costs and in enhancing its appeal to skilled IT personnel.

CDR Year to 30 June	2004	2005
Revenues ($mn)	479.1	599.9
Network services (%)	48	42
Data hardware & services (%)	27	36
Voice hardware & services (%)	25	22
EBIT ($mn)	10.6	31.5
EBIT margin (%)	2.2	5.2
Gross margin (%)	23.6	19.2
Profit before tax ($mn)	7.3	27.5
Profit after tax ($mn)	9.5	23.6
Earnings per share (¢)	6.5	14.5
Cash flow per share (¢)	15.5	24.0
Dividend (¢)	2	6
Percentage franked	100	100
Net tangible assets per share ($)	~	0.31
Interest cover (times)	3.2	7.9
Return on equity (%)	7.8	14.3
Debt-to-equity ratio (%)	40.8	10.5
Current ratio	1.0	1.3

Commonwealth Bank of Australia

Share price ($)	37.41	
12-month high ($)	39.64	
12-month low ($)	28.79	
Market capitalisation ($mn)	47 728.8	
Price-to-NTA-per-share ratio	2.4	
5-year share price return (% pa)	12.1	
Sector: Financials	**Company**	**Sector**
Price-earnings ratio (times)	11.9	14.3
Dividend yield (%)	5.3	4.5

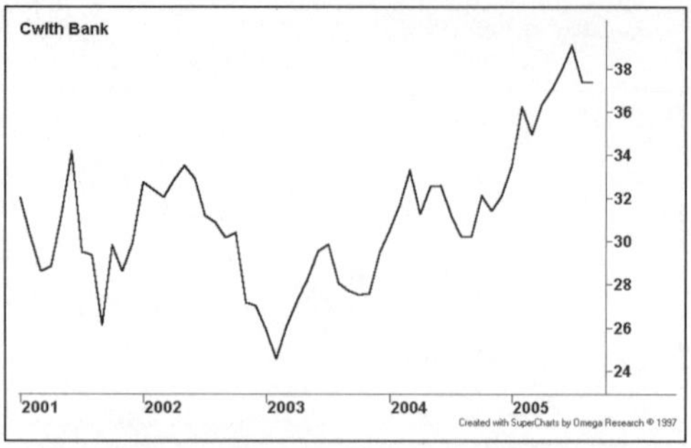

www.commbank.com.au

Australia's second-largest bank, with over seven million retail customers, the CBA is the country's top provider of home loans, personal loans and credit cards, and the largest holder of deposits. It is also Australia's largest funds manager, through Commonwealth Financial Services and Colonial First State, and the third-largest life insurer. Commonwealth Securities has become Australia's largest online stockbroker. It has significant interests in New Zealand through ASB Bank.

Latest business results (June 2005, full year)

The Commonwealth Bank reported an excellent result, with profits higher than much of the market had expected. Most areas of operation were strong, with the core banking business recording an after-tax profit increase of 11%, driven by continuing good growth in home lending and despite a decline in the net interest margin. The funds management business reported a 28% jump in profit, with funds under administration rising 12% to $123 billion. Insurance business profit rose 21%. Much of the excellent result was attributed to the CBA's three-year, $1.5-billion 'Which new Bank' restructuring program, which delivered $724 million in benefits and helped bring about a substantial reduction in the bank's cost to income ratio. New Zealand business was also strong, the bank reporting increased market share across all segments.

Outlook

Fears that CBA's strong exposure to home lending—it holds an estimated 20% of the national market—would be damaging in the event of a housing slowdown have so far not materialised, with buoyant levels of business lending offsetting a slowing of demand for housing credit. The 'Which new Bank' program remains on track to deliver annual net benefits of at least $900 million from 2006. However, the bank anticipates that strong competition—particularly for deposits—will bring about continuing declines in the interest margin. The new CommSee program, designed to enhance customer service, has been implemented for more than half the bank's customers. CBA plans to develop a financial service presence in select Asian markets, and has announced a series of acquisitions, including the private banking arm of a leading Singapore stockbroker, and equity stakes in two of China's leading commercial banks.

CBA Year to 30 June	2004	2005
Operating income ($mn)	10 491.0	11 354.0
Net interest income ($mn)	5410.0	5966.0
Operating expenses ($mn)	6249.0	5847.0
Profit before tax ($mn)	3843.0	5638.0
Profit after tax ($mn)	2572.0	3991.0
Earnings per share (¢)	204.8	313.5
Dividend (¢)	183	197
Percentage franked	100	100
Non-interest income to total income (%)	48.4	47.5
Net tangible assets per share ($)	14.00	15.53
Cost to income ratio (%)	59.6	51.5
Return on equity (%)	12.1	17.1
Return on assets (%)	0.9	1.3

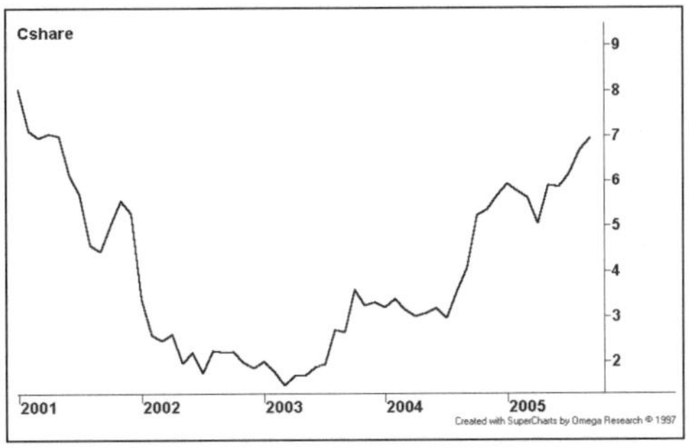

www.computershare.com.au

Computershare Ltd

Share price ($)	6.70	
12-month high ($)	6.74	
12-month low ($)	3.14	
Market capitalisation ($mn)	3902.5	
Price-to-NTA-per-share ratio	na	
5-year share price return (% pa)	–2.5	
Sector: Information technology	**Company**	**Sector**
Price-earnings ratio (times)	45.0	34.4
Dividend yield (%)	1.6	1.7

Melbourne-based Computershare, established in 1978, is one of the world's leading financial services and technology providers for the global securities industry, offering services to listed companies, investors, employees, exchanges and other financial institutions. It is the world's only global share registry/transfer agent, managing more than 90 million shareholder accounts for over 14 000 corporations in 21 countries. In Australia it arranges registry services for more than half of all companies, as well as 80% of those in New Zealand, 60% in Canada, 50% in Germany and significant proportions in Britain, Ireland, South Africa, the United States and Hong Kong. More recently it has moved into Russia, and it is launching a joint venture operation in Japan.

Latest business results (June 2005, full year)

Computershare enjoyed another surge in sales and profits as it continued its global expansion. North American revenues were up 32%, and now represent more than 40% of company turnover, thanks to growing demand for share-registry services and some major new customers. However, North American profits fell, and profitability in the region remains lower than elsewhere. Asia Pacific revenues (31% of the total) rose 25%, with profits surging more than 50%, thanks to buoyant stock market activity and new business wins. European and South African revenues fell, though profits edged up.

Outlook

Computershare appears to be back on a high-growth trajectory, and it is forecasting that June 2006 revenues will grow to around $1.5 billion, with EPS up by more than 20%. It expects to see significant benefits from its biggest-ever acquisition, EquiServe, announced in 2004 but being integrated into the company from mid-2005. EquiServe provides share-registry and employee plan administration services to about 1300 US clients, including more than half of the 30 corporations in the Dow Jones Industrial Average index. Computershare expects high growth in the management of employee share plans for companies, seeing this becoming a market as big as its share-registry business. It has expressed its desire to be a major participant in Japanese share-registry services, and has initiated talks with potential partners. Its share-registry business — often involving the holding of money in trust for customers — means that Computershare would be a big beneficiary of any rise in US interest rates.

CPU Year to 30 June	2004	2005
Revenues ($mn)	871.2	1063.5
EBIT ($mn)	116.1	127.4
EBIT margin (%)	13.3	12.0
Profit before tax ($mn)	110.7	117.7
Profit after tax ($mn)	77.8	83.2
Earnings per share (¢)	14.2	14.9
Cash flow per share (¢)	25.2	27.8
Dividend (¢)	8	11
Percentage franked	100	5
Net tangible assets per share ($)	~	~
Interest cover (times)	21.4	13.2
Return on equity (%)	13.2	12.4
Debt-to-equity ratio (%)	36.6	69.7
Current ratio	1.0	1.0

Corporate Express Australia Ltd

Share price ($)	6.24	
12-month high ($)	6.75	
12-month low ($)	5.11	
Market capitalisation ($mn)	1128.0	
Price-to-NTA-per-share ratio	14.1	
4-year share price return (% pa)	12.6	
Sector: Industrials	**Company**	**Sector**
Price-earnings ratio (times)	20.5	16.2
Dividend yield (%)	2.4	3.6

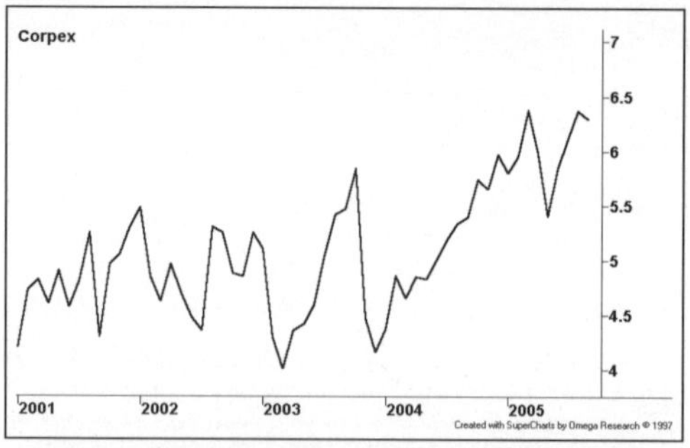

www.ce.com.au

Sydney-based Corporate Express, a 52%-owned subsidiary of the Dutch-based office provisions giant Buhrmann, has become Australia's largest distributor of office supplies to business. As well as basic office provisions, its products and services include information technology (IT) equipment and supplies, business furniture, janitorial supplies, print services, promotional marketing, and liquor, coffee and kitchen supplies. It services some 38 000 corporate customers from a string of 45 regional offices throughout Australia and New Zealand.

Latest business results (June 2005, half year)

The company recorded another firm gain in sales and profits, even after revising up its June 2004 profit figures, in order to restate previous figures in accord with the new Australian International Financial Reporting Standards. The large contract office-products customer sector was relatively flat, but the small and mid-sized customer sectors remained strong. IT-related sales—both hardware and software—were especially buoyant. Part of the good result came through the acquisition during the period of five new businesses in office products, machine services and facilities management. These five businesses have total annualised revenues of around $11.5 million. The company realised good business from the continued roll-out of its janitorial services and from its new facilities supplies division.

CXP Year to 31 December	2003	2004
Revenues ($mn)	896.3	982.6
EBIT ($mn)	68.7	85.6
EBIT margin (%)	7.7	8.7
Gross margin (%)	23.2	26.4
Profit before tax ($mn)	67.5	85.6
Profit after tax ($mn)	45.7	58.2
Earnings per share (¢)	24.0	30.4
Cash flow per share (¢)	30.6	37.9
Dividend (¢)	13	15
Percentage franked	100	100
Interest cover (times)	57.3	~
Return on equity (%)	28.4	31.1
Half year to 30 June	**2004**	**2005**
Revenues ($mn)	470.0	537.2
Profit before tax ($mn)	43.2	46.0
Profit after tax ($mn)	30.0	32.0
Earnings per share (¢)	15.7	17.2
Dividend (¢)	7	8.5
Percentage franked	100	100
Net tangible assets per share ($)	0.48	0.44
Debt-to-equity ratio (%)	~	7.9
Current ratio	1.3	1.2

Outlook

Corporate Express has achieved strong growth over an extended period through an aggressive policy of corporate acquisition. Many of the more than 45 businesses it has acquired have been small, niche office-supply distributors, lacking the capital to expand, but with solid customer bases. The company has said that it will continue this acquisition policy, though some concerns have been expressed that quality takeover targets are now becoming scarce. The company also continues to expand the range of products and services it is able to offer its corporate customers, and specialty businesses—such as janitorial services, promotional marketing, printing services, business furniture, canteen supplies and liquor—now represent 46% of total sales. Management believe these businesses present the best potential for long-term growth. The company has conceded that it is being hurt by rising fuel costs, and it is working on counter-measures, including improved efficiencies and price adjustments.

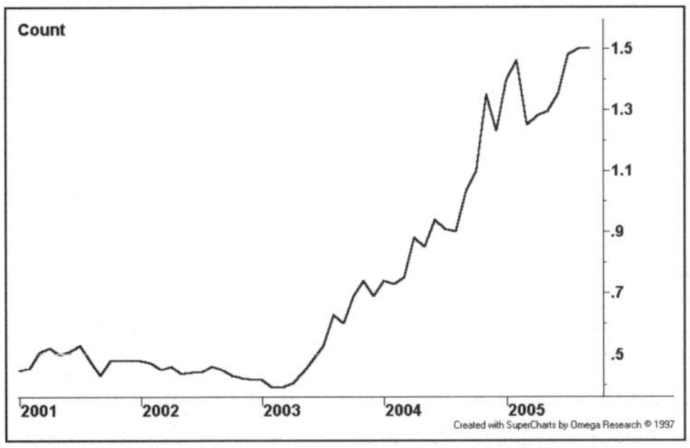

www.count.com.au

Count Financial Ltd

Share price ($)	1.48	
12-month high ($)	1.55	
12-month low ($)	0.86	
Market capitalisation ($mn)	340.9	
Price-to-NTA-per-share ratio	21.0	
4-year share price return (% pa)	35.6	
Sector: Financials	**Company**	**Sector**
Price-earnings ratio (times)	27.1	14.3
Dividend yield (%)	3.0	4.5

Sydney-based financial services specialist Count Financial was established in 1980, and has since grown into Australia's largest independently owned network of financial planning accountants and advisers. It consists of a franchise network of around 460 (mainly accountancy) practices, employing more than 1000 financial advisers. It provides financial planning services and holds investment funds under management.

Latest business results (June 2005, full year)

With the stock market and the financial services industry booming, Count Financial achieved an excellent result. Fees and commission income rose 9% to $12.25 million, thanks especially to increasing fees from lending and insurance businesses. Asset-based income soared 29% to $13.6 million. Profits were also helped by a steady lowering of costs, including a contribution from a head office move to smaller premises and a slight reduction in staff numbers. At year-end, funds under management were up 36% to $8.62 million, with loans outstanding totalling $1.66 billion, which was up 34%.

Outlook

With growing numbers of baby boomers worried about their retirement and superannuation, the Australian financial planning industry continues to boom, and Count is a leading beneficiary. It is already forecasting June 2006 EBIT growth of at least 30%, with a projected full-year dividend of 4.5¢ per share. It also continues to lower costs, with its expense-to-income ratio falling sharply from 64% in the June 2002 year to 45% in June 2005, and expected to fall below 40% in June 2006. Its three-pronged strategy for continued growth involves boosting the number of franchisees, boosting their productivity—particularly through the introduction of new computer systems—and adding new services. It has introduced commercial loans and a salary packaging service, and plans a new margin-lending broking service. It is also devising new strategies to assist high-net-worth individuals. It sees good prospects from new rules allowing employees to choose their superannuation scheme. It continues to attract more accountancy firms to its network and, as it is able to slot each new member company into its existing systems, its profitability could increase as the company grows larger. It also actively lends money to its franchisees in order to help them grow, and believes it will be able to fund loan growth of around $5 million annually for some years.

COU Year to 30 June	2004	2005
Revenues ($mn)	69.0	83.5
EBIT ($mn)	12.1	16.9
EBIT margin (%)	17.6	20.3
Profit before tax ($mn)	12.5	17.4
Profit after tax ($mn)	9.0	12.3
Earnings per share (¢)	4.1	5.5
Cash flow per share (¢)	4.6	5.8
Dividend (¢)	3.5	4.5
Percentage franked	100	100
Net tangible assets per share ($)	0.06	0.07
Interest cover (times)	~	~
Return on equity (%)	69.0	85.3
Debt-to-equity ratio (%)	~	~
Current ratio	1.8	1.8

CSL LTD

Share price ($)	35.51
12-month high ($)	35.85
12-month low ($)	23.86
Market capitalisation ($mn)	6465.6
Price-to-NTA-per-share ratio	5.0
5-year share price return (% pa)	1.3

Sector: Health care	Company	Sector
Price-earnings ratio (times)	23.4	28.0
Dividend yield (%)	1.3	1.7

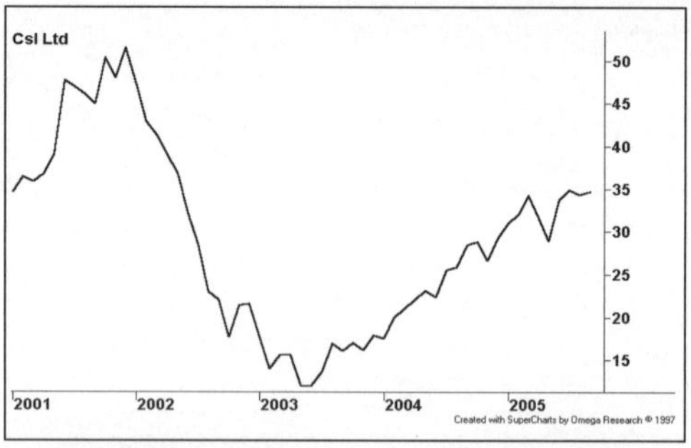

www.csl.com.au

Melbourne-based CSL, formerly the state-owned Commonwealth Serum Laboratories, was founded in 1916. It is one of Australia's largest investors in pharmaceutical research, operating principally through three broad groupings — CSL Bioplasma, CSL Pharmaceutical and ZLB Behring, which incorporates ZLB Plasma Services. Its plasma products include immunoglobulins to treat infections, autoimmune diseases and for preventing haemolytic disease in newborn babies; plasma volume expanders to treat acute blood loss and severe burns; and clotting factors to treat bleeding disorders. Its pharmaceutical products include paediatric and adult vaccines; treatments for infections and severe pain; products for skin disorders; and antivenoms for poisonous bites and stings. It operates from major facilities in Australia, Germany, Switzerland, America and Japan. It has high market shares for many of its products, and exports to numerous countries.

Latest business results (June 2005, full year)

Sales and profits soared, thanks to the positive impact from the inclusion of a full 12 months of trading by ZLB Behring, which was acquired in March 2004. The results were also boosted by good volume growth in the sale of the haemophilia drug Helixate. Research and development expenditure of $146 million was up 44% on the previous year. An after-tax profit of $250 million from the sale of JRH Biosciences, CSL's cell culture business, was treated as a significant item.

Outlook

CSL has become one of Australia's most successful pharmaceuticals company, with a global reach for its products. With integration of ZLB Behring virtually accomplished, the company is now starting to reap substantial synergies. In particular, during the June 2006 year and beyond, CSL expects to benefit from the sale of surplus ZLB Behring inventory. It views the plasma therapeutics industry as being in the final stages of consolidation, with supply and demand moving into balance, and it expects to be able to gain from the lower-cost manufacturing base that it has put into place. US pharmaceuticals giant Merck is well-advanced in its phase III clinical trial program on the human papillomavirus vaccine for cervical cancer that it has licensed from CSL, and a substantial flow of royalty payments to CSL is expected. The company has announced that it expects June 2006 sales revenues to be roughly the same as June 2005, but margin growth would push EPS up by about 10%.

CSL Year to 30 June	2004	2005
Revenues ($mn)	1650.2	2749.9
EBIT ($mn)	268.8	386.7
EBIT margin (%)	16.3	14.1
Gross margin (%)	35.2	38.7
Profit before tax ($mn)	254.6	362.2
Profit after tax ($mn)	144.6	296.9
Earnings per share (¢)	81.2	151.5
Cash flow per share (¢)	154.1	238.6
Dividend (¢)	38	47
Percentage franked	100	100
Net tangible assets per share ($)	6.18	7.07
Interest cover (times)	18.9	15.8
Return on equity (%)	8.6	14.3
Debt-to-equity ratio (%)	35.4	14.5
Current ratio	2.9	4.2

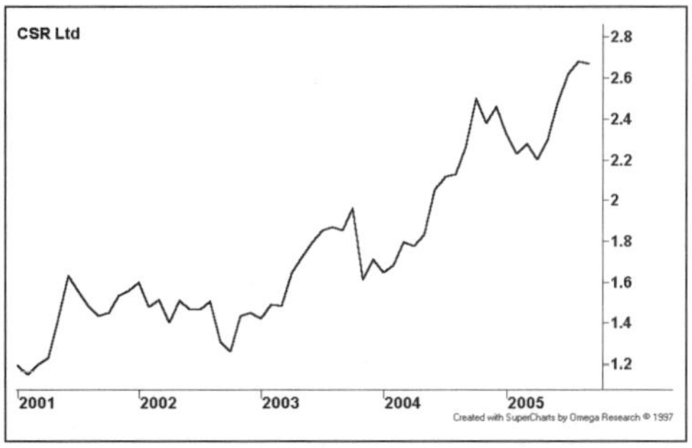

www.csr.com.au

CSR Ltd

Share price ($)	2.72	
12-month high ($)	2.80	
12-month low ($)	2.05	
Market capitalisation ($mn)	2394.3	
Price-to-NTA-per-share ratio	2.1	
5-year share price return (% pa)	29.6	
Sector: Materials	**Company**	**Sector**
Price-earnings ratio (times)	12.4	17.0
Dividend yield (%)	4.4	2.2

CSR, founded in 1855 as a sugar refiner, returned to its roots with the 2003 demerger of its Rinker construction materials business into a separate company, also listed on the stock exchange. CSR now operates principally in three separate industries: it is one of the world's leading sugar producers; it makes building products, such as bricks, pavers, plasterboard and roofing tiles; and it owns 70% of Gove Aluminium Finance, which holds more than a third of the equity of NSW's Tomago Aluminium Smelter, responsible for the production of about a quarter of Australia's aluminium output. Most recently, CSR has been working to establish a property development business.

Latest business results (March 2005, full year)

A recovery in world sugar prices helped push CSR to a big gain in revenues and profits. Sugar revenues were up 60% and profits more than doubled. Productivity initiatives and improved weather conditions boosted the sugarcane crop, and the company was also helped by accounting changes and by payments from the government's sugar reform programme. Building product revenues edged up, but higher costs meant that profits dipped. Higher sales prices boosted aluminium revenues, but increased alumina costs depressed profits. Nevertheless, aluminium contributes nearly 40% of company profit, despite representing just 20% of sales. Property EBIT soared 80% to $28.6 million, following the handover of land for a major residential development in Woodcroft, Sydney.

Outlook

CSR is working to restructure and rationalise its remaining businesses. Having apparently been unsuccessful in finding a buyer for its sugar operations, it is now boosting this business, including the construction of a $160-million electricity plant at its Pioneer sugar mill in North Queensland, to generate renewable electricity from sugarcane waste fibre. It expects a slowing home construction market to reduce demand for building products, but expects operational improvements and sales to the commercial sector to sustain profits. CSR expects the redevelopment of surplus industrial property assets to provide a growing stream of profits in coming years. It has approved $32 million to redevelop a 100-hectare former quarry site at Erskine Park, Sydney, and also expects significant income from continuing residential developments at Ferntree Gully, Melbourne.

CSR Year to 31 March	2004	2005
Revenues ($mn)	1970.8	2367.5
Building products (%)	46	39
Sugar—milling (%)	27	26
Aluminium (%)	23	20
Sugar—ethanol & refining (%)	3	13
EBIT ($mn)	262.7	322.0
EBIT margin (%)	13.3	13.6
Gross margin (%)	28.9	26.7
Profit before tax ($mn)	249.7	303.1
Profit after tax ($mn)	160.2	200.8
Earnings per share (¢)	17.1	21.9
Cash flow per share (¢)	28.5	34.6
Dividend (¢)	11	12
Percentage franked	70	100
Net tangible assets per share ($)	1.13	1.31
Interest cover (times)	20.2	17.0
Return on equity (%)	14.9	17.4
Debt-to-equity ratio (%)	14.3	19.7
Current ratio	1.2	1.7

CVC Ltd

Share price ($)	1.40	
12-month high ($)	2.28	
12-month low ($)	1.03	
Market capitalisation ($mn)	184.8	
Price-to-NTA-per-share ratio	1.3	
5-year share price return (% pa)	17.0	
Sector: Financials	**Company**	**Sector**
Price-earnings ratio (times)	5.5	14.3
Dividend yield (%)	3.6	4.5

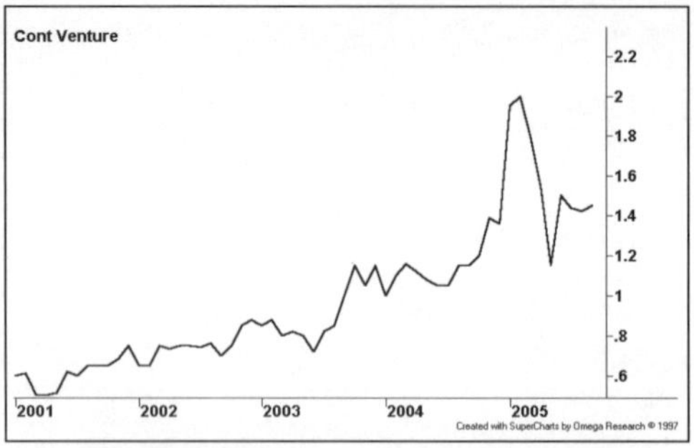

www.cvcltd.com.au

Sydney finance company CVC was founded in 1984 as Continental Venture Capital. It provides venture capital to new businesses. It also seeks investment opportunities in profitable, high-growth companies, and typically invests between $1 million and $5 million, then works with company managers in developing the business. Through its investment company CVC Sustainable Investments and its CVC Renewable Energy Equity Fund, it has a particular interest in environmentally friendly ventures. In addition, it assists management buyouts of companies, and it is also involved in property development.

Latest business results (June 2005, full year)

CVC enjoyed an excellent year, with a big leap in its profits. A major contribution came from the sale of the Chevron Renaissance shopping centre on the Gold Coast, in which CVC held a 50% stake. The sale netted CVC a profit of approximately $10 million. A further $9 million profit derived from the sale of shares in the Surfers Paradise property development and management company Sunland Group. There was also a $3 million profit from the sell-down of shares into the public listing of Pro-Pac Packaging. At the end of June 2005, CVC still held 13% of the equity of Sunland Group and 15% of Pro-Pac Packaging.

Outlook

CVC is a finance company, and its profits can be quite dependent on issues of timing. Thus, it is difficult to forecast whether profits will rise or fall in any particular financial year. Nevertheless, the company has been steadily building its recurrent earnings base — including a series of new initiatives during the June 2005 year — and the long-term outlook is favourable. Together with Winten Property Group it is undertaking a 200-lot property development in NSW known as Fern Bay Seaside Village, and sees this as providing a significant revenue stream for many years. In another joint venture, it has bought land at Belrose in Sydney for development as a bulky goods centre. It is working with Ron Finemore, former executive chairman of the listed Finemore Holdings, in the development of a new road-freight transportation venture, and has acquired the leading livestock transporter Lewingtons, as the first of an expected series of acquisitions. Another of CVC's investments, the functional food and natural health supplement maker Probiotec, could seek a public listing.

CVC Year to 30 June	2004	2005
Revenues ($mn)	47.6	61.8
EBIT ($mn)	9.3	27.5
EBIT margin (%)	19.6	44.6
Profit before tax ($mn)	12.2	30.5
Profit after tax ($mn)	10.1	29.0
Earnings per share (¢)	9.4	25.4
Cash flow per share (¢)	10.0	26.4
Dividend (¢)	3	5
Percentage franked	100	100
Net tangible assets per share ($)	0.73	1.04
Interest cover (times)	~	~
Return on equity (%)	12.6	26.1
Debt-to-equity ratio (%)	~	~
Current ratio	2.0	36.6

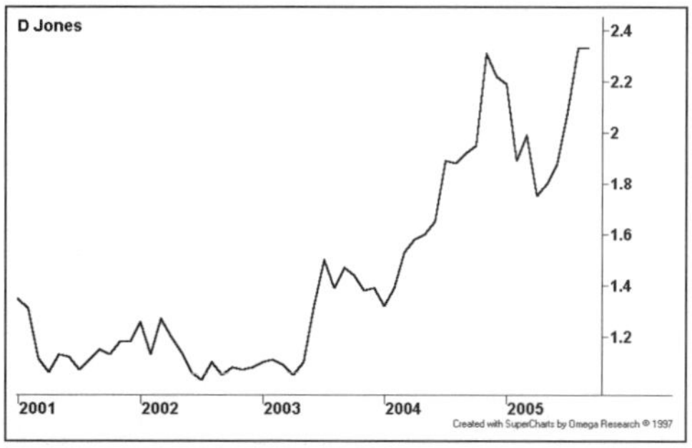

www.davidjones.com.au

David Jones Ltd

Share price ($)	2.19
12-month high ($)	2.40
12-month low ($)	1.63
Market capitalisation ($mn)	957.0
Price-to-NTA-per-share ratio	2.1
5-year share price return (% pa)	19.7

Sector: Consumer discretionary	Company	Sector
Price-earnings ratio (times)	13.8	24.2
Dividend yield (%)	5.0	1.2

Sydney-based retailer David Jones dates back to 1838 and the opening of the David Jones & Company general store in Sydney. It is Australia's oldest department store chain, and claims to be the oldest in the world still trading under its original name. It operates 36 stores, with representation in every state and in the ACT.

Latest business results (January 2005, half year)

David Jones was yet to announce its July 2005 full-year results as this book was going to press, and the latest figures in the tables on this page are the interim results to January 2005. However, the company had released its full-year sales figures, which were up 1.7% from the previous year, or 3.3% on a like-for-like basis, as the July 2004 year was 53 weeks, and the July 2005 year 52 weeks. There was good business for the company's core categories of womenswear, cosmetics, accessories, footwear and menswear. However, furniture and consumer electronics suffered in a highly competitive and deflationary environment. The company said its credit card business had shown good growth, its stock management program led to a 5.5% decline in its stock position during the year and its cost-efficiency program had achieved its targets earlier than expected. It expected a full-year after-tax profit of $77.5 million to $78.0 million.

Outlook

The company's drive to restructure and cut costs made it a significant beneficiary of the rise over many years in consumer spending, which was reflected in the share price. However, the company now faces the possibility of a slowdown in consumer spending, particularly for the upmarket items in which it specialises. In addition, it is facing intensified competition, not only from the low-cost chains like Kmart and Target, but also from its main rival Myer, which has increasingly been resorting to discounting to boost its sagging business. Coles Myer has flagged the possibility of selling the Myer stores, which could lead to a big upheaval in the Australian department store environment. David Jones sees its large credit card and financial services operation as providing a particular stimulus for future long-term profit growth.

DJS Year to 31 July*	2003	2004
Revenues ($mn)	1711.2	1769.5
EBIT ($mn)	65.3	95.3
EBIT margin (%)	3.8	5.4
Gross margin (%)	36.4	37.1
Profit before tax ($mn)	62.0	94.7
Profit after tax ($mn)	37.5	65.3
Earnings per share (¢)	9.2	15.9
Cash flow per share (¢)	20.8	26.3
Dividend (¢)	6	11
Percentage franked	100	100
Interest cover (times)	19.8	157.0
Return on equity (%)	8.6	15.1

* 26 July 2003

Half year to 29 January**	2004	2005
Revenues ($mn)	926.3	977.7
Profit before tax ($mn)	62.3	77.3
Profit after tax ($mn)	43.4	52.9
Earnings per share (¢)	9.9	12.1
Dividend (¢)	5	6
Percentage franked	100	100
Net tangible assets per share ($)	0.98	1.03
Debt-to-equity ratio (%)	~	~
Current ratio	1.8	1.9

** 24 January 2004

Downer EDI Ltd

Share price ($)	5.97	
12-month high ($)	5.98	
12-month low ($)	3.20	
Market capitalisation ($mn)	1723.9	
Price-to-NTA-per-share ratio	3.1	
5-year share price return (% pa)	24.4	
Sector: Industrials	**Company**	**Sector**
Price-earnings ratio (times)	16.4	16.2
Dividend yield (%)	3.0	3.6

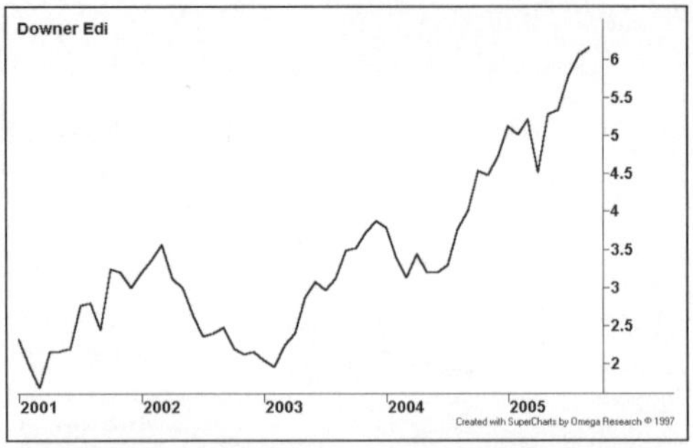

www.downeredi.com.au

Sydney-based Downer EDI—Australia's second-largest listed engineering, infrastructure and resource services company, after Leighton Holdings—has grown through a long series of mergers in Australia and New Zealand. It provides engineering and infrastructure management services to the public and private power, rail, road, telecommunications, mining and mineral processing sectors in Australia, New Zealand, Asia and the Pacific. It operates through five broad divisions: Works Infrastructure, Downer Engineering, Roche Mining, Century Resources and EDI Rail.

Latest business results (June 2005, full year)

Downer EDI continued to ride the infrastructure boom, reporting its eighth straight year of gains in sales and profits. All businesses were strong apart from rail, which saw sales and profits down following the completion of Stage 2 of the Millennium Train contract in Sydney. Mining and resources provided the best growth, with revenues up 31% and profits surging 87%. There was a noteworthy doubling of revenues from the company's Century Resources subsidiary, which is engaged in oil and gas drilling activities, and it moved out of the red into profit. Engineering division turnover was up 10%, but profits fell due to weakness in telecommunications. The infrastructure division saw revenues up 31% and profits rising 16%, with strong performances in both Australia and New Zealand.

Outlook

Downer EDI is ideally placed to take full advantage of a growing number of major rail and transport infrastructure projects that are being promoted in Australia and New Zealand. The company is also well-positioned to benefit from the continued buoyancy of the resources sector with a continuing stream of major new projects. It maintains a policy of seeking bolt-on acquisitions to broaden the scope of its businesses. It sees India emerging as a significant growth market for its new Singapore-based engineering consultancy, CPG, and it also hopes to expand this business in China. The company has flagged 2006 as a year in which it will improve earnings quality, rather than pursuing sales growth, through boosting the services side of its businesses and pursuing contract renewals and extensions. It also wishes to develop alliance-style contracts with clients, with risk and rewards shared and jointly managed. It forecasts modest 8% sales growth in the June 2006 year, though with profit rising by a higher percentage.

DOW Year to 30 June	2004	2005
Revenues ($mn)	3112.3	3724.9
Mining & resources (%)	29	34
Engineering (%)	34	33
Infrastructure services (%)	21	23
Rail (%)	13	9
EBIT ($mn)	138.6	170.6
EBIT margin (%)	4.5	4.6
Profit before tax ($mn)	109.2	131.6
Profit after tax ($mn)	81.5	104.0
Earnings per share (¢)	29.6	36.3
Cash flow per share (¢)	72.3	78.5
Dividend (¢)	13.6	18
Percentage franked	50	63
Net tangible assets per share ($)	1.75	1.92
Interest cover (times)	4.7	4.4
Return on equity (%)	10.3	12.0
Debt-to-equity ratio (%)	40.9	37.5
Current ratio	1.4	1.5

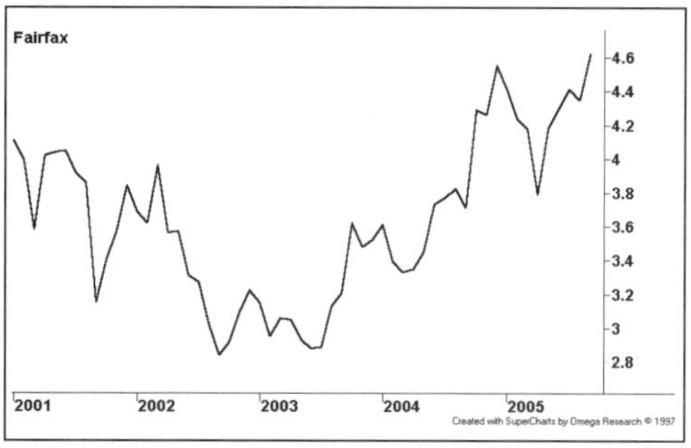

www.fxj.com.au

Fairfax (John) Holdings Ltd

Share price ($)	4.42
12-month high ($)	4.69
12-month low ($)	3.65
Market capitalisation ($mn)	4030.7
Price-to-NTA-per-share ratio	na
5-year share price return (% pa)	3.5

Sector: Consumer discretionary	Company	Sector
Price-earnings ratio (times)	16.1	24.2
Dividend yield (%)	4.2	1.2

John Fairfax Holdings is one of Australia's leading media companies. It publishes *The Sydney Morning Herald*, Melbourne's *The Age*, *The Australian Financial Review* and *BRW* magazine, as well as local and specialist newspapers and magazines. It also provides a range of online services through its Fairfax Digital subsidiary. It operates New Zealand's largest publishing business, including a string of metropolitan and regional newspapers and many magazine titles. Fairfax also owns the publishing house Text Media and 43% of AAP Information Services.

Latest business results (June 2005, full year)

Strong economic conditions in Australia and New Zealand handed Fairfax another excellent result, with declining real estate markets more than offset by buoyant conditions for most other areas of business. Australian revenues were up 5%, with advertising revenues up 4.6% and the company achieving particular success in containing costs. EBIT for this business was up 7.3%. New Zealand business, now representing 28% of the total, was strong across the board, with revenues and advertising income both up 9% and EBIT surging 19%. New Zealand is now responsible for nearly 40% of the company's profit. The Fairfax Digital operation achieved a 38% increase in revenues to $54.9 million, and was profitable at the EBIT level for the first time.

Outlook

The publishing business has high fixed costs and profits are greatly affected by economic conditions. Small increases in advertising and circulation can translate into a big rise in profits, and the reverse is also true. However, thanks in particular to the NZ acquisition in 2003, the company's operations have become more balanced than previously and far less geared to the volatile Sydney and Melbourne real estate markets. Fairfax continues to realise cost efficiencies in New Zealand and is experiencing advertising and circulation growth. Domestically, the company is seeing excellent growth from its magazine business and its regional and community newspapers. There has also been good growth for its business magazines, although the company now plans a restructure of these. The digital operation has been expanded with the addition in July 2005 of the RSVP online dating service. There has been considerable speculation that the government might change the country's cross-media ownership laws and Fairfax has said it is ready to pursue any new business opportunities that might present themselves.

FXJ Year to 30 June	2004	2005
Revenues ($mn)	1765.9	1855.1
EBIT ($mn)	368.2	425.8
EBIT margin (%)	20.9	23.0
Gross margin (%)	67.1	68.4
Profit before tax ($mn)	296.3	347.4
Profit after tax ($mn)	207.6	252.6
Earnings per share (¢)	23.4	27.5
Cash flow per share (¢)	33.1	36.5
Dividend (¢)	16.5	18.5
Percentage franked	100	100
Net tangible assets per share ($)	~	~
Interest cover (times)	5.1	5.4
Return on equity (%)	10.8	11.8
Debt-to-equity ratio (%)	52.7	1.4
Current ratio	1.0	1.0

Fantastic Holdings Ltd

Share price ($)	3.80	
12-month high ($)	5.40	
12-month low ($)	3.34	
Market capitalisation ($mn)	310.5	
Price-to-NTA-per-share ratio	8.4	
5-year share price return (% pa)	29.9	
Sector: Consumer discretionary	**Company**	**Sector**
Price-earnings ratio (times)	17.9	24.2
Dividend yield (%)	2.9	1.2

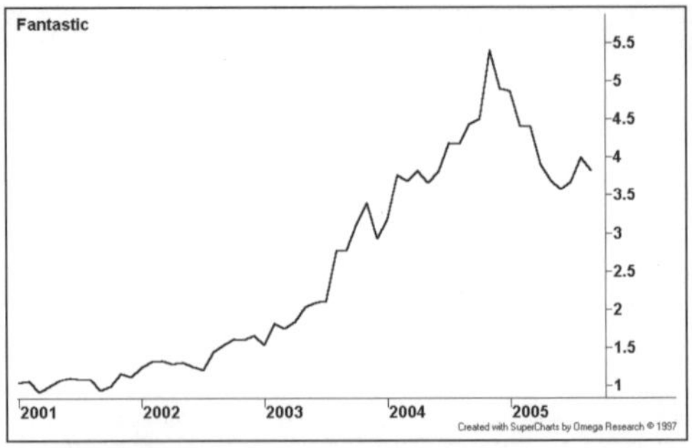

www.fantasticfurniture.com.au

Sydney-based furniture manufacturer and retailer Fantastic Holdings evolved from a struggling furniture chain that was acquired in 1996 by a group of partners, including managing director Julian Tertini, who earlier had helped launch Freedom Furniture. Today, Fantastic is one of Australia's leading budget furniture chains, with a total of 46 company-owned and franchised Fantastic Furniture stores in NSW, ACT, Victoria and Tasmania, and 14 Plush leather-goods stores in Victoria, NSW and South Australia.

Latest business results (June 2005, full year)

Fantastic achieved another surge in profits, its sixth consecutive earnings increase since listing on the ASX in 1999. Company and franchised store retail sales were up 16%, or 9% on a like-for-like basis. The good result came despite a slowdown in the housing market, rising petrol prices and increased discounting by rivals, especially in the second half of the financial year. Six new stores—two Fantastic Furniture outlets and four Plush stores—were opened during the year and contributed to the result. The company also acquired five Fantastic Furniture franchised stores, and these now operate as company stores.

Outlook

Fantastic has achieved great success in the budget furniture sector through a policy of careful planning and strict cost containment. It has slowed its policy of expansion—opening two fewer new stores in the June 2005 year than originally planned—as it believes that bulky good store rentals have risen too high in some locations. It has stated that it expects a correction in the bulky good property market, and it believes it will be able to take advantage of this. It now plans ten new store openings during the June 2006 year, including the first Fantastic Furniture stores in Queensland and South Australia. Looking to the longer term, it envisages a total of 92 Fantastic Furniture stores, in all states and territories, and 43 Plush stores. It is also considering an expansion into New Zealand. The company plans a major bulky goods value centre and testing ground in Dandenong, Victoria, and is waiting for approval from the relevant local council. Thanks to its emphasis on the budget sector, the company believes it will weather the effects of any slowdown in consumer spending on furniture if interest rates rise.

FAN Year to 30 June	2004	2005
Revenues ($mn)	183.0	221.0
EBIT ($mn)	21.9	25.4
EBIT margin (%)	12.0	11.5
Gross margin (%)	40.5	41.6
Profit before tax ($mn)	22.3	25.5
Profit after tax ($mn)	15.7	17.7
Earnings per share (¢)	21.0	21.2
Cash flow per share (¢)	22.2	22.7
Dividend (¢)	10.3	11
Percentage franked	100	100
Net tangible assets per share ($)	0.39	0.45
Interest cover (times)	~	~
Return on equity (%)	56.8	48.2
Debt-to-equity ratio (%)	~	~
Current ratio	2.1	2.2

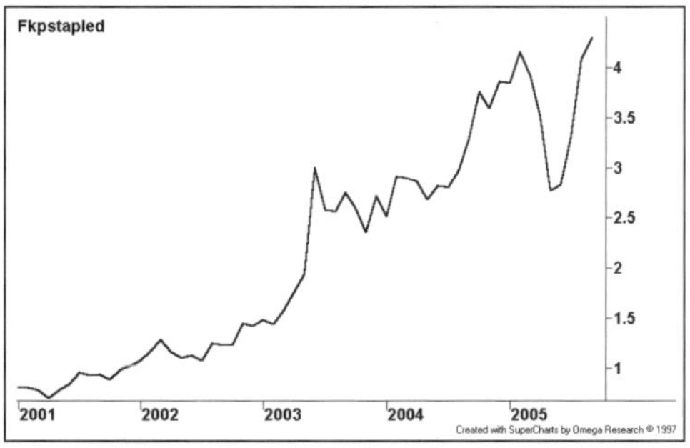

www.fkp.com.au

FKP Property Group

Share price ($)	3.85	
12-month high ($)	4.38	
12-month low ($)	2.61	
Market capitalisation ($mn)	664.0	
Price-to-NTA-per-share ratio	1.9	
5-year share price return (% pa)	46.6	
Sector: Financials	**Company**	**Sector**
Price-earnings ratio (times)	11.2	14.3
Dividend yield (%)	6.5	4.5

FKP, formerly called Forrester Kurts Properties, is a leading Queensland-based property developer, with activities that encompass construction, residential developments, commercial and retail projects, master planned residential communities and the ownership and management of retirement villages. It is active in all eastern states. Its subsidiary Australian Retirement Homes has become a leader in the aged care industry, with 28 retirement community properties, making FKP one of Australia's largest owner-operators of retirement villages. The company also manages two property trusts.

Latest business results (June 2005, full year)

FKP overcame the housing slowdown to post an excellent result, with a strong rise in profit, and strength across all its businesses. There was a particularly powerful contribution from the property investments and funds management division, which completed its first full year of operation, with EBIT soaring more than 12 times. The property development division, responsible for more than half of company turnover, saw EBIT up 11%, with good growth in residential and retirement sectors offsetting higher construction costs. The land subdivision business recorded a 20% rise in EBIT, though this mainly reflected the one-off sale of a school site to the Queensland government. The retirement investments business recorded a 35% increase in profits, partly reflecting a full year contribution from Forest Place Group, now controlled by FKP.

Outlook

In the June 2005 year, FKP generated 35% of its earnings from recurring income streams such as retirement villages and funds management—up from 18% a year earlier—with the aim of raising this to 50% by 2008. Its property investment and funds management division owns office and retail assets worth $140 million, and also manages two property trusts. As yields fall, property trusts are finding it increasingly hard to source attractive properties, and the company believes its ability to develop its own properties will become a competitive advantage. Its retirement village portfolio comprises nearly 4000 units, and with the average age of residents now 80 years old it expects a growing number of unit resales, which will boost this business. FKP's property development division has reduced its exposure to the residential sector, and expects a higher concentration on commercial development to underpin further earnings growth in 2006.

FKP Year to 30 June	2004	2005
Revenues ($mn)	263.7	299.7
Property development (%)	64	57
Land subdivision (%)	25	22
Retirement investments (%)	9	13
Investments & funds management (%)	1	8
EBIT ($mn)	59.2	78.3
EBIT margin (%)	22.4	26.1
Gross margin (%)	27.2	26.0
Profit before tax ($mn)	53.0	71.3
Profit after tax ($mn)	36.7	54.9
Earnings per share (¢)	30.8	34.5
Cash flow per share (¢)	32.3	36.2
Dividend (¢)	15	25.03
Percentage franked	100	74
Net tangible assets per share ($)	1.80	2.01
Interest cover (times)	9.6	11.2
Return on equity (%)	17.5	18.2
Debt-to-equity ratio (%)	51.4	26.4
Current ratio	2.0	2.4

Fleetwood Corporation Ltd

Share price ($)	6.77
12-month high ($)	9.54
12-month low ($)	5.75
Market capitalisation ($mn)	302.7
Price-to-NTA-per-share ratio	4.0
5-year share price return (% pa)	42.3

Sector: Consumer discretionary	Company	Sector
Price-earnings ratio (times)	12.4	24.2
Dividend yield (%)	3.0	1.2

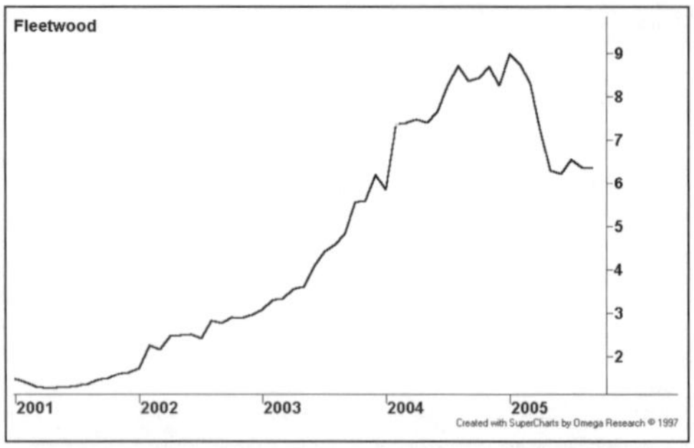

www.fleetwood.com.au

Western Australian company Fleetwood, established in 1964, is a leader in the caravan, recreational vehicle and portable accommodation businesses. Its Coromal Caravans division is the second-largest caravan manufacturer in Australia and its Windsor Caravans business is the fourth-largest. Its Camec Group is Australia's largest caravan spare parts and accessories manufacturer and retailer. Fleetwood Durabuilt is one of the largest park home and transportable home manufacturers in Western Australia, and Fleetwood Rainbow manufactures park homes and cabins in Melbourne and sells to Victoria, South Australia and southern NSW. Fleetwood Portables is one of Australia's largest providers of portable accommodation to the resources industry, and Flexiglass Challenge is Australia's largest manufacturer of canopies for utility vehicles.

Latest business results (June 2005, full year)

Profits rose to another record high. However, this was largely due to a $7.8 million after-tax profit from the sale of the company's parks division, which was not recorded as a significant item. Excluding this, the after-tax profit fell. The best result came from the manufactured accommodation division, with sales up 26% to $101.9 million, and EBITA (earnings before interest, tax and goodwill amortisation) up 13% to $9.1 million. By contrast, the recreational vehicle division saw sales dip 1%, to $167.5 million, with EBITA down 4% to $21.9 million.

FWD Year to 30 June	2004	2005
Revenues ($mn)	231.1	255.1
Recreational vehicles (%)	65	56
Manufactured accommodation (%)	31	34
EBIT ($mn)	31.2	37.0
EBIT margin (%)	13.5	14.5
Gross margin (%)	26.8	24.1
Profit before tax ($mn)	29.4	36.1
Profit after tax ($mn)	20.2	25.1
Earnings per share (¢)	44.8	54.6
Cash flow per share (¢)	61.8	71.2
Dividend (¢)	18	20
Percentage franked	100	100
Net tangible assets per share ($)	1.47	1.68
Interest cover (times)	17.1	41.2
Return on equity (%)	22.9	24.9
Debt-to-equity ratio (%)	26.3	17.6
Current ratio	1.8	1.8

Outlook

Fleetwood's superb profit growth of recent years seems to have stalled, and this has hit the share price. However, the company has announced that much of the slowdown has come because of a major restructuring of its operations to facilitate future growth, and that this was largely completed by mid-2005. It has included an expansion of caravan manufacturing facilities, the relocation of Fleetwood Rainbow to larger premises in Victoria with increased production capacity, and the relocation of Camec's NSW and Auckland businesses to new warehouse-style premises. The long-term outlook for the company remains very positive. With most caravan purchasers aged over 55, Fleetwood is a big beneficiary of this growing demographic. The company's other major source of revenue — on-site manufactured accommodation for resource project workers — is also flourishing, thanks to the ongoing resources boom, with a string of profitable new contracts in prospect.

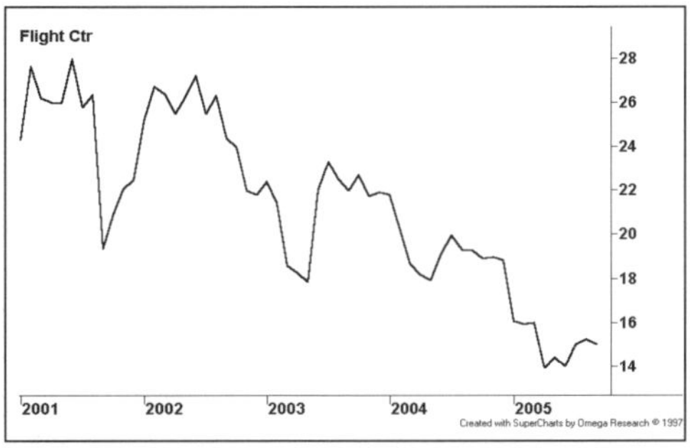

www.flightcentre.com.au

FLIGHT CENTRE LTD

Share price ($)	15.58	
12-month high ($)	20.14	
12-month low ($)	12.81	
Market capitalisation ($mn)	1344.3	
Price-to-NTA-per-share ratio	6.2	
5-year share price return (% pa)	–3.9	
Sector: Consumer discretionary	**Company**	**Sector**
Price-earnings ratio (times)	21.7	24.2
Dividend yield (%)	3.2	1.2

Brisbane-based Flight Centre is the largest independent retail travel agency in Australia and New Zealand, and has an estimated 20% market share. It operates under various brands, including Escape Travel, Student Flights, Travel Associates, Overseas Working Holidays, Cruiseabout, FCm Travel Solutions and Campus Travel, as well as various online brands. It has expanded to South Africa, Britain, Canada and the US, with a total of 1500 sales outlets.

Latest business results (June 2005, full year)

Sales revenues continued to rise, but Flight Centre suffered its first profit decline as its business was hit by a contraction in retail margins, reduced profitability on low-cost airfares and higher staffing and technology costs. Altogether, the company achieved 17% growth in total transaction value, increasing to $6.9 billion. All major regions experienced growth in turnover, with a particularly good result from the company's fast-growing British operation. South Africa too saw good profit growth. But New Zealand profits were stagnant, and losses mounted in the US. Canada, too, remained in the red.

Outlook

For some years after its 1995 stock market listing, Flight Centre was a stellar performer, with its continuing spectacular profit growth making it one of the market's top-performing stocks. However, as doubts began to arise about whether the performance could continue, the share price started to slide and, in recent years, the stock has been delivering negative returns. The latest result—the company's first-ever decline in earnings, despite initial forecasts of continuing profit growth—sent the shares into further decline, especially as the company was unwilling to make an earnings forecast for the June 2006 year. Nevertheless, at the end of June 2005, Flight Centre had net cash holdings of more than $200 million, and it continues its campaign of expansion. It opened a net total of 57 new stores in the June 2005 year, mainly under the Flight Centre and Escape Travel banners and is eyeing a medium-sized corporate acquisition in the US. In order to address its earnings stagnation it is working to slice away some of the layers of bureaucracy within its organisational structure, and it is trying to move more strongly into higher-margin businesses, such as package tours, hotel bookings, cruises and car hire.

FLT Year to 30 June	2004	2005
Revenues ($mn)	774.3	870.3
EBIT ($mn)	117.8	97.7
EBIT margin (%)	15.2	11.2
Profit before tax ($mn)	121.3	107.0
Profit after tax ($mn)	81.9	67.9
Earnings per share (¢)	87.4	71.9
Cash flow per share (¢)	129.3	120.9
Dividend (¢)	61	50.5
Percentage franked	100	100
Net tangible assets per share ($)	2.73	2.52
Interest cover (times)	~	~
Return on equity (%)	20.7	16.7
Debt-to-equity ratio (%)	~	~
Current ratio	1.3	1.3

Foodland Associated Ltd

Share price ($)	27.06
12-month high ($)	27.79
12-month low ($)	16.65
Market capitalisation ($mn)	3174.3
Price-to-NTA-per-share ratio	10.2
5-year share price return (% pa)	35.1

Sector: Consumer staples	Company	Sector
Price-earnings ratio (times)	22.2	15.6
Dividend yield (%)	3.5	3.3

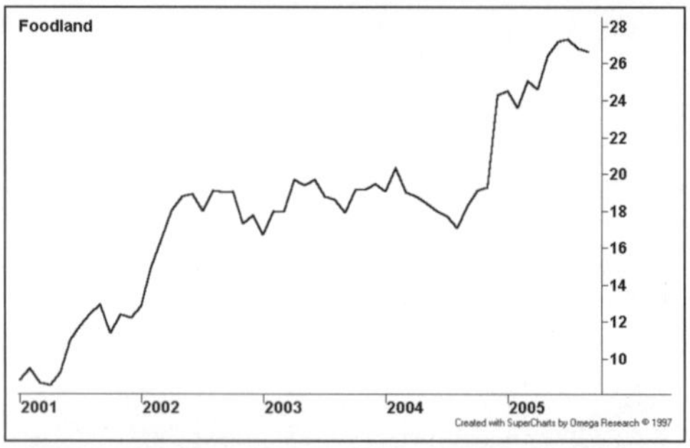

www.fal.com.au

Perth-based Foodland is one of Australia's leading grocery retailers and wholesalers. Its Australian supermarket division, Action, operates 80 supermarkets across Western Australia, Queensland and northern NSW. In Western Australia, the group is a leading grocery wholesaler, with four Cash & Carry branches. It also operates 16 Quickstop fuel and convenience store outlets. In New Zealand, it operates 150 supermarkets in the Countdown, Foodtown, Woolworths and Price Chopper banner groups and 22 Woolworths outlets at Gull convenience stores. Foodland has been the object of a takeover bid by Woolworths and Metcash, who look set to acquire its assets, probably before the end of 2005.

Latest business results (January 2005, half year)

Foodland had yet to announce its full-year financial results as this book was going to press, and the latest figures in the tables on this page are the first-half results to January 2005. However, the company has announced that total sales for the 31 July 2005 year were up 5.1% from the previous year, at $6.3 billion. The best result came from the company's franchise and supply businesses, with sales up 10.4%. New Zealand supermarkets were also strong, up 8.5%. However, domestic supermarkets saw sales increase just 2.6%, hurt by the aggressive petrol discount offers of rival chains.

FOA Year to 1 August*	2003	2004
Revenues ($mn)	6385.8	6026.5
EBIT ($mn)	256.2	260.1
EBIT margin (%)	4.0	4.3
Gross margin (%)	17.0	15.7
Profit before tax ($mn)	191.4	225.9
Profit after tax ($mn)	120.1	142.7
Earnings per share (¢)	103.3	122.0
Cash flow per share (¢)	225.1	234.1
Dividend (¢)	85	96
Percentage franked	100	100
Interest cover (times)	4.0	7.6
Return on equity (%)	13.2	14.4

* 3 August 2003

Half year to 30 January**	2004	2005
Revenues ($mn)	3090.4	3197.2
Profit before tax ($mn)	125.6	87.8
Profit after tax ($mn)	77.8	53.2
Earnings per share (¢)	66.6	45.3
Dividend (¢)	43	43
Percentage franked	100	25
Net tangible assets per share ($)	2.23	2.66
Debt-to-equity ratio (%)	37.2	22.4
Current ratio	1.3	1.0

** 1 February 2004

Outlook

Foodland's rapid growth of previous years seems to have ground to a halt, with much of the damage coming from the petrol discount schemes of Woolworths and Coles Myer. Nevertheless, the company has been continuing a program of refurbishing its existing stores and the opening of new outlets. At the time of writing, the company management had recommended—in the absence of a superior bid—that shareholders accept Woolworths' and Metcash's offers of a total of $3.3 billion to $3.4 billion for the company's businesses. Under this agreed transaction, Woolworths will acquire Foodland's New Zealand businesses, along with 19 Action stores and three development sites, in Western Australia, Queensland and NSW, worth $2.5 billion. Metcash will acquire the remainder of Foodland's Australian businesses. Foodland plans to convene meetings of its shareholders to explain the proposal and seek their approval.

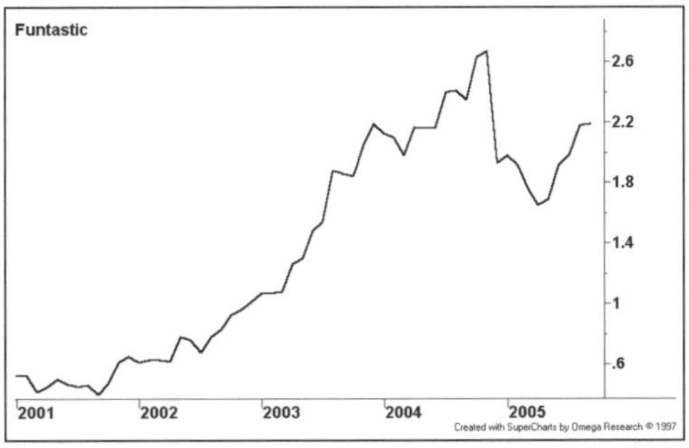

www.funtastic.com.au

Funtastic Ltd

Share price ($)	2.20
12-month high ($)	2.79
12-month low ($)	1.51
Market capitalisation ($mn)	280.8
Price-to-NTA-per-share ratio	5.6
5-year share price return (% pa)	48.1

Sector: Consumer discretionary	Company	Sector
Price-earnings ratio (times)	15.9	24.2
Dividend yield (%)	3.9	1.2

Melbourne-based Funtastic, founded in 1944, is Australia's leading distributor of toys and other children's products. It also markets and distributes a wide range of other consumer products, and its businesses are divided into eight main product areas: toys, apparel, publishing, confectionary, accessories, nursery, footwear and homewares. Its brands include Spider-Man, Barbie, Thomas the Tank Engine, Bob the Builder, The Wiggles and Winnie the Pooh.

Latest business results (June 2005, half year)

Profits soared on a solid increase in sales thanks to continuing demand for the company's toys, with particular strength in the Bratz, LeapFrog and Tamagotchi products. The company's publishing business was strong as a result of the addition of Disney master publishing rights, but its electronics products business showed weakness. The company reported the emergence of what it believes to be sustainable cost synergies from the successful integration of acquired businesses. There was a maiden contribution from the acquisition of Planet Fun in New Zealand, which achieved sales of $8 million and an after-tax profit of $0.5 million. The results were Funtastic's first under new reporting standards. The company said that under the old standards its after-tax profit would have been only $4.1 million, instead of the reported $5.3 million.

Outlook

Funtastic has shown exceptional growth since listing in 1999, due to both underlying organic expansion and a series of acquisitions. The company's own target is for annual sales of $0.5 billion by December 2007. Its portfolio of popular children's brands has seen it develop close ties with all the leading retail chains. It has been able to leverage this relationship to move into the supply of a wide range of other consumer products, and this has been a key factor in its growth. It is now looking to grow overseas, and it hopes to use the Planet Fun acquisition to expand in New Zealand in the same way it has developed in Australia. The bulk of Funtastic's profits come in the December half, and it has announced that it expects a full-year after-tax profit of between $21.4 million and $21.9 million.

FUN Year to 31 December	2003	2004
Revenues ($mn)	223.5	311.3
EBIT ($mn)	22.4	25.3
EBIT margin (%)	10.0	8.1
Gross margin (%)	36.9	34.9
Profit before tax ($mn)	20.8	23.1
Profit after tax ($mn)	14.0	16.9
Earnings per share (¢)	12.8	13.8
Cash flow per share (¢)	13.6	14.9
Dividend (¢)	7	8.5
Percentage franked	100	100
Interest cover (times)	14.2	11.7
Return on equity (%)	20.0	18.3
Half year to 30 June	**2004**	**2005**
Revenues ($mn)	127.0	138.5
Profit before tax ($mn)	5.5	7.9
Profit after tax ($mn)	3.6	5.3
Earnings per share (¢)	2.9	4.2
Dividend (¢)	3.5	4
Percentage franked	100	100
Net tangible assets per share ($)	0.40	0.39
Debt-to-equity ratio (%)	43.7	38.5
Current ratio	1.8	2.6

GAZAL CORPORATION LTD		
Share price ($)	2.93	
12-month high ($)	3.80	
12-month low ($)	2.69	
Market capitalisation ($mn)	184.8	
Price-to-NTA-per-share ratio	4.0	
5-year share price return (% pa)	13.9	
Sector: Consumer discretionary	**Company**	**Sector**
Price-earnings ratio (times)	14.0	24.2
Dividend yield (%)	5.5	1.2

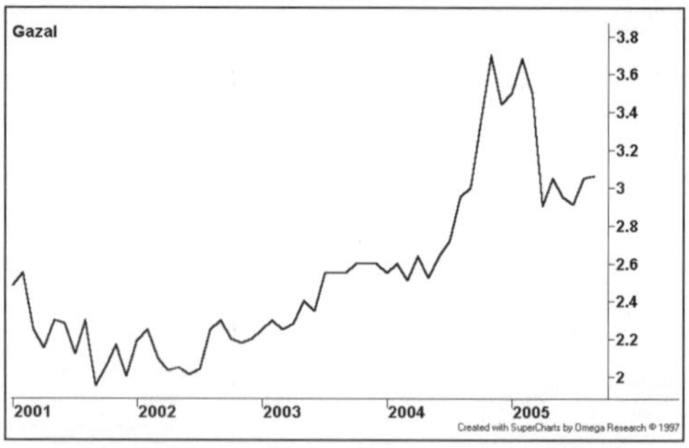

www.gazal.com.au

Sydney-based Gazal, founded in 1958, is one of Australia's largest publicly listed clothing companies, specialising mainly in business shirts, men's casual wear and surf wear, women's intimate apparel and school wear. It owns the Mambo label, and in Australia it is a licence holder for such well-known brands as Calvin Klein, Trent Nathan, Nautica, Kenneth Cole, Van Heusen, Playboy, Lovable, Virginware, Crystelle, Maui and Sons, Bisley, Midford, Oroton, Mariner and Kookai. It also makes house-brand merchandise for major retailers, and it has some sales in Europe. The controlling Gazal family hold more than 60% of the shares.

Latest business results (June 2005, full year)

A strong first half propelled Gazal to a full-year rise in sales, despite a second-half slowdown caused by an easing in consumer spending and the late arrival of cold weather. Higher promotional costs meant profits were essentially flat, though a lower tax charge led to a good rise in the after-tax profit figure. The company's key brands all performed well, with a particularly good contribution from the Bisley workwear business. The American sportswear brand Kenneth Cole was launched during the year, and Gazal opened its sixth Trade Secret factory outlet store in Hillsdale, Sydney, in December 2004. Mambo showed an improvement over the previous year. The company's small European operation—about 7% of turnover—saw sales down, but it made a small profit.

Outlook

Gazal is starting to feel the pinch of a slowdown in consumer spending. In response, it has boosted its advertising and promotional spending, which is having a negative impact on costs. It is also working to improve inventory management and boost supply-chain efficiencies, and reported a 3% reduction in inventory at the end of June 2005 compared to a year earlier. It hopes to embark on a strategy of acquiring its own high-profile brands and developing these as intellectual assets with long-term value and, with the assistance of Rothschild Australia, it is assessing several strategic growth opportunities. In August 2005, it announced the acquisition of the Bracks Apparel Group, a market leader in menswear with operations in Australia and New Zealand. Gazal continues to struggle to boost sales and profits for the iconic Mambo brand, with the medium-term goal of establishing it as a global surf brand.

GZL Year to 30 June	2004	2005
Revenues ($mn)	193.0	212.6
EBIT ($mn)	18.4	18.8
EBIT margin (%)	9.5	8.9
Gross margin (%)	50.4	52.0
Profit before tax ($mn)	16.2	16.5
Profit after tax ($mn)	10.8	12.5
Earnings per share (¢)	18.8	20.9
Cash flow per share (¢)	26.2	29.1
Dividend (¢)	14	16
Percentage franked	100	100
Net tangible assets per share ($)	0.81	0.74
Interest cover (times)	8.4	8.0
Return on equity (%)	11.9	13.6
Debt-to-equity ratio (%)	36.5	38.2
Current ratio	2.0	2.0

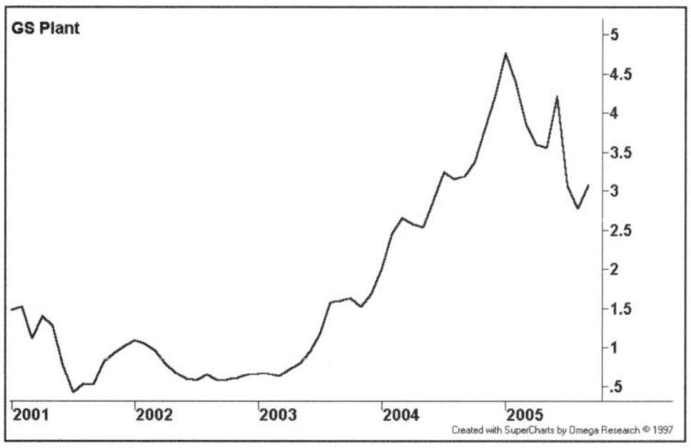

www.great-southern.com.au

Great Southern Plantations Ltd

Share price ($)	3.07
12-month high ($)	5.03
12-month low ($)	2.75
Market capitalisation ($mn)	874.6
Price-to-NTA-per-share ratio	1.3
5-year share price return (% pa)	21.6

Sector: Materials	Company	Sector
Price-earnings ratio (times)	6.5	17.0
Dividend yield (%)	4.6	2.2

Perth-based Great Southern Plantations, founded in 1987, is an agribusiness investment manager, providing investors with tax-effective investment products. It manages more than 110 000 hectares of eucalypt plantations, mainly in Western Australia, Victoria and Queensland. It also manages a viticulture project on 170 hectares of land in the Frankland River wine region of Western Australia, and in 2005 it launched its first organic olive project in the Preston Valley region of Western Australia.

Latest business results (June 2005, full year)

Great Southern achieved another major increase in profits. Sales of eucalypt plantation products totalled approximately $304 million — up from $227 in the previous year — though not all this revenue was recognised in the June 2005 year. The 2005 organic olives project closed in May 2005 fully subscribed, raising $19 million. Two new vineyard projects also closed during the year fully subscribed, raising $32 million. During the year Great Southern began harvesting its own timber for the first time and, in February 2005, the first of three shipments of woodchip left Western Australia for Japan. Harvested timber delivered $7 million in revenues to the company, with a profit of $0.1 million.

Outlook

Great Southern Plantations is a big beneficiary of growing investor interest in managed schemes targeting agriculture. It has bought the rights to acquire 55 000 hectares of plantable land, in Western Australia and Victoria, and this will form the base of future long-term growth. In 2004 it announced its first hardwood woodchip contract — a three-year deal with Japan's Nichimen Corporation to export more than 500 000 tonnes of woodchip over three years — and it expects further similar contracts as its plantations mature. The company's olive plantation is now the country's largest organic olive grove, with over 80 000 trees, and Great Southern plans to expand its olives project offerings in 2006. In April 2005, Great Southern acquired Sylvatech Limited, a company involved in the development and management of forestry projects on the Tiwi Islands in the Northern Territory, providing the company with access to extensive plantation land for use in future projects. And, in July 2005, it acquired for $55 million from Environinvest its beef cattle managed investment scheme business, including prime grazing land and 55 000 head of cattle on King Island.

GTP Year to 30 June	2004	2005
Revenues ($mn)	204.2	309.5
EBIT ($mn)	131.1	175.0
EBIT margin (%)	64.2	56.5
Profit before tax ($mn)	132.7	175.6
Profit after tax ($mn)	93.2	124.3
Earnings per share (¢)	44.1	47.0
Cash flow per share (¢)	44.3	47.7
Dividend (¢)	10	14
Percentage franked	100	100
Net tangible assets per share ($)	1.84	2.44
Interest cover (times)	~	~
Return on equity (%)	27.6	20.5
Debt-to-equity ratio (%)	~	1.8
Current ratio	1.0	1.2

GUD Holdings Ltd

Share price ($)	8.41	
12-month high ($)	11.42	
12-month low ($)	5.31	
Market capitalisation ($mn)	496.7	
Price-to-NTA-per-share ratio	6.8	
5-year share price return (% pa)	44.7	
Sector: Consumer discretionary	**Company**	**Sector**
Price-earnings ratio (times)	13.5	24.2
Dividend yield (%)	5.9	1.2

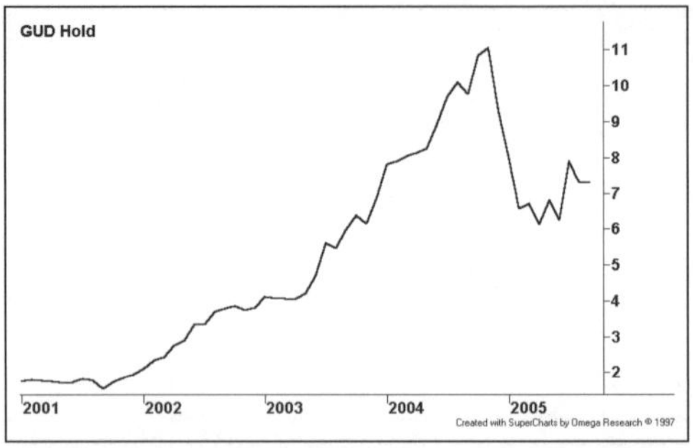

www.gud.com.au

GUD, based in Melbourne and founded in 1940, is a diversified manufacturer and distributor with five broad product lines: Sunbeam small electrical appliances; Victa lawnmowers; Ryco, Wesfil and Goss automotive filtration and associated products; Davey water pumps, pump sets and water pressure systems; and Lock Focus security products and associated hardware. It exports to more than 50 countries.

Latest business results (June 2005, full year)

The once high-flying company saw profits fall for the first time in five years due to flat sales. There was a particularly bad performance from the Victa lawnmower business, hit by competition from low-cost Chinese rivals. By contrast, Sunbeam realised generally excellent business, with enhanced market share and higher margins. Victa and Sunbeam are included within consumer products in the table on this page. The water products business was also strong, with growing demand for Davey water conservation products and good sales and profitability from the new Spa-Quip pool products acquisition. However, automotive product profits sagged, hurt by weakness in the car parts after-market. The company reported a $12.6 million pre-tax significant loss from the restructuring of its Ryco business.

Outlook

Having restructured its Victa operation to meet local competition, the company has been hurt by Chinese rivals. It is now finalising arrangements with Chinese suppliers to provide components for assembly in Australia. GUD expects a good contribution from the mid-2005 acquisition of the Oates household and commercial cleaning products business, which has leading market shares for floor cleaning accessories in both consumer and commercial market segments. GUD expects Oates to generate $65 million in sales and $6 million in EBIT in the June 2006 year. The acquisition in April 2005 of New Zealand-based Contamination Control hands GUD a new range of water cooling and purification products, with the potential to use the Davey dealer networks to boost sales in Australia and abroad. GUD has closed its domestic Ryco automotive components plant and now sources all product offshore. With a lower cost structure it is now looking to boost its product range. With modest debt levels, GUD plans a continuing series of bolt-on acquisitions, and management have expressed confidence that June 2006 profits will be higher than June 2005.

GUD Year to 30 June	2004	2005
Revenues ($mn)	393.8	394.4
Consumer products (%)	56	55
Water products (%)	19	22
Automotive products (%)	22	20
Security products (%)	3	3
EBIT ($mn)	62.6	58.0
EBIT margin (%)	15.9	14.7
Gross margin (%)	39.3	39.1
Profit before tax ($mn)	60.2	54.9
Profit after tax ($mn)	41.7	37.8
Earnings per share (¢)	68.6	62.5
Cash flow per share (¢)	88.1	78.5
Dividend (¢)	40	50
Percentage franked	100	100
Net tangible assets per share ($)	1.39	1.24
Interest cover (times)	25.8	18.8
Return on equity (%)	31.0	27.2
Debt-to-equity ratio (%)	12.3	27.7
Current ratio	1.7	1.9

Share price (\$)	3.65		
12-month high (\$)	4.80		
12-month low (\$)	3.31		
Market capitalisation (\$mn)	1214.0		
Price-to-NTA-per-share ratio	1.8		
5-year share price return (% pa)	43.1		

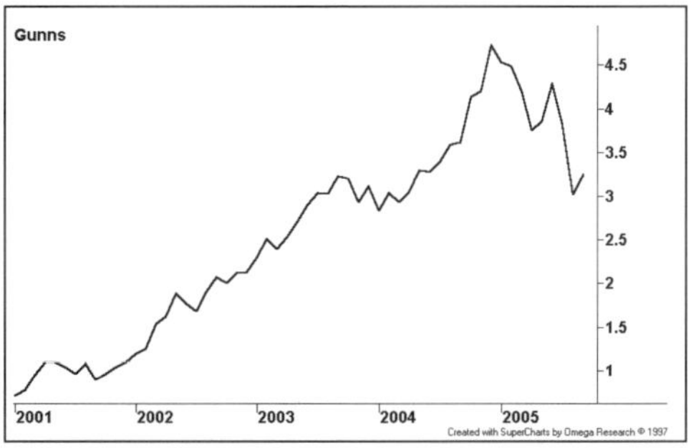

www.gunns.com.au

Gunns Ltd

Sector: Materials	Company	Sector
Price-earnings ratio (times)	12.2	17.0
Dividend yield (%)	3.4	2.2

Launceston timber company Gunns was founded in 1875 and claims to be one of Australia's oldest companies. It owns 175 000 hectares of land, manages over 90 000 hectares of plantations, and is Australia's largest hardwood producer, with five sawmills around Tasmania. It also maintains two veneer factories in Tasmania and one in New Zealand. It operates four woodchip export ports in Tasmania, and woodchip sales to Asian pulp mills are a major activity. Other businesses include six Gunns Mitre 10 hardware stores in northern Tasmania, the building contracting company Hinman Wright and Manser, and Tamar Ridge Wines. The Gunns Plantations subsidiary offers managed investment products in timber plantations to the public.

Latest business results (June 2005, full year)

Sales were up, but profits dipped. Forest product revenues were steady but profits edged down, hurt by a reduction in sales volumes in the second half of the financial year. In addition, the continuing strength of the Australian dollar eroded the company's competitive position in some of its export markets. The managed investments business saw revenues up 10%, with over 11 000 hectares planted during the year, though profits were flat. Its other businesses—notably its Tasmanian-based construction and merchandising activities which represent about 13% of total company turnover—achieved a 25% rise in sales from continuing strength in the Tasmanian building and construction sector.

Outlook

The forestry industry has enjoyed buoyant conditions over several years and this is reflected in the soaring Gunns share price. The outlook remains firm, with Asian demand for Australian wood fibre continuing to rise, and Gunns one of the key suppliers. Nevertheless, the strength of the dollar remains a concern, along with rising fuel and labour costs. Gunns sees its planned \$1.1 billion Bell Bay Pulp Mill as playing a major role in its long-term future. Due to become operational in 2008, it could have the capacity to add over \$350 million annually to the company's export revenues. In the shorter term, the company is placing a particular emphasis on its newly acquired West Australian jarrah business, thanks to the premium price obtainable for this product from the furniture and fit-out markets. Gunns also plans a significant expansion of its managed investment program in 2006, including the start of development activity outside Tasmania.

GNS Year to 30 June	2004	2005
Revenues (\$mn)	649.7	668.5
EBIT (\$mn)	174.4	172.0
EBIT margin (%)	26.8	25.7
Gross margin (%)	21.8	20.0
Profit before tax (\$mn)	151.5	144.7
Profit after tax (\$mn)	105.3	101.3
Earnings per share (¢)	31.3*	29.9
Cash flow per share (¢)	36.2*	35.0
Dividend (¢)	12.5*	12.5
Percentage franked	100	100
Net tangible assets per share (\$)	1.30*	1.97
Interest cover (times)	7.6	6.3
Return on equity (%)	26.4	18.1
Debt-to-equity ratio (%)	64.5	53.1
Current ratio	1.0	1.0

* adjusted for a four-for-one share split

GWA International Ltd

Share price ($)	3.10
12-month high ($)	3.39
12-month low ($)	2.52
Market capitalisation ($mn)	879.4
Price-to-NTA-per-share ratio	2.0
5-year share price return (% pa)	18.5

Sector: Industrials	Company	Sector
Price-earnings ratio (times)	13.7	16.2
Dividend yield (%)	5.8	3.6

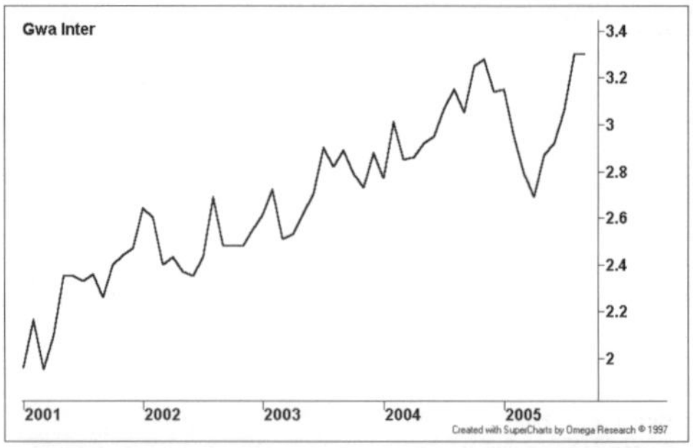

www.gwail.com.au

Brisbane-based GWA is a manufacturer of a wide range of household products, including 90% of Australia's toilets. Its Caroma division is a leading supplier of bathroom fittings, and has operations in Asia, Europe and America. The Sebel contract furniture business provides seating for stadiums and auditoriums, and also operates in several countries. In addition, the company makes Rover lawnmowers, Dorf Clark tapware, Dux hot water systems and Gainsborough door fittings, and it owns the Wisa Beheer cistern producer in the Netherlands.

Latest business results (June 2005, full year)

Profits edged up, despite a drop in sales which reflected the slowdown in the residential property market. The key was GWA's largest business, Caroma, which posted record profits—despite a dip in sales—thanks to the company's drive to boost efficiencies. In a highly competitive market, the smaller Dorf Clark tapware business saw sales down 10%, but profits up 15%. The Gainsborough door business and the Dux water heater operation also saw profits rise. However, sales and profits were down for the Sebel commercial furniture division, which was hit by the strong dollar and by problems with a major contract. The Rover mower business was hurt by strong competition and unfavourable weather and it, too, saw sales and profits decline.

Outlook

Over 80% of GWA's sales are geared to the residential and commercial construction and renovation markets, and the company is now experiencing the impact of a slowdown. Its initial forecast is for little growth in the June 2006 year. In response, it is engaged in a restructuring of many of its operations in order to cut costs, including the opening of a new office in Shanghai, which is aimed at developing strategic partnerships with suppliers in the region. It is also striving to move Caroma, Dorf and Dux up-market into new, high-tech products with an emphasis on water and energy conservation. Its new Caroma Smartflush water-saving toilet has won a series of awards. It has also begun a major upgrade of its Wetherill Park sanitaryware plant, aimed at boosting capacity and cutting costs, and it expects the benefits to start to arrive in the June 2006 year.

GWT Year to 30 June	2004	2005
Revenues ($mn)	667.9	626.9
Building fixtures & fittings (%)	83	84
Commercial furniture (%)	10	10
EBIT ($mn)	99.5	102.5
EBIT margin (%)	14.9	16.4
Gross margin (%)	46.3	47.3
Profit before tax ($mn)	88.4	91.5
Profit after tax ($mn)	62.1	63.2
Earnings per share (¢)	22.3	22.7
Cash flow per share (¢)	33.3	32.5
Dividend (¢)	18	18
Percentage franked	100	100
Net tangible assets per share ($)	0.25	1.53
Interest cover (times)	9.0	9.3
Return on equity (%)	14.7	14.8
Debt-to-equity ratio (%)	37.2	38.0
Current ratio	3.1	3.5

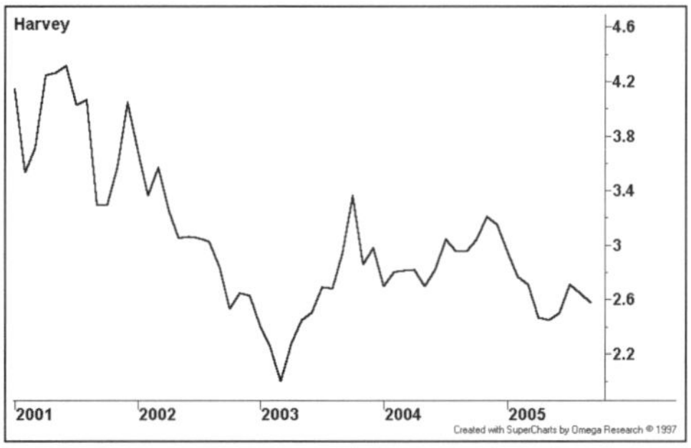

www.harveynorman.com.au

Harvey Norman Holdings Ltd

Share price ($)	2.66	
12-month high ($)	3.29	
12-month low ($)	2.30	
Market capitalisation ($mn)	2845.4	
Price-to-NTA-per-share ratio	2.2	
5-year share price return (% pa)	–6.2	
Sector: Consumer discretionary	**Company**	**Sector**
Price-earnings ratio (times)	16.4	24.2
Dividend yield (%)	2.4	1.2

Sydney-based Harvey Norman, established in 1982, operates a chain of more than 200 retail stores specialising in electrical and electronic goods, home appliances, furniture, flooring, carpets and manchester, throughout Australia, New Zealand and Singapore, and three in Slovenia and Ireland, under the Harvey Norman, Domayne and Joyce Mayne banners. Many of the stores are independently held as part of a franchise operation, from which Harvey Norman receives income for advisory and advertising services. It also receives rental income from property investments, from its own stores and from the provision of finance to franchisees and customers. It has bought controlling stakes in Rebel Sport and in the Singapore retailer Pertama Holdings.

Latest business results (June 2005, full year)

In an environment of slowing consumer spending, Harvey Norman saw sales up, but profits edged down. The second half of the year saw a notable slowdown, as rising fuel prices and the housing downturn hit household spending patterns. The company was also hurt by continuing price deflation for many of its big-ticket items, putting pressure on margins. Total group sales, including franchised stores but excluding Pertama Holdings and Rebel Sport, rose 10.6% to $4.1 billion, or a 5.3% rise on a like-for-like basis. Nine new stores were opened in Australia during the year and two in New Zealand. The company's best result came from New Zealand, where pre-tax profit jumped 41% to $35.5 million. Asian pre-tax profit rose 16% to $10.2 million. But domestic business saw profits down. The small Slovenian operation fell into the red.

Outlook

Harvey Norman is a major beneficiary of the continuing Australian appetite for the latest high-tech gadgets, and it sees great long-term potential from the development and convergence of products where it enjoys strength, including digital imaging and recording, home networking, plasma and LCD displays, portable media players and personal computers. In November 2005 it launches its inaugural audio visual/information technology (AV/IT) concept store at Castle Hill, Sydney. It plans two new stores in Singapore and is investigating sites in Malaysia. It also plans a second store in Slovenia, as well as six more in Ireland over the coming four years. It is also investigating moves elsewhere in Europe, as well as expansion into China and India.

HVN Year to 30 June	2004	2005
Revenues ($mn)	1751.7	1933.8
Franchising operations (%)	29	28
Retail — New Zealand (%)	19	23
Retail — Rebel Sport (%)	17	17
Retail — Asia (%)	18	16
Non-franchised retail (%)	9	9
Property (%)	5	4
EBIT ($mn)	296.3	306.5
EBIT margin (%)	16.9	15.8
Gross margin (%)	25.1	25.1
Profit before tax ($mn)	269.3	269.7
Profit after tax ($mn)	176.1	171.4
Earnings per share (¢)	16.6	16.2
Cash flow per share (¢)	23.7	24.2
Dividend (¢)	7.5	6.5
Percentage franked	100	100
Net tangible assets per share ($)	1.09	1.19
Interest cover (times)	11.0	8.3
Return on equity (%)	16.6	14.1
Debt-to-equity ratio (%)	36.3	42.8
Current ratio	1.7	1.9

HGL Ltd

Share price ($)	1.75	
12-month high ($)	2.13	
12-month low ($)	1.72	
Market capitalisation ($mn)	87.7	
Price-to-NTA-per-share ratio	1.4	
5-year share price return (% pa)	15.7	
Sector: Industrials	**Company**	**Sector**
Price-earnings ratio (times)	8.2	16.2
Dividend yield (%)	5.1	3.6

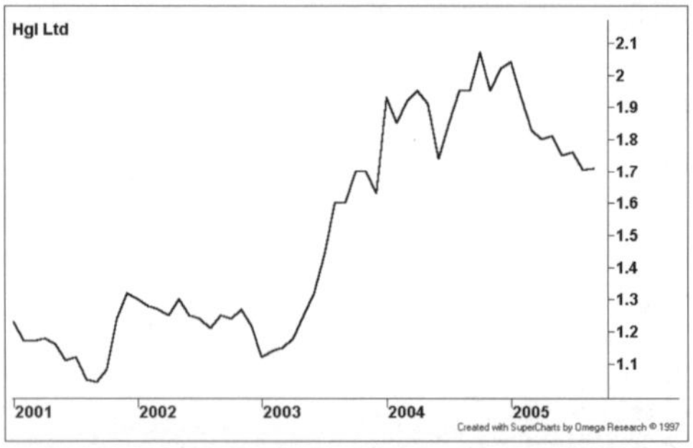

www.hgl.com.au

Sydney-based HGL is a small diversified investment group that specialises in acquiring and rejuvenating underperforming niche companies. In recent years, it has been targeting those in the import and distribution business, and it is now part-owner of ten of these, including firms that specialise in fabrics, cosmetics, headwear and imaging equipment. Generally, the companies are partially owned by their management or other industry experts, who work in partnership with HGL executives. HGL also participates in public company investing and the funds management sector, including a 39% interest in the boutique funds manager MMC Asset Management and a 6% stake in the listed investment company Hunter Hall International. It also owns 7% of Calliden Group (formerly Reinsurance Australia).

Latest business results (March 2005, half year)

Profits were up, despite a fall in earnings from the company's import and distribution businesses. This followed a $0.5 million loss from a service contract initiated by the Anitech imaging-equipment business unit and a $0.6 million bad debt incurred by the Thalgo cosmetics business. EBIT from MMC more than doubled to $1.1 million, due mainly to growth in funds under management from MMC Contrarian. Dividend income from HGL's investment portfolio doubled to $0.6 million. Revaluations and capital gains rose 19% to $4.4 million.

HNG Year to 30 September	2003	2004
Revenues ($mn)	116.2	123.1
EBIT ($mn)	15.2	18.3
EBIT margin (%)	13.1	14.9
Gross margin (%)	45.3	48.0
Profit before tax ($mn)	14.9	18.7
Profit after tax ($mn)	9.9	10.5
Earnings per share (¢)	21.2	21.3
Cash flow per share (¢)	25.2	25.6
Dividend (¢)	8.6	9
Percentage franked	100	100
Interest cover (times)	42.3	~
Return on equity (%)	19.5	17.2
Half year to 30 March	**2004**	**2005**
Revenues ($mn)	50.7	55.3
Profit before tax ($mn)	11.1	11.9
Profit after tax ($mn)	6.3	7.4
Earnings per share (¢)	13.0	14.6
Dividend (¢)	4.2	4.4
Percentage franked	100	100
Net tangible assets per share ($)	1.09	1.22
Debt-to-equity ratio (%)	~	~
Current ratio	3.6	4.2

Outlook

HGL's growth prospects depend to a large degree on management's success in identifying high-potential, underperforming niche businesses that require fresh capital and business know-how. HGL management must also then negotiate a satisfactory partnership deal with the entity's owners. The company's target is businesses where the return on capital employed is likely to exceed 20% in a reasonably short period of time, and it hopes to invest $25 million in these businesses over the next few years. In April 2005 it acquired AMCLA, an importer and distributor of pharmaceutical products. The price was $4 million, with a further $1 million payable if certain earnings targets are met. In June 2005 it sold its 50% stake in OP's Optical Products, yielding an after-tax profit of $0.2 million.

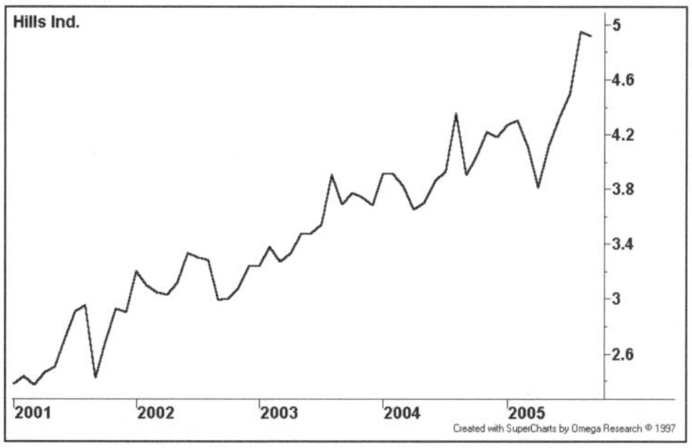

www.hills.com.au

Hills Industries Ltd

Share price ($)	4.78	
12-month high ($)	4.87	
12-month low ($)	3.60	
Market capitalisation ($mn)	791.3	
Price-to-NTA-per-share ratio	3.8	
5-year share price return (% pa)	21.5	
Sector: Industrials	**Company**	**Sector**
Price-earnings ratio (times)	20.3	16.2
Dividend yield (%)	5.0	3.6

Adelaide-based Hills, founded in 1946, is famous for its clothes hoists. However, it also manufactures a diverse range of other products, including garden equipment, structural tubing, a wide range of commercial and industrial steel products, closed-circuit TV systems, satellite dishes, electronic security systems and television antennas. It owns 47% of the listed metal products manufacturer Korvest.

Latest business results (June 2005, full year)

The company's electronics and building products businesses powered Hills to another excellent rise in sales and profits. The building and industrial products division saw EBIT jump ahead 23%, on a 16% sales rise, thanks to a buoyant domestic construction industry. There were strong performances from Korvest Ezy-Strut construction support systems, from Fielders roll-forming products and from Orrcon industrial pipes and tubing. The electronic security and entertainment division realised a 27% surge in EBIT on a 21% increase in sales as a result of a stream of new products, growing demand for security systems and good sales of supplies for Foxtel's new digital television offering. However, despite a small increase in sales, profits from the home and hardware products division slumped 29%, hurt by higher raw materials costs and strong competition from Chinese imports.

Outlook

Hills has overcome higher steel prices to remain a major beneficiary of the strength in the domestic construction industry, with a nearly fourfold surge in profits for its building and industrial products division over four years, and sales revenues more than doubling. While the domestic non-residential and engineering construction sectors remain strong, this division should prosper. The electronics business is also booming again, with the Foxtel and Austar digitalisation programs a particular incentive. The company is also working to boost earnings through a series of bolt-on acquisitions. In 2005 these included commercial audio specialist Audio Telex, automation systems company Crestron Control Solutions, water storage tank manufacturer Team Poly and the remaining 50% of steel tubing maker Orrcon. However, the home and hardware business continues to struggle, with the company's iconic Hills-brand products facing rising expenses—particularly for steel—and increased competition. Though the company is working to cut costs, it believes the recovery for this division will be only modest in the short term.

HIL Year to 30 June	2004	2005
Revenues ($mn)	713.6	810.2
Building & industrial (%)	54	53
Electronic security & entertainment (%)	24	25
Home & hardware (%)	22	20
EBIT ($mn)	58.5	64.0
EBIT margin (%)	8.2	7.9
Gross margin (%)	34.8	33.6
Profit before tax ($mn)	54.0	60.7
Profit after tax ($mn)	31.1	36.2
Earnings per share (¢)	22.5	23.5
Cash flow per share (¢)	36.8	37.1
Dividend (¢)	22.5	24
Percentage franked	100	100
Net tangible assets per share ($)	1.31	1.24
Interest cover (times)	12.9	19.3
Return on equity (%)	16.6	14.6
Debt-to-equity ratio (%)	26.9	27.1
Current ratio	2.0	1.9

Housewares International Ltd

Share price ($)	1.67	
12-month high ($)	2.70	
12-month low ($)	1.37	
Market capitalisation ($mn)	199.7	
Price-to-NTA-per-share ratio	2.4	
5-year share price return (% pa)	19.5	
Sector: Consumer discretionary	**Company**	**Sector**
Price-earnings ratio (times)	10.9	24.2
Dividend yield (%)	7.8	1.2

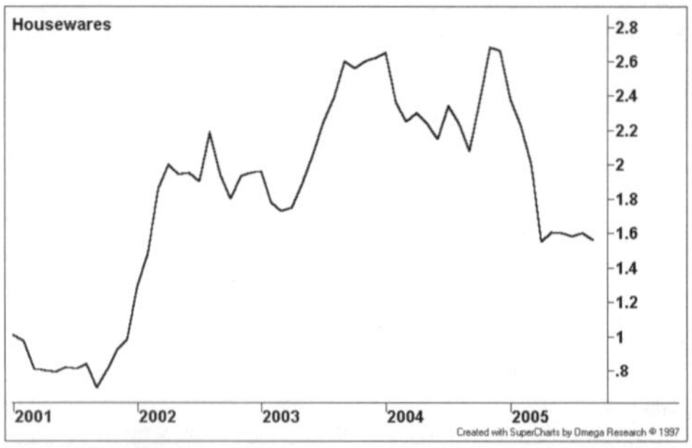

www.housewares.com.au

Melbourne-based Housewares International has evolved from its 1957 beginnings as a small local importer into a large distributor of household products in several countries. Its wholly-owned brands include Breville, Kambrook, Ronson and Goldair for home appliances, and Arcosteel, alex liddy, Baccarat, Forum, Mayfair & Jackson and Pronto for kitchenware. It also owns the Sabco household cleaning good company. Its distribution companies include Metro Marketing in the US and a 50% stake in Anglo Canadian in Canada.

Latest business results (June 2005, full year)

Sales edged down and profits fell sharply, as the company was hit by a second-half slowdown in consumer spending, as well as by intense competition for many of its product categories. There were particular problems with the company's homewares business, with domestic sales down 16% and overseas business falling 22%. Profit for this division plunged 74%. By contrast, the electrical division saw domestic sales down 5%, but achieved a healthy 38% jump in overseas turnover, and profits for the division were up 16%.

Outlook

In a deflationary environment for many of its products, Housewares International has embarked on a major upheaval of its operations, designed to cut costs and built a new base for long-term profitability. In particular, it is working to boost its brands, in order to differentiate them from the flood of cheap Chinese imports in local stores. It is also slimming down its distribution channels, allowing Australian retailers in some cases to buy directly from its Chinese office, rather than from an Australian warehouse. A restructuring of the homewares business was launched in April 2005, and will see the number of products cut in half, as well as reducing the number of customers, rationalising production and cutting staff numbers. Its electrical division continues to face cost and competitive pressures in Australia. However, it is seeing noteworthy success abroad, particularly in America, where sales more than doubled in the June 2005 year to $16.8 million. The company has aimed for an upscale image in the US, and selected Breville products have been accepted by retailers that include Williams and Sonoma, Federated Stores and Bed Bath and Beyond. New Zealand has also become a strong market, and new markets have opened in France and Russia.

HWI Year to 30 June	2004	2005
Revenues ($mn)	457.6	441.0
Electrical (%)	65	70
Homewares (%)	35	30
EBIT ($mn)	39.0	30.4
EBIT margin (%)	8.5	6.9
Gross margin (%)	40.8	42.1
Profit before tax ($mn)	34.0	24.5
Profit after tax ($mn)	22.9	18.1
Earnings per share (¢)	19.7	15.3
Cash flow per share (¢)	24.2	20.0
Dividend (¢)	10.5	13
Percentage franked	100	100
Net tangible assets per share ($)	0.69	0.69
Interest cover (times)	7.9	5.1
Return on equity (%)	15.2	11.4
Debt-to-equity ratio (%)	39.8	46.5
Current ratio	3.1	3.3

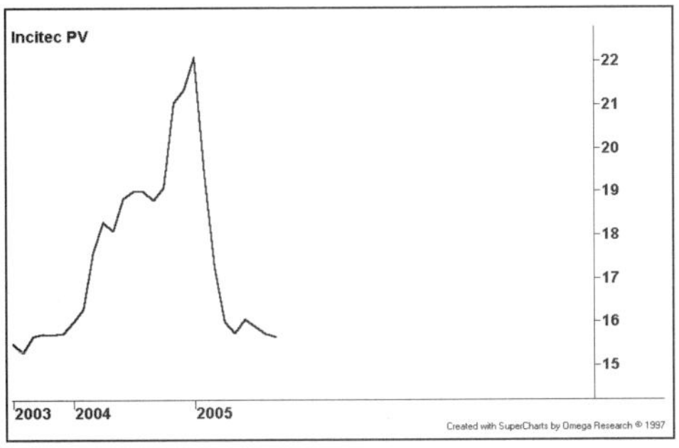

www.incitecpivot.com.au

Incitec Pivot Ltd

Share price ($)	15.78	
12-month high ($)	22.50	
12-month low ($)	15.00	
Market capitalisation ($mn)	923.2	
Price-to-NTA-per-share ratio	2.3	
5-year share price return (% pa)	na	
Sector: Materials	**Company**	**Sector**
Price-earnings ratio (times)	12.3	17.0
Dividend yield (%)	5.7	2.2

Melbourne-based Incitec Pivot was formally established in June 2003 from the merger of two of Australia's largest fertiliser manufacturers and distributors—the listed company Incitec and its unlisted rival Pivot, both with histories dating back more than 80 years. With manufacturing facilities in Queensland, Victoria and New South Wales, major distribution facilities throughout the eastern seaboard of Australia, and annual production of around three million tonnes, the new company is a major force in the rural economy. Incitec's former parent, Orica, owns 70% of the company, and much of the balance is held by the farming community. The shares are very thinly traded.

Latest business results (March 2005, half year)

The full-year results, as released by the company—and as presented in the table on this page—are for Pivot only until May 2003, then for the new company from June 2003. No dividend was officially recorded for the company for the September 2003 year, even though Incitec paid one to its own shareholders, and it is Incitec's financial record which forms the basis for the company's continuing inclusion in this book. In the March 2005 half year, profits fell quite substantially, despite a small uptick in sales revenues. This resulted from increased phosphate rock costs—including higher shipping charges and a less favourable currency hedging rate—and from strong competition, which hampered the company's ability to pass on the higher costs.

Outlook

The new company has become the dominant force in the Australian fertiliser industry, with roughly a 50% national market share and more than 70% of the eastern seaboard market. With the merger completed, and with low debt levels, it is now looking for expansion opportunities—including in Western Australia; however, with many small farmer shareholders, it has also expressed its desire to maintain high dividend payouts. Despite this, it remains quite dependent on domestic weather patterns and on global commodities prices. It has also been affected by enhanced competition from rival Hi-Fert, which has acquired Summit Fertilisers to deliver it a 20% share of the east coast fertiliser market.

IPL Year to 30 September*	2003	2004
Revenues ($mn)	686.3	1107.1
EBIT ($mn)	59.3	112.5
EBIT margin (%)	8.6	10.2
Gross margin (%)	31.4	30.4
Profit before tax ($mn)	52.4	107.1
Profit after tax ($mn)	35.1	75.0
Earnings per share (¢)	112.7	128.8
Cash flow per share (¢)	191.0	206.5
Dividend (¢)	0	90
Percentage franked	~	100
Interest cover (times)	8.7	20.8
Return on equity (%)	9.7	12.5

* Results are for Pivot only to May 2003 and for Incitec Pivot from June 2003

Half year to 31 March	2004	2005
Revenues ($mn)	420.3	423.2
Profit before tax ($mn)	28.9	18.5
Profit after tax ($mn)	20.2	12.4
Earnings per share (¢)	34.7	21.4
Dividend (¢)	20	15
Percentage franked	100	100
Net tangible assets per share ($)	7.02	6.98
Debt-to-equity ratio (%)	22.7	22.3
Current ratio	1.3	1.3

Infomedia Ltd

Share price ($)	0.58	
12-month high ($)	0.91	
12-month low ($)	0.45	
Market capitalisation ($mn)	187.1	
Price-to-NTA-per-share ratio	5.2	
5-year share price return (% pa)	–21.4	
Sector: Information technology	**Company**	**Sector**
Price-earnings ratio (times)	13.0	34.4
Dividend yield (%)	5.9	1.7

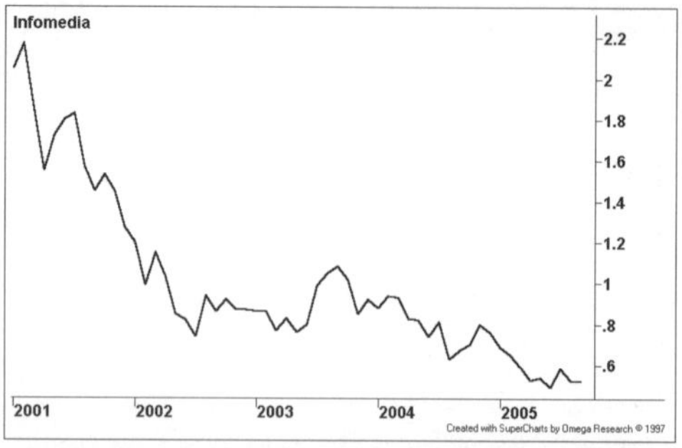

www.infomedia.com.au

Sydney software company Infomedia was formed in 1991, and has grown into a world leader in the development of specialised electronic catalogues. Its main product, Microcat, is an electronic parts catalogue for the automotive industry—with versions for most leading car companies, including General Motors, Ford, Toyota, Honda, Mitsubishi and Hyundai—and is shipped to customers in over 160 countries, in 25 languages. The company is also active in the provision of data management and business systems services. It operates support centres in Cologne, Utrecht, Troy, Cambridge, Melbourne, Mexico City, Tokyo and Toronto.

Latest business results (June 2005, full year)

Sales and profits fell as the company was hit by adverse exchange rates and by new competition for its Ford Europe business, which is its largest single market. At the end of the financial year the company had 46,732 Electronic Parts Catalogue (EPC) subscriptions, down from 51,524 a year before. This resulted from a decline in Ford Europe business, and the company's other EPC subscriptions experienced 12% growth during the year. There was noteworthy 370% sales growth for the company's Superservice Menus data management product, which provides automotive dealers with a range of browser-accessed service, repair, and warranty management tools. Nevertheless, its non-EPC business—representing about 12% of company turnover—remained in the red. A $9.1 million after-tax charge, recorded as a significant item, reflected a non-cash write-down of the PartsImager electronic catalogue business, which is being replaced by the Microcat product.

Outlook

Infomedia's EPC business enjoys extremely high margins—in the June 2004 year the company recorded a $32.1 million pre-tax profit on EPC sales of $63.4 million—and is attracting a growing number of competitors. Its Ford Europe business represents the company's largest market, and this is now under threat. North American General Motors dealers account for about 13% of Infomedia's EPC subscription base, and in August 2005 the company revealed that GM would phase out distribution of the catalogue and would launch its own EPC system from September 2006. As a result, Infomedia is now arranging its own direct representation for GM dealers, which will incur considerable start-up costs, with uncertain results. The company sees its small non-EPC business as offering great growth potential.

IFM Year to 30 June	2004	2005
Revenues ($mn)	69.6	59.1
EBIT ($mn)	29.6	20.8
EBIT margin (%)	42.5	35.2
Gross margin (%)	79.0	70.6
Profit before tax ($mn)	29.7	21.0
Profit after tax ($mn)	20.7	14.5
Earnings per share (¢)	6.4	4.5
Cash flow per share (¢)	8.2	6.3
Dividend (¢)	3.8	3.4
Percentage franked	100	100
Net tangible assets per share ($)	0.09	0.11
Interest cover (times)	~	~
Return on equity (%)	43.7	30.1
Debt-to-equity ratio (%)	~	~
Current ratio	1.9	2.3

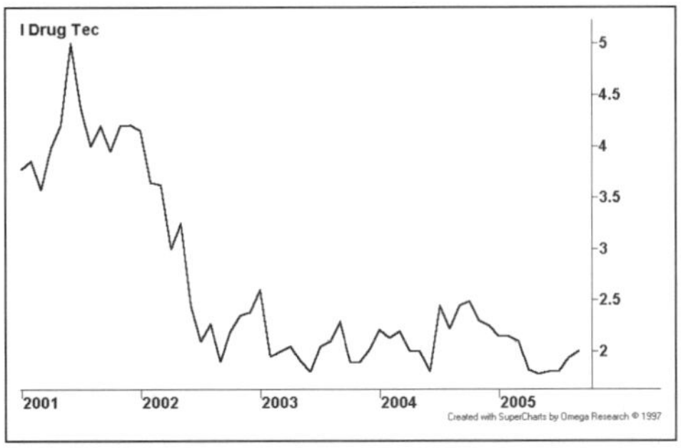

www.idtaus.com.au

Institute of Drug Technology Australia Ltd

Share price ($)	1.77	
12-month high ($)	2.60	
12-month low ($)	1.72	
Market capitalisation ($mn)	76.3	
Price-to-NTA-per-share ratio	2.8	
5-year share price return (% pa)	−10.7	
Sector: Health care	**Company**	**Sector**
Price-earnings ratio (times)	17.0	28.0
Dividend yield (%)	4.5	1.7

The Melbourne-based Institute of Drug Technology Australia (IDT), established in 1975, is a small, well-regarded developer and manufacturer of active pharmaceutical ingredients (APIs) for local and international companies. It also provides technical consulting and clinical trial services to the pharmaceuticals, chemical and biotechnology industries. In addition, it operates a research and development business for clients. Its Melbourne manufacturing facilities and laboratories have been licensed by the Australian Therapeutic Goods Administration and the United States Food and Drug Administration for production of APIs, and the company has developed a strong reputation for its dedicated facilities for the development and production of anti-cancer drugs. Through its CMAX division, IDT offers early-stage clinical trial services from a base at the Royal Adelaide Hospital.

Latest business results (June 2005, full year)

Sales edged up, and the company also announced its 11th straight rise in profits. Significant progress was reported on three major contracts with US pharmaceuticals companies which were announced in mid-2004. The company also said it had undertaken a number of important development and manufacturing projects with leading Australian biotechnology companies, aimed at producing new chemical entities for use in pre-clinical and early clinical development programs. The company also revealed that API manufacturing now represented a little over 10% of total revenues, down from over 50% in 2001.

Outlook

IDT continues to expand, despite the steady fall-off in demand for its generic API products. One of its three major projects for US companies involves the development of a novel drug for Pfizer, including the construction of specialised facilities, and this has already realised significant fee-for-service work. The second project — for an unnamed company — has also involved the construction of new facilities, and technical work is said to be progressing satisfactorily. The third project involves the supply of thalidomide capsules for Celgene Corporation, with IDT's facilities approved by the FDA in June 2005. The company announced that, thanks to growing demand for its CMAX clinical trial service, this business is expanding into Melbourne in a new, purpose-built facility and with several projects already contracted. IDT has confidence that recent new projects with leading biotechnology companies will provide further development opportunities in future.

IDT Year to 30 June	2004	2005
Revenues ($mn)	25.2	26.5
EBIT ($mn)	6.0	6.3
EBIT margin (%)	23.9	23.7
Gross margin (%)	72.9	79.7
Profit before tax ($mn)	6.1	6.4
Profit after tax ($mn)	4.3	4.5
Earnings per share (¢)	10.0	10.4
Cash flow per share (¢)	15.7	16.3
Dividend (¢)	7	8
Percentage franked	100	100
Net tangible assets per share ($)	0.61	0.64
Interest cover (times)	~	~
Return on equity (%)	15.7	15.7
Debt-to-equity ratio (%)	~	~
Current ratio	3.2	3.4

INTEGRATED GROUP LTD

Share price ($)	1.83
12-month high ($)	2.87
12-month low ($)	1.32
Market capitalisation ($mn)	130.4
Price-to-NTA-per-share ratio	4.3
5-year share price return (% pa)	19.2

Sector: Industrials	Company	Sector
Price-earnings ratio (times)	13.1	16.2
Dividend yield (%)	6.0	3.6

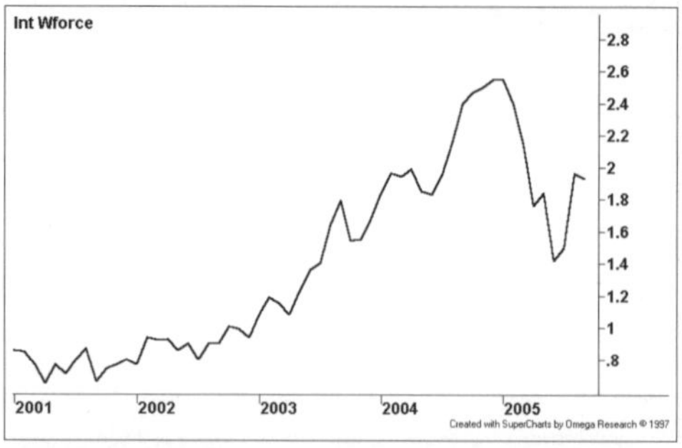

www.intgroup.com.au

Perth-based Integrated Group, founded in 1992 as Integrated Workforce, is a labour hire company, with a particular specialty in the supply of blue-collar workers for industry. It has expanded rapidly, through acquisition and organic growth, and now does business nationwide. It has also branched into the provision of support and maintenance services for the oil and gas sector, through its marine services division and its Integrated Maintenance Services subsidiary.

Latest business results (June 2005, full year)

Profits fell, despite good sales revenue growth, in a poor result for the company. The key factor was a 10% decline in revenues and a 13% drop in profits for the marine services division, due to problems with several contracts and generally sluggish levels of activity in the marine workforce market. By contrast, the workforce services division recorded 17% growth in sales revenues, with profits up 14%, following the successful tender for some significant national contracts. However, the company reported that a drop in activity levels late in the financial year meant that the result for this division was less than expected. Integrated Group boosted its stake in Integrated Maintenance Services from 50% to 100% from July 2004, and this business provided a solid contribution. There was also a maiden contribution from the company's new training services division, based on the acquisition in August 2004 of Corpfit Training Solutions.

Outlook

Integrated Group has been working to cut costs and boost efficiencies, and believes it is on track to resume growth. Its workforce services division — once more the primary driver of the company's business — has opened 11 new offices, and expects to achieve significant new penetration into the small and medium-sized markets. The company also believes that a slowdown in activity for the division late in the financial year has been reversed. It has established a national presence for its maintenance services division, and believes this will stimulate growth in 2006. Its new training services division is producing good margins and solid growth is expected in 2006. However, it continues to struggle with the slump in its marine services division, which in the June 2003 financial year represented over 60% of company profit, but in the latest result was less than 30%.

IWF Year to 30 June	2004	2005
Revenues ($mn)	331.2	395.4
Workforce division (%)	69	68
Marine division (%)	31	23
Maintenanance division (%)	0	6
EBIT ($mn)	17.6	17.4
EBIT margin (%)	5.3	4.4
Profit before tax ($mn)	16.4	15.7
Profit after tax ($mn)	11.8	9.9
Earnings per share (¢)	16.9	14.0
Cash flow per share (¢)	23.5	21.8
Dividend (¢)	10	11
Percentage franked	100	100
Net tangible assets per share ($)	0.44	0.43
Interest cover (times)	14.8	10.1
Return on equity (%)	24.0	18.4
Debt-to-equity ratio (%)	17.9	50.5
Current ratio	1.4	1.1

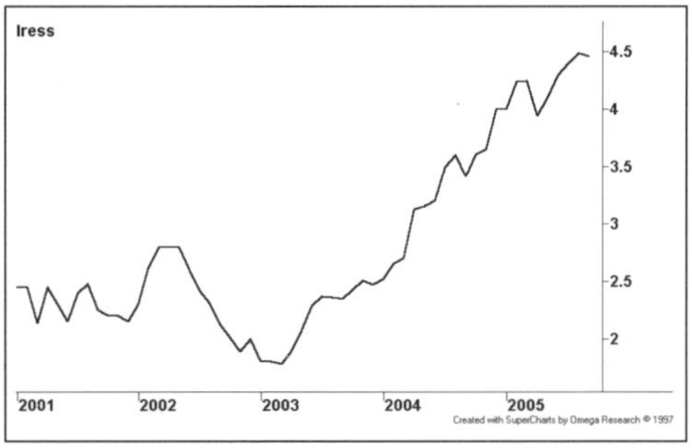

www.iress.com.au

IRESS Market Technology Ltd

Share price ($)	4.54
12-month high ($)	4.65
12-month low ($)	3.31
Market capitalisation ($mn)	479.3
Price-to-NTA-per-share ratio	14.4
4-year share price return (% pa)	23.6

Sector: Information technology	Company	Sector
Price-earnings ratio (times)	29.1	34.4
Dividend yield (%)	3.4	1.7

Melbourne-based IRESS was founded in 1993, and was formerly called BridgeDFS. It produces the prominent IRESS (integrated real-time equity system) sharemarket information system. Within the IRESS system it offers a range of trading products, including the IRESS Order System, the IRESS Equity Trading System, the IRESS Funds Trading System and the IRESS Risk Management System. It also produces the webIRESS and htmlIRESS equity information systems, and its XPLAN Technology division provides software for the financial planning industry. IRESS has operations in New Zealand and operates a joint venture in Canada. The Australian Stock Exchange owns 14% of the equity.

Latest business results (June 2005, half year)

A buoyant stock market environment helped power IRESS to a big gain in profits, although part of the increase came about through a restating of the June 2004 results in accord with the new Australian International Financial Reporting Standards. Demand for the company's mainstream information services continued to grow in both Australia and New Zealand. The XPLAN business more than doubled its revenues, to represent nearly 6% of company turnover, and it moved into profit for the first time. The small Canadian operation also saw strong revenue growth, and a break-even profit performance.

Outlook

IRESS is heavily geared to levels of stock market activity, which has fuelled some strong growth for the company. The provision of real-time stock market data and order processing systems is a very competitive business, and IRESS must continually upgrade its products to maintain a market advantage. Its IPS integrated tax-based retail portfolio system has been fully implemented in its broker configuration at several significant clients, and the electronic trade confirmation service also continues to grow. The company has been developing a range of enhancements to its key products and services in response to the ASX move to an anonymous market. Thanks to product enhancements introduced during the year, it is seeing expansion in New Zealand. Its Canadian joint venture is also progressing well, with the company confident of strong medium-term profits. The XPLAN division is expected to make a growing contribution to company profits.

IRE Year to 31 December	2003	2004
Revenues ($mn)	53.8	61.1
EBIT ($mn)	21.7	23.7
EBIT margin (%)	40.4	38.8
Profit before tax ($mn)	22.6	24.9
Profit after tax ($mn)	15.6	16.3
Earnings per share (¢)	15.3	15.6
Cash flow per share (¢)	19.1	19.3
Dividend (¢)	12.5	15.5
Percentage franked	100	100
Interest cover (times)	~	~
Return on equity (%)	72.0	51.7
Half year to 30 June	**2004**	**2005**
Revenues ($mn)	29.5	35.0
Profit before tax ($mn)	8.6	13.4
Profit after tax ($mn)	4.4	8.8
Earnings per share (¢)	4.2	8.3
Dividend (¢)	5.5	6.5
Percentage franked	100	100
Net tangible assets per share ($)	0.25	0.32
Debt-to-equity ratio (%)	~	~
Current ratio	4.1	4.3

K&S CORPORATION LTD

Share price ($)	3.46	
12-month high ($)	3.73	
12-month low ($)	2.51	
Market capitalisation ($mn)	224.3	
Price-to-NTA-per-share ratio	2.7	
5-year share price return (% pa)	41.3	
Sector: Industrials	**Company**	**Sector**
Price-earnings ratio (times)	10.4	16.2
Dividend yield (%)	3.9	3.6

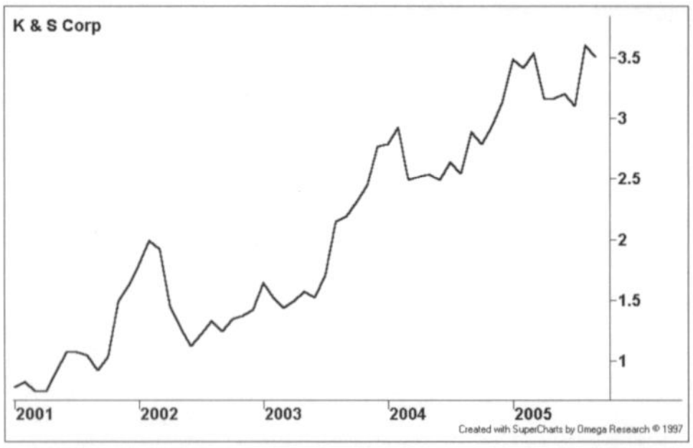

www.ksgroup.com.au

Based in Mt Gambier, and with a history stretching back more than 55 years, K&S is one of Australia's leading transport, warehousing and logistics companies and has a strategy directed towards large national contracts. It controls one of the largest company-owned fleets in Australia, as well as owning over 160 000 square metres of warehousing and a large range of rail and sea containers. It operates through four divisions: K&S Freighters is involved in road, rail and coastal sea forwarding; K&S Integrated Distribution handles warehousing, storage and local distribution; K&S Agencies manages Ampol fuel distribution throughout regions of South Australia and Victoria; and K&S (NZ) provides distribution throughout New Zealand. The company chairman, Allan Scott, owns more than 60% of the equity.

Latest business results (June 2005, full year)

K&S enjoyed another excellent year, although a large part of the profit gain—$6.4 million before tax—derived from the favourable settlement of fraud-related legal actions against two online betting agencies. There was strong organic growth from existing customers and a solid contribution from new contracts with Capral, Orrcon and Coca-Cola, together with the full-year effect of the acquisition of Cochrane's Transport in New Zealand. The company reported that organic growth from existing contracts provided $22.2 million in additional revenues, new contracts contributed an extra $11.3 million and New Zealand operations—which grew 73%—an additional $11.6 million.

Outlook

The ongoing strength of the domestic economy has provided a strong boost to K&S, which at the same time has been expanding its operations. It has made a series of strong moves into New Zealand, winning a major contract with timber giant Fletcher Challenge, and its acquisition of Cochrane's Transport has turned it into a key provider of logistics services to the dairy, kiwifruit and paper industries. The purchase of two additional transport businesses in New Zealand in February 2005 will provide further growth opportunities. A new transport terminal at Coopers Plains in Brisbane is providing upgraded infrastructure to support future growth. In April 2005, K&S began construction of a major new $28.3 million transport terminal and warehouse at Laverton in Melbourne. Due to be operational by April 2006, it is intended to provide scope for a substantial boost to Melbourne business.

KSC Year to 30 June	2004	2005
Revenues ($mn)	295.7	340.8
EBIT ($mn)	20.1	31.1
EBIT margin (%)	6.8	9.1
Gross margin (%)	8.8	8.0
Profit before tax ($mn)	17.6	28.4
Profit after tax ($mn)	12.2	19.9
Earnings per share (¢)	20.3	33.2
Cash flow per share (¢)	43.0	57.4
Dividend (¢)	11	13.5
Percentage franked	100	100
Net tangible assets per share ($)	0.95	1.26
Interest cover (times)	8.1	11.6
Return on equity (%)	19.5	26.4
Debt-to-equity ratio (%)	52.7	37.7
Current ratio	0.9	1.1

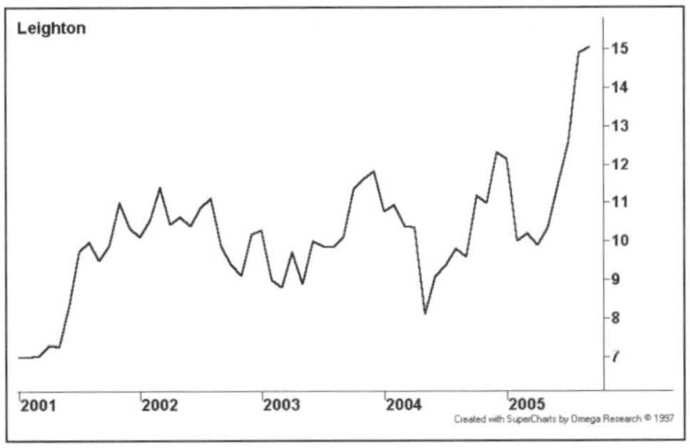

www.leighton.com.au

Leighton Holdings Ltd

Share price ($)	13.30	
12-month high ($)	13.37	
12-month low ($)	8.80	
Market capitalisation ($mn)	3763.1	
Price-to-NTA-per-share ratio	4.2	
5-year share price return (% pa)	24.0	
Sector: Industrials	**Company**	**Sector**
Price-earnings ratio (times)	17.7	16.2
Dividend yield (%)	3.8	3.6

Founded in 1949, Leighton is Australia's largest project development and contracting group. It incorporates Leighton Contractors, Thiess Contractors, Leighton Asia, Leighton Properties and John Holland, and employs more than 10 000 people at sites around the Asia-Pacific region and in South America. The German construction company Hochtief owns 53% of Leighton's shares.

Latest business results (June 2005, full year)

Leighton enjoyed a massive recovery from the slump of the previous year, when it experienced major cost blow-outs. The Australia-Pacific region — responsible for about 85% of turnover — was the key, with revenues up 36% and pre-tax profit soaring nearly fourfold. Engineering and infrastructure work was the prime contributor, with revenues of $2.4 billion, up 45%. Mining and resources revenue was also strong, up 32% to $1.4 billion. Building and property revenue jumped 38% to $1.8 billion. In contrast, Asian revenues rose moderately, but pre-tax profit plunged 33%, hurt by losses on the North Luzon Expressway and problems with a contract in Sri Lanka. The company also received a $38.5 million boost from a new policy recognising profits earlier in a contract's life than previously. Work in hand at the end of the financial year was $15.5 billion, up from $13.0 billion a year earlier.

Outlook

Leighton sees transport infrastructure work as the driving force for an expected further solid lift in profits in the June 2006 year. In particular, the acceleration of work on the $2.5 billion EastLink Mitcham-Frankston freeway in Melbourne is expected to provide a considerable boost to earnings, and the company is actively pursuing work on the $1.5 billion North-South Bypass Tunnel and the $1.5 billion Gateway Bridge duplication, both in Brisbane. Leighton also anticipates good growth in contract coal mining and in resources-related process engineering projects. However, building and property activity is not expected to grow. With some large infrastructure and building projects in Hong Kong, Macau and Malaysia, and major Indonesian coal mining contracts, the company also expects to see an improved result from its Asian operations. Leighton's huge net cash holdings of more than $400 million have given rise to speculation that it is seeking a major acquisition. The shares have been boosted by speculation that majority shareholder Hochtief might make a full takeover bid.

LEI Year to 30 June	2004	2005
Revenues ($mn)	4834.4	6257.8
Civil & building (%)	58	59
Mining & resources (%)	31	28
Telecommunications	3	5
Property development	2	4
EBIT ($mn)	164.6	303.3
EBIT margin (%)	3.4	4.8
Profit before tax ($mn)	161.4	289.1
Profit after tax ($mn)	110.0	205.4
Earnings per share (¢)	40.6	75.3
Cash flow per share (¢)	148.4	211.4
Dividend (¢)	45	50
Percentage franked	100	50
Net tangible assets per share ($)	3.02	3.19
Interest cover (times)	50.2	21.4
Return on equity (%)	12.9	23.6
Debt-to-equity ratio (%)	~	~

Macquarie Bank Ltd

Share price ($)	63.45	
12-month high ($)	64.64	
12-month low ($)	31.96	
Market capitalisation ($mn)	14 403.4	
Price-to-NTA-per-share ratio	4.4	
5-year share price return (% pa)	22.5	
Sector: Financials	**Company**	**Sector**
Price-earnings ratio (times)	16.9	14.3
Dividend yield (%)	2.5	4.5

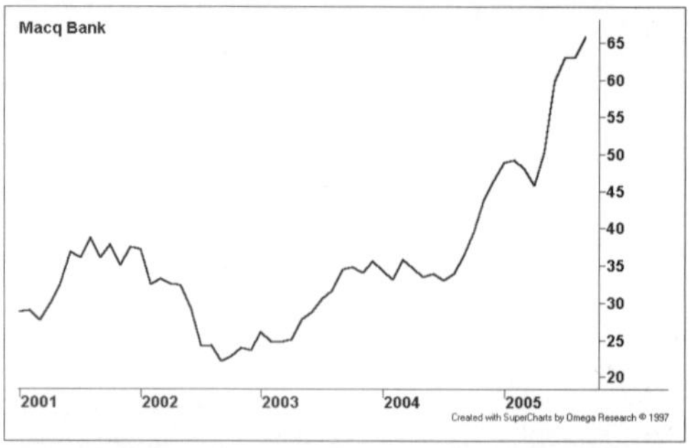

www.macquarie.com.au

Macquarie — established in 1969 as Hill Samuel Australia, a subsidiary of a British merchant bank — is Australia's leading locally owned investment bank. Its activities are divided into six operating groups that span four broad business segments: Asset and Wealth Management involves the distribution and manufacture of funds management products; Financial Markets incorporates the bank's trading in fixed income, equities, currency, commodities and derivative products; Investment Banking encompasses corporate finance, advisory, underwriting, facilitation, broking and real estate/property development activities; and Lending includes banking activities, mortgages, margin lending and leasing. Its extensive international business accounts for more than one third of company income.

Latest business results (March 2005, full year)

Macquarie delivered another powerhouse result, with strength in all major business areas. Net interest income was up 37%. Fee and commission income jumped 44%. Trading income was up 31%, based largely on favourable equity market trading. There was a $300 million profit relating to the merger of Macquarie Goodman Industrial Trust and Macquarie Goodman Management. Assets under management rose 42% to $89 billion. Despite considerable growth in expenses, including the addition of 447 staff from the acquisition of the ING cash equities sales business in Asia, the bank achieved an impressive reduction in its cost to income ratio.

Outlook

Macquarie continues to race ahead, and its shares have been stellar performers. Thanks to a growing number of initiatives overseas, it is possible that half the bank's income will be derived offshore within a few years. In particular, the roll-out of a succession of infrastructure and other specialist funds around the world is expected to provide a steady and stable source of management fee income. Domestically, the bank is part of the ConnectEast Group, that will build and manage the $2.5 billion Mitcham-Frankston freeway, and it has bought 92 radio stations to form a new specialist fund. The new Macquarie Securities Asia — formerly the ING cash equities sales business — is already profitable and growing. Also in Asia, the bank has concluded the largest initial public offering in Philippines history, and has been awarded a Malaysian stockbroking licence. In Europe, the bank has established the Macquarie European Infrastructure Fund, and its London-based Global Energy Markets team has been recording strong growth.

MBL Year to 31 March	2004	2005
Operating income ($mn)	2465.0	3749.0
Net interest income ($mn)	270.0	370.0
Operating expenses ($mn)	1780.0	2588.0
Profit before tax ($mn)	685.0	1161.0
Profit after tax ($mn)	494.0	823.0
Earnings per share (¢)	233.0	374.6
Dividend (¢)	122	161
Percentage franked	90	90
Non-interest income to total income (%)	89.0	90.1
Net tangible assets per share ($)	13.03	14.44
Cost to income ratio (%)	72.2	69.0
Return on equity (%)	19.8	25.8
Return on assets (%)	1.3	1.8

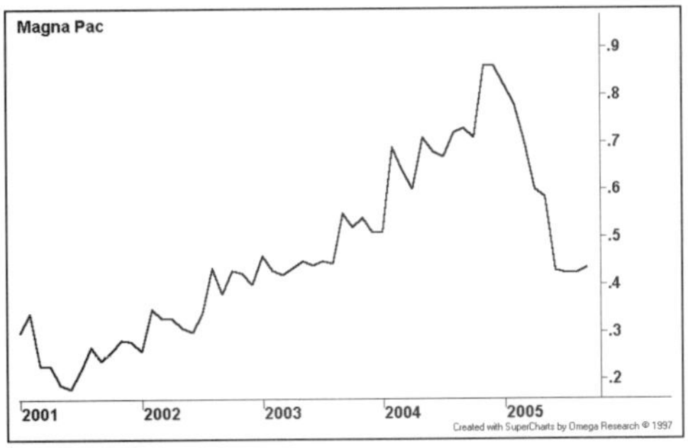

www.magnapacific.com.au

Magna Pacific (Holdings) Ltd

Share price ($)	0.43
12-month high ($)	0.94
12-month low ($)	0.39
Market capitalisation ($mn)	52.3
Price-to-NTA-per-share ratio	1.9
5-year share price return (% pa)	8.1

Sector: Consumer discretionary	Company	Sector
Price-earnings ratio (times)	6.6	24.2
Dividend yield (%)	7.0	1.2

Brisbane-based Magna Pacific is a leading wholesale distributor of DVDs and videos to retailers and rental outlets throughout Australia and New Zealand. It owns a 2300-square-metre facility in Brisbane capable of round-the-clock manufacture/packaging of six million DVDs and one million videos annually. It has also recently moved into cinema distribution of movies. Magna Pacific shares are listed on the ASX and also on German stock exchanges.

Latest business results (June 2005, full year)

Sales revenues fell, due to an increase in low-price budget DVD sales, but profits surged, thanks to buoyant Australian demand for DVDs. There was also a $2 million profit—treated as a significant item—from the sale of the company's shareholding in the Becker Group.

Outlook

Magna Pacific has grown to become one of the leaders in Australia and New Zealand in the highly fragmented DVD distribution business, and is a major beneficiary of the continuing boom in demand for DVD products. As the market grows, the company will benefit further from growing economies of scale. Nevertheless, its future is also very dependent on its ability to continue to make available popular DVD content. It has a back catalogue of 3000 titles, of which it has to date released fewer than half. It is already a leading distributor of documentaries and children's titles, and is placing a new emphasis on music DVDs. It is achieving noteworthy success with its new line of DVD singles, launched in February 2005. These contain 30 minutes of children's television programing and retail for under $5. They are sold through major chains such as Woolworths and Kmart and, by being located at the retailers' point of purchase rather than in the DVD section, target impulse buyers. With 56 titles already available, some 400 000 units were sold between February and June 2005, with a forecast of more than one million units in the June 2006 year and two million in June 2007. Magna Pacific has acquired the 49% of its New Zealand subsidiary that it did not own previously, and is restructuring its operations there. Magna Pacific has no debt and, with cash holdings of over $10 million, it is seeking further investment opportunities. It is building a new $14 million warehouse in Brisbane.

MPH Year to 30 June	2004	2005
Revenues ($mn)	39.4	36.7
EBIT ($mn)	9.1	10.3
EBIT margin (%)	23.0	28.1
Gross margin (%)	46.6	54.8
Profit before tax ($mn)	10.0	11.3
Profit after tax ($mn)	3.5	7.3
Earnings per share (¢)	4.1	6.6
Cash flow per share (¢)	5.3	7.8
Dividend (¢)	2	3
Percentage franked	100	100
Net tangible assets per share ($)	0.34	0.22
Interest cover (times)	~	~
Return on equity (%)	12.0	18.8
Debt-to-equity ratio (%)	~	~
Current ratio	6.3	4.3

MaxiTRANS Industries Ltd

Share price ($)	0.84	
12-month high ($)	1.08	
12-month low ($)	0.67	
Market capitalisation ($mn)	142.5	
Price-to-NTA-per-share ratio	4.4	
5-year share price return (% pa)	42.3	
Sector: Industrials	**Company**	**Sector**
Price-earnings ratio (times)	12.8	16.2
Dividend yield (%)	4.8	3.6

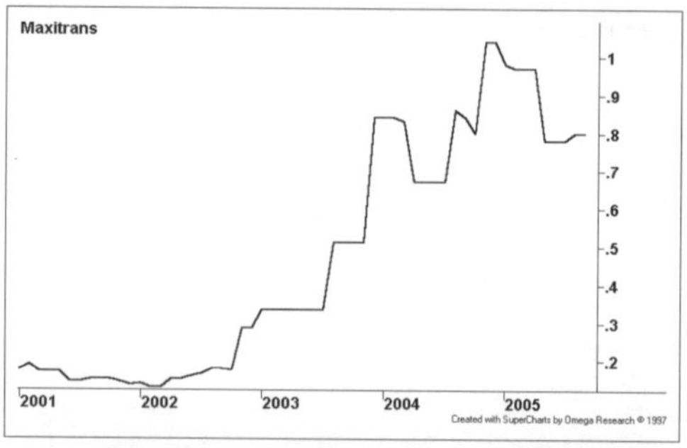

www.maxitrans.com.au

Based in Melbourne, MaxiTRANS was formed in 1998 from the merger of Freighter Industries (which had been established in 1946) and Maxi-CUBE (started in 1972). It is today a leading manufacturer of a wide range of specialised truck trailers for the road transportation industry, and they are mainly produced in Ballarat and Auckland. It operates MTC, a Chinese joint venture operation with THT, a major Chinese transport equipment manufacturer. MTC produces fibreglass wall panels which are sold throughout China, including in the manufacture of insulated and refrigerated trailers. The acquisition in 2004 of Hamelex-White made MaxiTRANS Australia's largest manufacturer of tip trailers. The company also operates a significant truck and trailer parts business, boosted by the acquisition in December 2004 of a 70% stake in the Colrain parts venture.

Latest business results (June 2005, full year)

The buoyant domestic economic helped MaxiTRANS achieve a strong gain in revenues and profits, and an increased market share. The good result came despite a shortage of skilled labour, which held back production. Revenues from the sale of new trailer and tipper units rose 25% to $166 million, though pre-tax profit rose just 5%. Van unit sales rose 25%, Lusty EMS-brand tipper unit sales rose 46%, Hamelex White-brand tipper sales rose 8% and trailer unit sales were up 5%. Revenues from servicing and the sale of parts jumped 145% to $46 million, thanks partially to the Colrain acquisition, with profits surging more than threefold.

Outlook

MaxiTRANS is working to restructure its operations, with the aim of powering long-term growth. It has reported that the June 2006 year has begun well, with several major new contracts already received, and more expected. It is implementing strategies to boost production capacity and is introducing a series of robotic systems to address the problem of skill shortages. It is also hiring significant numbers of new apprentices. The Colrain parts acquisition provides an opportunity for growth in complementary markets in the transport equipment industry, along with synergies with existing businesses. The sale of the TraileRentals business will help MaxiTRANS boost trailer sales to other companies that had been competitors in the rental segment. The company's Chinese operation is making a solid contribution, and a 50% factory expansion is expected to boost business.

MXI Year to 30 June	2004	2005
Revenues ($mn)	158.9	223.2
EBIT ($mn)	13.1	17.4
EBIT margin (%)	8.2	7.8
Gross margin (%)	21.8	16.9
Profit before tax ($mn)	11.6	15.2
Profit after tax ($mn)	8.8	11.3
Earnings per share (¢)	5.7	6.6
Cash flow per share (¢)	8.7	9.9
Dividend (¢)	3.5	4
Percentage franked	100	100
Net tangible assets per share ($)	0.20	0.19
Interest cover (times)	8.9	7.9
Return on equity (%)	15.7	16.2
Debt-to-equity ratio (%)	28.6	56.7
Current ratio	1.7	1.9

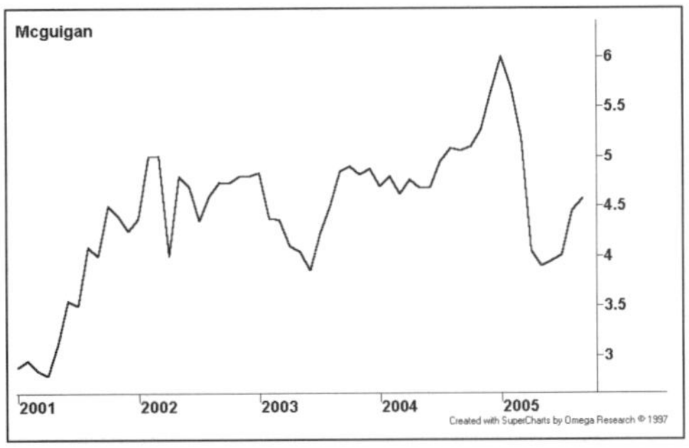

www.mcguiganwines.com.au

McGuigan Simeon Wines Ltd

Share price ($)	4.01
12-month high ($)	6.23
12-month low ($)	3.58
Market capitalisation ($mn)	452.3
Price-to-NTA-per-share ratio	1.5
5-year share price return (% pa)	12.9

Sector: Consumer staples	Company	Sector
Price-earnings ratio (times)	12.5	15.6
Dividend yield (%)	5.9	3.3

McGuigan Simeon Wines was formed from the 2002 merger of Brian McGuigan Wines — founded ten years earlier — with Simeon Wines. It is now one of Australia's largest listed wineries, with vineyards in many premium viticulture regions. Its labels include the Harvest range and the Black Label range, as well as Miranda Wines. It is also Australia's largest seller of bulk wine and it manages vineyards. Exports are more than 40% of sales.

Latest business results (June 2005, full year)

Sales rose, but McGuigan Simeon was hit by a global glut of grapes, and profits tumbled. The best result came from the company's high-margin bulk wine business, where McGuigan has particular strengths, with domestic sales up 4% and exports soaring 49%, and profits also up. Bottled wine revenues rose 15% domestically and 8% overseas, with a significant expansion of British sales, but earnings fell, with the continuing strength of the dollar a factor. The worst result was from McGuigan's owned and leased vineyards, with revenues down and profits more than halving, as the company struggled to manage a significant decline in the price of grapes. Altogether, British sales rose 40% to $86.5 million, American sales were up 28% to $48.8 million and New Zealand sales soared 73% to $9.9 million.

Outlook

The company announced in September 2005 that the industry remained highly competitive, with unfavourable exchange rates and oversupply hurting it in all market sectors, especially exports. It did not see this situation changing significantly for one or two years and it forecast a June 2006 profit in line with the previous year, or even slightly down. Nevertheless, the company has good — and growing — market shares for its products and is financially stable. It continues to seek acquisitions. It expects the January 2005 acquisition of a bottling and warehousing operation in Victoria from Beringer Blass Wines to further lower its cost base. The company has reported that the 2005 vintage was of excellent quality, with tonnage from its vineyards 5% above budget. The company has also taken some heart from the fact that there had been two consecutive small vintages in the US, and a relatively small vintage in South America, which is becoming a major export rival to Australian wineries.

MGW Year to 30 June	2004	2005
Revenues ($mn)	305.7	368.1
Bottled wine (%)	41	39
Bulk wine & processing (%)	31	32
Bulk in bottle (%)	14	18
Vineyard development (%)	14	11
EBIT ($mn)	61.6	54.1
EBIT margin (%)	20.1	14.7
Gross margin (%)	17.3	13.6
Profit before tax ($mn)	51.3	45.1
Profit after tax ($mn)	40.2	35.9
Earnings per share (¢)	38.2	32.1
Cash flow per share (¢)	50.2	43.8
Dividend (¢)	23.5	23.5
Percentage franked	100	100
Net tangible assets per share ($)	2.57	2.75
Interest cover (times)	6.0	6.0
Return on equity (%)	13.3	10.3
Debt-to-equity ratio (%)	44.7	45.7
Current ratio	2.2	3.0

Metcash Ltd

Share price ($)	4.08	
12-month high ($)	4.32	
12-month low ($)	3.08	
Market capitalisation ($mn)	1757.6	
Price-to-NTA-per-share ratio	na	
5-year share price return (% pa)	61.2	
Sector: Consumer staples	**Company**	**Sector**
Price-earnings ratio (times)	26.1	15.6
Dividend yield (%)	2.3	3.3

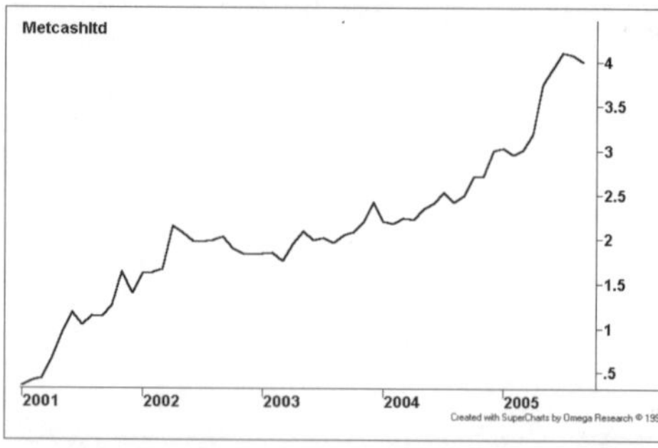

www.metcash.com

Sydney-based Metcash, a 74%-owned subsidiary of South Africa's Metro Cash and Carry, is one of Australia's leading grocery retail and wholesale companies. Its principal business is IGA Distribution, which operates from eight distribution centres and supplies some 4500 independent grocery stores on the eastern seaboard and in South Australia. Its Australian Liquor Marketers division supplies liquor to more than 13 000 outlets throughout Australia and New Zealand. The Campbells Cash and Carry business operates from 41 warehouses, and supplies groceries to convenience stores, petrol stations and other smaller outlets. As this book was being published, Metcash expected to acquire many of Foodland's businesses.

Latest business results (April 2005, full year)

Profits edged up on a dip in sales, in a competitive grocery environment. The core IGA food distribution business—responsible for more than half the company's turnover and for about three-quarters of company profit—saw EBIT up nearly 10%, despite a small decline in total sales revenues. A change in the product mix for the Campbells Cash and Carry division, along with cost reductions, helped this business to an 18% jump in EBIT. However, the liquor business saw EBIT down by nearly 15%, primarily due to the loss of business from Australian Leisure and Hospitality.

Outlook

Since being acquired by South African interests in 1998, Metcash has been undergoing a major restructuring that is now realising steady increases in profits. It expects—subject to shareholder approval—to acquire Foodland's 60 Australian supermarkets and its Western Australian wholesale business, and believes this will create significant synergies with existing businesses. Like its rivals, Metcash is boosting its percentage of own-brand products at its supermarkets, with generally higher margins than for branded grocery items. In the April 2005 year, its corporate brands of Black & Gold, Way of Life and IGA realised 26.5% growth compared to the previous year. Campbells Cash and Carry is gaining strength in the booming convenience store business. A new supply agreement with 350 7-Eleven stores is expected to add $200 million in sales. Its newly created Independent Brands of Australia is working to consolidate more than 1200 independent liquor stores under three main brands—Cellarbrations, Cheers and Liquor Force.

MTS Year to 30 April	2004	2005
Revenues ($mn)	7173.9	6993.7
Food distribution (%)	55	55
Liquor distribution (%)	31	31
Cash & carry distribution (%)	14	14
EBIT ($mn)	163.2	165.3
EBIT margin (%)	2.3	2.4
Gross margin (%)	2.3	2.0
Profit before tax ($mn)	155.7	163.8
Profit after tax ($mn)	101.8	104.9
Earnings per share (¢)	15.8	15.6
Cash flow per share (¢)	23.2	24.4
Dividend (¢)	11	9.5
Percentage franked	100	100
Net tangible assets per share ($)	0.36	~
Interest cover (times)	21.5	113.6
Return on equity (%)	22.7	10.5
Debt-to-equity ratio (%)	7.5	14.5
Current ratio	1.1	1.4

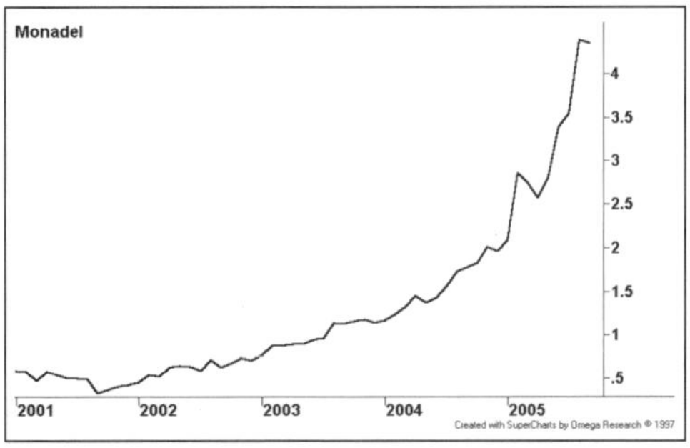

www.monadel.com.au

Monadelphous Group Ltd

Share price ($)	3.93
12-month high ($)	4.00
12-month low ($)	1.49
Market capitalisation ($mn)	317.2
Price-to-NTA-per-share ratio	7.1
5-year share price return (% pa)	56.8

Sector: Industrials	Company	Sector
Price-earnings ratio (times)	18.6	16.2
Dividend yield (%)	3.6	3.6

Perth-based Monadelphous is an engineering company that provides project management, construction, maintenance and support services to the mining, mineral processing, chemicals and associated industries. It operates from branches at key mining and mineral processing centres throughout Australia, with a client base that includes most of the country's resource majors.

Latest business results (June 2005, full year)

Monadelphous unleashed another stunning result, with sales and profits rocketing upwards. The engineering construction division was the star, with revenues up 137% to $239 million, as the company won increasingly larger construction contracts associated with some of Australia's leading resource development projects. Major projects completed included structural, mechanical and electrical construction works for the expansion of Comalco's bauxite operations at Weipa in Queensland, the design and construction of coal handling facilities for Xstrata's Rolleston coal project in Queensland, and a major expansion of Rio Tinto's Yandi iron ore plant in Western Australia. The maintenance and industrial services division saw revenues up 26% to $151 million, thanks to a number of new long-term contracts and new major customers. The division achieved particular growth in Queensland, as a result of contracts for the Comalco alumina refinery and Boyne smelter in Gladstone.

Outlook

As one of Australia's leading resource development contractors, Monadelphous is gaining enormous benefits from the ongoing resources boom, and this has been reflected in its surging share price. The company has said that it sees record levels of investment continuing in new resources projects for at least two or three more years. In particular, it sees significant opportunities from some major iron ore and coal development projects in Western Australia and Queensland and in July 2005 it announced that it had won a $65 million contract from BHP Billiton for construction work on its iron ore project at Port Hedland in Western Australia. The company announced in mid-2005 the acquisition of Queensland-based Murray Instrumentation and Electrical, a step to encourage support future growth. It believes this will help its maintenance and industrial services division broaden its services capability. Monadelphous has also flagged its interest in further acquisitions in order to diversify its revenue streams. A share split in mid-2005 was intended to boost liquidity of the shares. The company has conceded that skilled-labour shortages remain a major challenge.

MND Year to 30 June	2004	2005
Revenues ($mn)	220.8	390.6
EBIT ($mn)	11.9	23.8
EBIT margin (%)	5.4	6.1
Gross margin (%)	9.7	9.3
Profit before tax ($mn)	12.2	23.9
Profit after tax ($mn)	8.5	16.7
Earnings per share (¢)	11.1*	21.1
Cash flow per share (¢)	16.6*	28.0
Dividend (¢)	7.5*	14.25
Percentage franked	100	100
Net tangible assets per share ($)	0.50*	0.55
Interest cover (times)	~	~
Return on equity (%)	23.2	39.0
Debt-to-equity ratio (%)	~	~
Current ratio	1.5	1.4

* adjusted for a four-for-one share split

National Australia Bank Ltd

Share price ($)	31.36	
12-month high ($)	32.04	
12-month low ($)	26.23	
Market capitalisation ($mn)	49 241.3	
Price-to-NTA-per-share ratio	1.7	
5-year share price return (% pa)	9.1	
Sector: Financials	**Company**	**Sector**
Price-earnings ratio (times)	12.1	14.3
Dividend yield (%)	5.3	4.5

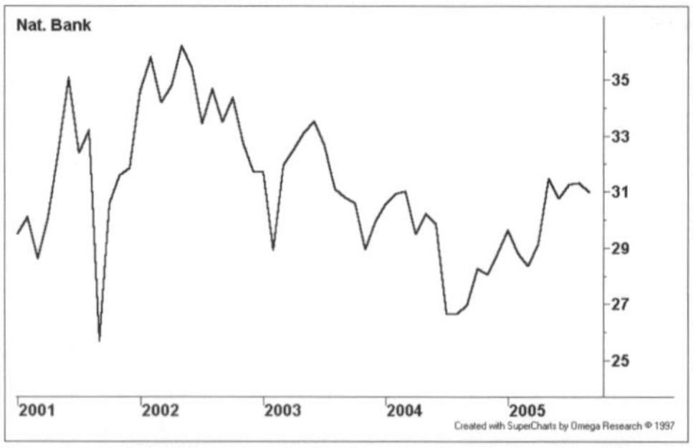

www.national.com.au

The National Australia Bank is Australia's largest bank and has a history dating back to 1858. It is a world-class operation with a wide spread of financial activities; it owns the Clydesdale Bank and Yorkshire Bank in Britain, and the Bank of New Zealand. Its MLC business is one of Australia's leading funds management operations. In 2005 it sold its two Irish banks, Northern Bank and National Irish Bank.

Latest business results (March 2005, half year)

Profits fell, culminating in a dismal result for the once high-flying bank. Locally, banking profits fell nearly 10%, with higher costs offsetting a slight improvement in some businesses. Wealth management profits rose 7%, thanks to improved returns on retained earnings and capital, more than offsetting lower insurance profits and higher regulatory and compliance costs. British profits fell 10%, hurt by higher costs and strong competition. New Zealand profits were flat from the March 2004 half, with strong growth—particularly in home lending—offset by margin contraction brought about by competitive pressures. The bank made a $1.1 billion profit—treated as a significant item—on the sale of the Northern Bank and National Irish Bank.

NAB Year to 30 September	2003	2004
Operating income ($mn)	12 873.0	13 034.0
Net interest income ($mn)	7419.0	7191.0
Operating expenses ($mn)	6612.0	8718.0
Profit before tax ($mn)	5628.0	5039.0
Profit after tax ($mn)	3947.0	3935.0
Earnings per share (¢)	260.4	259.7
Dividend (¢)	163	166
Percentage franked	100	100
Non-interest income to total income (%)	42.4	44.8
Cost to income ratio (%)	51.4	66.9
Return on equity (%)	16.6	13.9
Return on assets (%)	1.0	1.0
Half year to 31 March	**2004**	**2005**
Operating income ($mn)	6496.0	6601.0
Profit before tax ($mn)	2909.0	2748.0
Profit after tax ($mn)	2102.0	1714.0
Earnings per share (¢)	129.2	104.1
Dividend (¢)	83	83
Percentage franked	100	80
Net tangible assets per share ($)	15.81	18.03

Outlook

NAB believes that its problems have bottomed and that a profit recovery is under way. Nevertheless, concerned about escalating costs—which have increased to a level out of line with competitors—the bank has embarked on a massive $800 million restructuring of many of its operations. This includes significant staff redundancies and the closure of many of its British branches. It believes that it has started to gain market share domestically in home lending and business banking, with particularly strong growth in lending to medium-sized businesses. It has strengthened its wealth management business with a new leadership team and a realignment with its banking businesses to create single customer-focused products and services. It is working to build on its considerable strengths in New Zealand with new products and services in retail banking. However, it also faces the challenge of a slowdown in Australia in home and personal lending, and the bank's own forecast is for slowing economies in Australia and New Zealand.

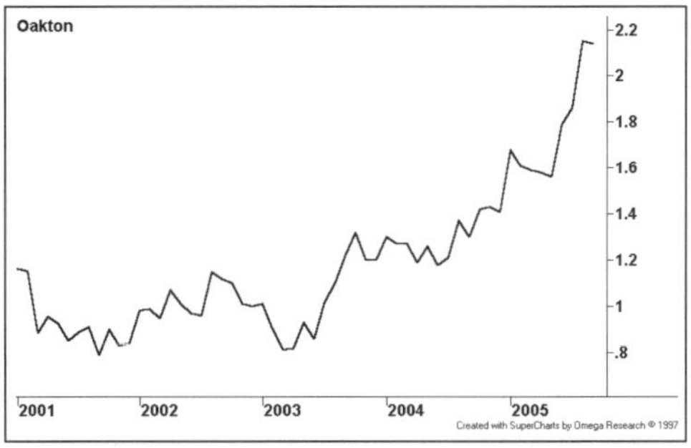

www.oakton.com.au

Oakton Ltd

Share price ($)	1.89
12-month high ($)	1.94
12-month low ($)	1.20
Market capitalisation ($mn)	173.3
Price-to-NTA-per-share ratio	12.3
5-year share price return (% pa)	18.2

Sector: Information technology	Company	Sector
Price-earnings ratio (times)	18.3	34.4
Dividend yield (%)	5.3	1.7

Melbourne-based technology consultant Oakton was established in 1988. It has grown rapidly through acquisition, and now serves a wide variety of blue-chip corporate and government clients, providing guidance on IT requirements and covering the full life cycle of planning and design, custom software development, packaged software implementation, information management and system integration processes. It also provides a service for fully managing organisations' operational systems. Oakton has offices in Melbourne and Sydney.

Latest business results (June 2005, full year)

Sales and profits rose in an excellent result, with the company reporting that it had gained market share across all its businesses. Much of the growth came from the company's Sydney operations, where profits doubled. Sydney is now responsible for nearly a third of company profits.

Outlook

Oakton continues its rapid expansion, with staff numbers at 390 in August 2005, up from around 260 in July 2004, and fewer than 100 in mid-2000. It has also undergone a major restructuring. In particular, it has fully integrated all its acquired businesses, it has consolidated the range of different services being offered by each acquired business into one set of ten integrated service lines, it has sold its underperforming products division, reduced the number of trading brands from eight to one, consolidated all marketing activity and websites and established a new management team in Sydney. As a result, it now sees itself set for a period of strong sales and profit growth. Its customer numbers have grown from 160 to 202 in two years—nearly a third in financial services and a further one quarter in the resources industry—and the company has also achieved notable success in boosting the number of services provided to each customer. It continues to expand in Sydney, with the goal that its operations there be equal in size to Melbourne by 2007, and it is planning further geographical diversification during 2006. With no debt and more than $5.5 million in cash, it also expects to continue to grow by acquisition. The IT consulting industry comprises some 19 000 firms, but fewer than 100 of these have more than 100 employees, offering many opportunities for strategic acquisitions.

OKN Year to 30 June	2004	2005
Revenues ($mn)	44.5	54.0
EBIT ($mn)	9.9	12.3
EBIT margin (%)	22.3	22.7
Profit before tax ($mn)	10.1	12.4
Profit after tax ($mn)	6.8	8.3
Earnings per share (¢)	8.5	10.3
Cash flow per share (¢)	10.4	12.7
Dividend (¢)	8	10
Percentage franked	100	100
Net tangible assets per share ($)	0.12	0.15
Interest cover (times)	~	~
Return on equity (%)	26.7	30.0
Debt-to-equity ratio (%)	~	~
Current ratio	2.6	2.2

OAMPS Ltd

Share price ($)	2.91	
12-month high ($)	3.12	
12-month low ($)	2.38	
Market capitalisation ($mn)	412.3	
Price-to-NTA-per-share ratio	8.7	
5-year share price return (% pa)	32.1	
Sector: Financials	**Company**	**Sector**
Price-earnings ratio (times)	14.0	14.3
Dividend yield (%)	5.2	4.5

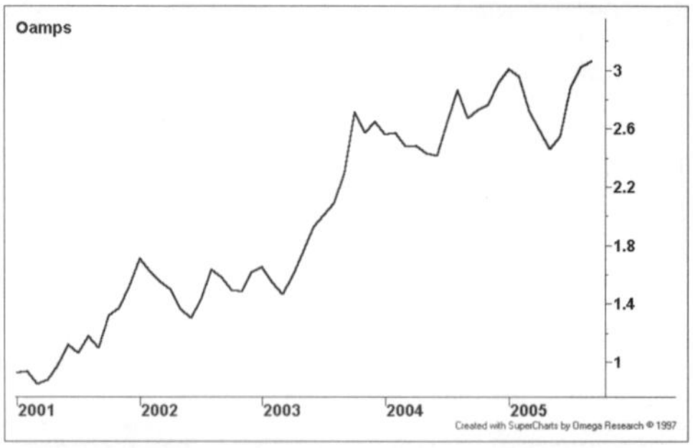

www.oamps.com.au

Melbourne-based OAMPS, established in 1976 as the Oil Agents Mutual Provident Society, is one of Australia's largest insurance brokers and underwriters. It also operates in various other related businesses: its premium funding arm is a lending facility for clients, it has a funds management business, it acts as trustee to superannuation funds and it provides clients with a range of other financial products, such as leasing facilities, warranty services and mortgage finance. It also operates an insurance broking and underwriting business in the United Kingdom, where it specialises in oil, tanker and hazardous goods risks. It has 29 offices in Australia and the Pacific.

Latest business results (June 2005, full year)

The company's strategy of expansion by acquisition meant another firm boost to revenues and profits, although growth was not at the same pace as in earlier years. Domestically, the company's insurance broking business continued to gain market share, with a 22% rise (to $627 million) in premiums processed, and a 20% gain in broking revenues to $88.7 million. Leveraging off the success of the broking business, the company's small premium funding operation also enjoyed a good year, with an 11% rise in insurance premiums funds to $133.5 million, and company revenues from this business of $8.1 million, also up 11%. The British broking business was strong, despite a softening in the motor and liability markets, with an 8% rise in insurance premiums processed, to $135 million, and revenues for the company up 13% to $16.9 million. Underwriting business, conducted through Australian International Insurance, also did well, with gross earned premium up 15% to $128.7 million. The underwriting agency business, operated by Australian Underwriting Services, saw its commission and fee income more than double to $31.9 million.

OMP Year to 30 June	2004	2005
Revenues ($mn)	222.8	280.5
Underwriting (%)	50	46
Broking—Australia (%)	33	32
Agencies (%)	6	11
Broking—UK (%)	5	6
EBIT ($mn)	32.2	38.1
EBIT margin (%)	14.5	13.6
Profit before tax ($mn)	36.8	45.0
Profit after tax ($mn)	24.6	29.2
Earnings per share (¢)	19.3*	20.8
Cash flow per share (¢)	26.5*	28.4
Dividend (¢)	12.8*	15.1
Percentage franked	100	100
Net tangible assets per share ($)	0.27*	0.33
Interest cover (times)	~	~
Return on equity (%)	19.3	17.1
Debt-to-equity ratio (%)	~	~
Current ratio	1.2	1.2

* adjusted for a one-for-four bonus issue

Outlook

OAMPS has opened three new broking branches following a string of further acquisitions, and growth continues. Nevertheless, the company has conceded that it is running out of potential acquisitions, due to the difficulty in finding businesses with earnings greater than the cost of capital for OAMPS. Consequently, the company has said that 2006 will largely be a period in which it addresses internal issues, including building and evolving its systems and processes in order to add value to its existing client relationships.

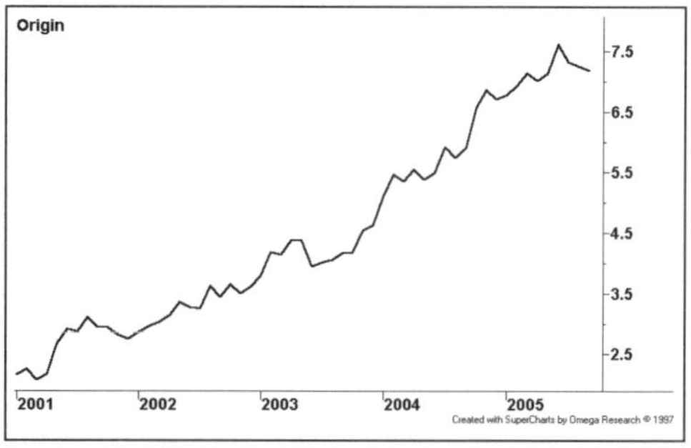

www.originenergy.com.au

Origin Energy Ltd

Share price ($)	7.47	
12-month high ($)	7.85	
12-month low ($)	5.62	
Market capitalisation ($mn)	5883.4	
Price-to-NTA-per-share ratio	3.4	
5-year share price return (% pa)	33.8	
Sector: Energy	**Company**	**Sector**
Price-earnings ratio (times)	20.1	17.7
Dividend yield (%)	2.0	1.9

Origin Energy, formerly the energy arm of the Boral group, was demerged in 2000. Today it is one of Australia's leading energy companies, supplying natural gas, electricity and liquefied petroleum gas to more than two million business and residential customers in Australia, New Zealand and the Pacific. It operates under five core business units: exploration and production, retail, generation, networks and the new Contact Energy business.

Latest business results (June 2005, full year)

Sales and profits jumped, though much of the good result came from the acquisition in October 2004 of 51% of the equity in New Zealand power company Contact Energy, which was responsible for 40% of company EBIT. Excellent growth came from the high-margin exploration and production division, with sales up 17% and EBIT ahead 28%, thanks to increased oil sales and higher prices. In a competitive environment, the retail business produced a creditable result, with EBIT up 13% on a small sales gain from reduced purchasing costs, which offset the adverse effects of mild weather and customer churn. The networks division saw profit little changed for the year, but the generation division reported a 34% EBIT decline, with increased development costs, a lower contribution from the Mt Stuart Power Station and the non-recurrence of one-off tax gains in the previous year.

Outlook

Origin's particular strength is that it operates across the entire energy supply chain, and it continues to expand. It believes that the introduction of new accounting rules has increased the volatility of its profit trends, and has increased the difficulty of making earnings forecasts. Nevertheless, it expects profits to rise by about 10% in the June 2006 year. One of the main drivers of earnings will be a full-year contribution from Contact Energy. It also expects strong revenue inflow from the start of a 15-year contract to supply Australian Gas Light Company with gas from the Spring Gully coal seam gas project in Queensland. The BassGas project in the Bass Strait is also expected to come on stream after a period of delays, and the Otway Gas project is also likely to be commissioned during 2006. On the negative side, the company envisages continuing challenging conditions for its retail business and further high costs for its generation division.

ORG Year to 30 June	2004	2005
Revenues ($mn)	3521.8	4860.6
EBIT ($mn)	329.2	615.2
EBIT margin (%)	9.3	12.7
Profit before tax ($mn)	283.8	480.1
Profit after tax ($mn)	204.9	266.0
Earnings per share (¢)	30.9	37.2
Cash flow per share (¢)	61.5	80.8
Dividend (¢)	13	15
Percentage franked	100	100
Net tangible assets per share ($)	1.68	2.21
Interest cover (times)	7.3	4.6
Return on equity (%)	11.1	11.4
Debt-to-equity ratio (%)	44.4	68.7
Current ratio	1.2	1.0

OrotonGroup Ltd

Share price ($)	2.25
12-month high ($)	3.00
12-month low ($)	1.80
Market capitalisation ($mn)	97.9
Price-to-NTA-per-share ratio	3.4
5-year share price return (% pa)	19.5

Sector: Consumer discretionary	Company	Sector
Price-earnings ratio (times)	10.8	24.2
Dividend yield (%)	6.7	1.2

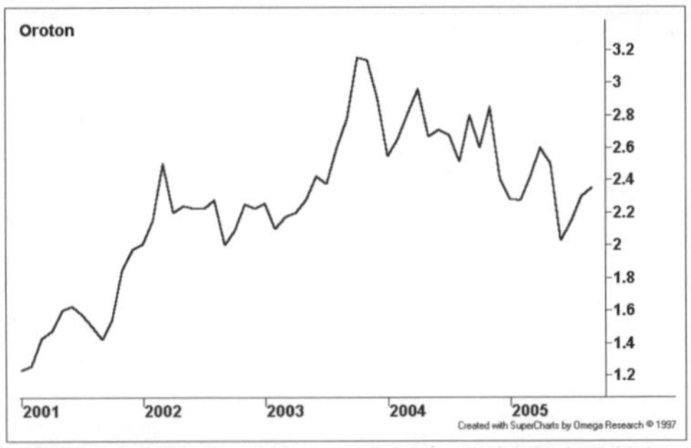

www.orotongroup.com.au

Sydney-based fashion company OrotonGroup was established in 1938. It operates through five premium brands—Polo Ralph Lauren, Oroton, Morrissey, Marcs and Aldo—with a total of 93 stores. The company is still majority-owned by the founding Lane family.

Latest business results (January 2005, half year)

Strong consumer spending boosted sales, but the company was hit by distribution problems. These had a significant negative impact on profits, which fell sharply. The disruptions, caused by the introduction of a new computer system, were particularly severe around the crucial Christmas trading season. The Oroton and Polo Ralph Lauren brands both performed at levels similar to previous periods. However, the company's two smaller brands, Morrissey and Marcs, were quite badly affected by the distribution delays, meaning sales were down. The newly acquired Aldo footwear brand did not make any contribution.

Outlook

The company is working to address its computer problems, including changes in its management structure, and it hopes that its business will bottom out during 2005. However, it is also being hurt by a slowdown in discretionary consumer spending and, in mid-2005, announced that it expected its full-year profits to show quite a sharp decline from the July 2004 year. The company has also announced a review of its balance sheet, notably capitalised expenses and inventory carrying values, and this might eventually lead to write-downs and a further decline in profit. OrotonGroup's problems have hurt the share price, and there has been further investor nervousness over reports that the company is in talks with Polo Ralph Lauren over its licence agreement—due to expire in 2010—and might be forced to make higher royalty payments. In mid-2005, company managers announced that they had ended talks with Catalyst Investment Managers concerning a potential privatisation of the company, incurring costs of about $1 million. The company sees great potential for its new Aldo footwear brand, and plans to open three or four stores annually, targeting the young, fashion-conscious consumer. It is also seeking further brands to add to its portfolio.

ORL Year to 31 July*	2003	2004
Revenues ($mn)	118.3	143.6
EBIT ($mn)	12.6	13.6
EBIT margin (%)	10.7	9.5
Gross margin (%)	61.8	62.5
Profit before tax ($mn)	11.6	12.3
Profit after tax ($mn)	8.3	8.4
Earnings per share (¢)	22.6	20.8
Cash flow per share (¢)	35.0	36.4
Dividend (¢)	11.5	15
Percentage franked	100	100
Interest cover (times)	12.7	10.6
Return on equity (%)	34.1	23.5

* 2 August 2003

Half year to 29 January**	2004	2005
Revenues ($mn)	74.1	77.6
Profit before tax ($mn)	6.3	4.9
Profit after tax ($mn)	4.3	3.3
Earnings per share (¢)	10.9	7.9
Dividend (¢)	5	5
Percentage franked	100	100
Net tangible assets per share ($)	0.62	0.67
Debt-to-equity ratio (%)	17.9	34.0
Current ratio	2.5	2.2

** 31 January 2004

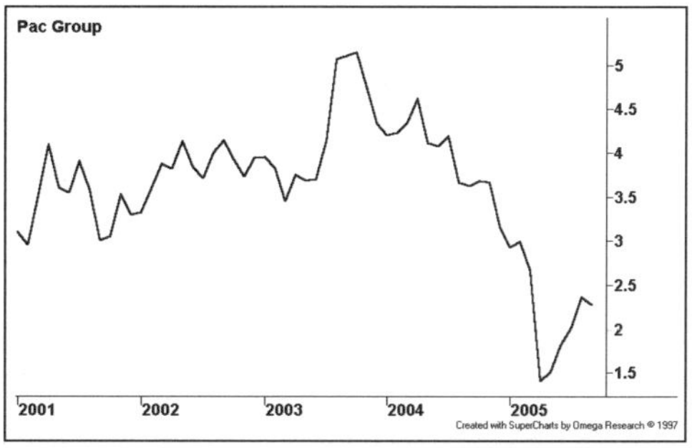

www.pacifica.com.au

Pacifica Group Ltd

Share price ($)	2.45	
12-month high ($)	3.92	
12-month low ($)	1.27	
Market capitalisation ($mn)	320.2	
Price-to-NTA-per-share ratio	1.6	
5-year share price return (% pa)	–6.0	
Sector: Consumer discretionary	**Company**	**Sector**
Price-earnings ratio (times)	7.4	24.2
Dividend yield (%)	8.4	1.2

Melbourne-based Pacifica is a major manufacturer of vehicle components and sells its innovative clutch and braking systems to top automobile makers around the world. It has overseas production facilities in America, Italy, Malaysia and Thailand. It also owns around half the equity of Friction Materials Pacific, a leading manufacturer in Australia and Asia of friction materials, disc brake pads, backing plates, clutch facings, truck blocks and drum brake linings. The company's small Melwire business manufactures woven wire, rubber and polyurethane products for mining, industrial and agricultural applications.

Latest business results (June 2005, half year)

Profits plunged, as the company was hit by higher steel costs, unfavourable currency movements and a 30% drop in sales for its Tennessee plant. The company's South Carolina plant recorded high sales, but margins were hurt by the cost of launching new production work. Domestic business was also weak, in part because of the relocation of certain operations to Asia. The company's European facility, AP Italia, saw sales rise 24%, with profits up even more. Malaysian and Thai sales and earnings were essentially the same as in the June 2004 half. The Friction Materials joint venture continued its poor performance, hurt by cheap imports, but Melwire posted a good result, buoyed by a strong resources sector.

Outlook

Pacifica's business is largely based on long-term contracts, and it can judge fairly well its profit outlook, although currency rate fluctuations introduce an element of uncertainty. The company has announced that it expects after-tax profit of $20 million to $25 million in 2005 and $35 million to $40 million in 2006, when car makers will be introducing new model ranges in most of its major markets. These include the major new GMT900 line of pick-up trucks and four-wheel drive vehicles from General Motors in the US. An important contribution will come from two new operations in China, which are intended to drive down costs. The first—a machining, plating and sub-assembly facility—launched production in July 2005. An adjoining iron foundry is expected to be ready by mid-2006. Pacifica has already won orders, for 2006 delivery, from Shanghai GM.

PBB Year to 31 December	2003	2004
Revenues ($mn)	923.8	872.1
EBIT ($mn)	96.3	89.5
EBIT margin (%)	10.4	10.3
Gross margin (%)	15.4	15.0
Profit before tax ($mn)	83.9	75.5
Profit after tax ($mn)	46.7	45.0
Earnings per share (¢)	34.0	33.1
Cash flow per share (¢)	71.9	71.5
Dividend (¢)	21.5	20.5
Percentage franked	100	93
Interest cover (times)	7.8	6.4
Return on equity (%)	16.8	17.0
Half year to 30 June	**2004**	**2005**
Revenues ($mn)	464.7	398.1
Profit before tax ($mn)	38.1	13.2
Profit after tax ($mn)	20.8	7.3
Earnings per share (¢)	15.3	5.4
Dividend (¢)	10.5	4
Percentage franked	100	55
Net tangible assets per share ($)	1.80	1.52
Debt-to-equity ratio (%)	50.5	65.8
Current ratio	1.7	1.7

Patrick Corporation Ltd

Share price ($)	5.81	
12-month high ($)	6.88	
12-month low ($)	5.00	
Market capitalisation ($mn)	3918.9	
Price-to-NTA-per-share ratio	2.9	
5-year share price return (% pa)	20.6	
Sector: Industrials	**Company**	**Sector**
Price-earnings ratio (times)	20.3	16.2
Dividend yield (%)	2.2	3.6

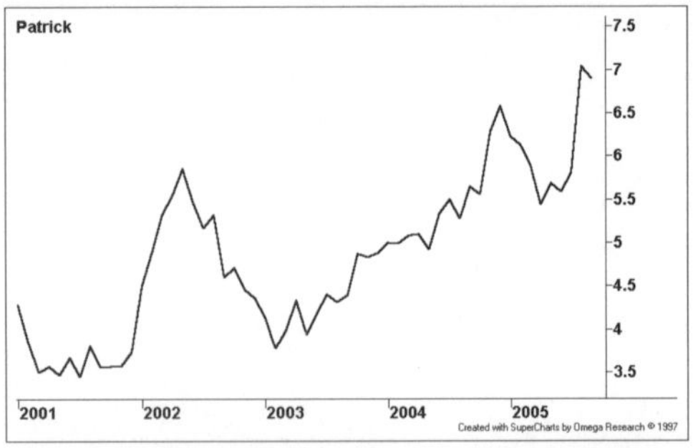

www.patrick.com.au

Sydney-based Patrick Corporation evolved out of Lang Corporation, which was incorporated in 1990. From an initial specialisation in the provision of stevedoring services, the company has grown into a leading Australian logistics enterprise. It is Australia's largest operator of container terminals, with facilities at all major ports, and is also the country's largest stevedore. Its shipping division offers cargo services between Tasmania and Melbourne and between Fremantle and Darwin, as well as a full range of land-based services to the shipping industry. The air services division provides international cargo-handling functions at all major transport hubs. With Toll Holdings it operates the Pacific National rail business, and it owns 62% of the Virgin Blue discount airline.

Latest business results (March 2005, half year)

The company recorded a strong half-year result. The rail division performed especially well, with revenues—including Patrick's share from its 50% stake in Pacific National—up 28% and profits before interest, tax and goodwill amortisation soaring 44%. The ports division recorded a 9% increase in revenues, with profits up 11%, thanks especially to continuing growth in international shipping volumes. The air division saw revenues up 15%, but profits fell 23%, depressed by higher jet fuel costs and rising airport charges.

PRK Year to 30 September	2003	2004
Revenues ($mn)	1100.7	1250.4
EBIT ($mn)	206.6	253.0
EBIT margin (%)	18.8	20.2
Profit before tax ($mn)	185.9	233.1
Profit after tax ($mn)	151.8	188.4
Earnings per share (¢)	23.4	28.6
Cash flow per share (¢)	35.5	41.0
Dividend (¢)	9.3	13
Percentage franked	100	100
Interest cover (times)	10.0	12.8
Return on equity (%)	11.4	11.3
Half year to 31 March	**2004**	**2005**
Revenues ($mn)	591.1	749.4
Rail (%)	37	40
Ports (%)	33	31
Air (%)	30	29
Profit before tax ($mn)	115.5	141.1
Profit after tax ($mn)	94.6	100.4
Earnings per share (¢)	16.8	15.3
Dividend (¢)	6	7
Percentage franked	100	100
Net tangible assets per share ($)	2.87	1.99
Debt-to-equity ratio (%)	14.0	42.7
Current ratio	1.2	1.5

Outlook

Patrick is steadily developing a formidable nationwide transportation network, and it is spending a lot on boosting capacity and reducing costs. It is doubling its handling capacity at both Sydney and Melbourne ports, and is restructuring its rail operations. One weakness is road transportation, though the 2005 acquisition of Melbourne's FCL Interstate Transport Services is seen as an attempt to develop this business. Higher oil prices mean that some freight customers are switching from road to rail, which benefits Patrick. However, its Virgin Blue operations are suffering from the oil price, as well as from a strong performance from its Qantas-owned rival Jetstar. In August 2005, Toll Holdings announced a $4.6 million takeover bid for Patrick, with the aim of creating a giant $8.6 billion transport and logistics company.

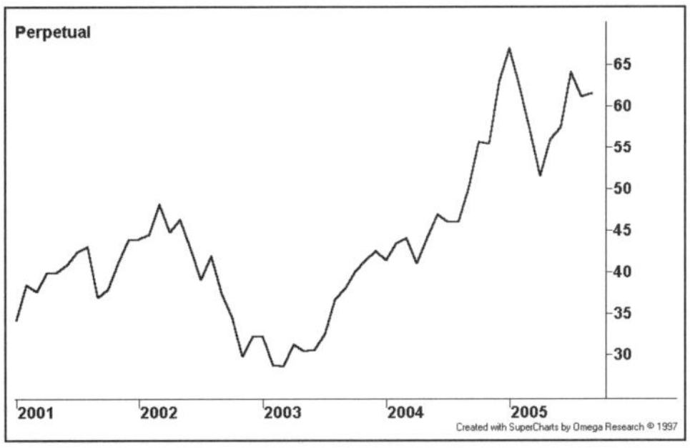

www.perpetual.com.au

Perpetual Trustees Australia Ltd

Share price ($)	65.65	
12-month high ($)	68.50	
12-month low ($)	45.80	
Market capitalisation ($mn)	2664.6	
Price-to-NTA-per-share ratio	8.2	
5-year share price return (% pa)	17.9	
Sector: Financials	**Company**	**Sector**
Price-earnings ratio (times)	22.7	14.3
Dividend yield (%)	4.0	4.5

Sydney-based Perpetual was established in 1885 and is now a dynamic financial services company. It is involved in trustee operations, funds management, estate administration, charitable planning, property management, financial planning and tax consulting. It has announced the sale of its share-registry business, ASX Perpetual Registrars, which it operated with the Australian Stock Exchange.

Latest business results (June 2005, full year)

Perpetual raced to another record profit, thanks especially to the strength of its core businesses in wealth management and corporate trust. Total funds under management grew 23% to $26.7 billion. Half of the increase came from fund performance, and half from new investment inflows into the funds. Funds under advice, administration and trust in the Perpetual Private Clients division rose 11% to $7.3 billion. Funds under administration in the Corporate Trust division swelled 28% to $144.3 billion, largely due to the continued strong demand for residential mortgage-backed securities.

Outlook

Perpetual continues to go from strength to strength and this has been reflected in its surging share price. With a strong focus on wealth management, it has been a prime beneficiary of strong markets and continuing high fund inflows from Australians working to build up their superannuation. However, its business success has become quite dependent on the local stock market, and the company itself has conceded that it could be hurt by any sharp fall in Australian equities. In order to diversify, in 2004 it established the Dublin-based PI Investment Management as a global equities firm. The new company began operations in 2005 and, among its early achievements, it was appointed by Irish Life plc as the third external investment manager on its $8.3 billion investment product platform. Other major new clients are AMP Hillross and the Van Eyk Blueprint International Share Fund. Perpetual has also launched two important new funds — the Credit Enhanced Cash Fund and the Credit Income Fund — and thanks to these, its credit operation has boosted its assets from $100 million early in the year to more than $1 billion. In mid-August, Perpetual and the Australian Stock Exchange announced the sale of their ASX Perpetual Registrars joint venture to Pacific Equity Partners for approximately $132 million, bringing Perpetual an after-tax profit of about $13.5 million.

PPT Year to 30 June	2004	2005
Revenues ($mn)	295.1	342.1
EBIT ($mn)	123.8	153.7
EBIT margin (%)	41.9	44.9
Profit before tax ($mn)	128.2	158.4
Profit after tax ($mn)	90.4	111.6
Earnings per share (¢)	237.8	289.4
Cash flow per share (¢)	282.5	323.1
Dividend (¢)	150	260
Percentage franked	100	100
Net tangible assets per share ($)	6.89	8.02
Interest cover (times)	~	~
Return on equity (%)	30.0	32.6
Debt-to-equity ratio (%)	~	~
Current ratio	2.5	2.4

Portman Ltd

Share price ($)	4.15	
12-month high ($)	4.33	
12-month low ($)	1.76	
Market capitalisation ($mn)	695.7	
Price-to-NTA-per-share ratio	3.4	
5-year share price return (% pa)	42.4	
Sector: Materials	**Company**	**Sector**
Price-earnings ratio (times)	22.0	17.0
Dividend yield (%)	1.1	2.2

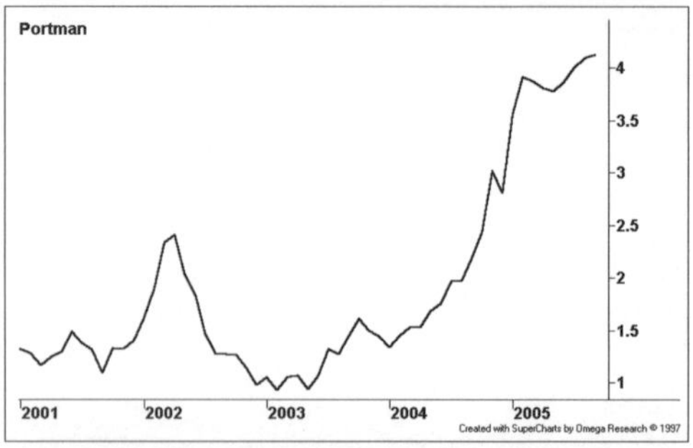

www.portman.com.au

Perth-based mining company Portman was originally formed in 1925 as Sturts Meadows Prospecting Syndicate. Today it is Australia's third-largest iron ore producer, behind BHP Billiton and Rio Tinto. It owns the Koolyanobbing project, located between Perth and Kalgoorlie in Western Australia, and has a 50% interest in the Cockatoo Island project, in the north of the state. About 75% of its output is shipped to China, and the remainder to Japan. Early in 2005, US iron ore producer Cleveland-Cliffs made a friendly takeover bid for Portman and it has acquired around 80% of the company's equity.

Latest business results (June 2005, half year)

The continuing strength of Chinese demand for iron ore and a 71% increase in the iron ore benchmark price for 2005 delivered Portman a massive rise in profits. Shipments from the Koolyanobbing iron ore operation were steady for the half, at 2.7 million tonnes. The Cockatoo Island operation increased its shipments from 0.3 million tonnes to 0.5 million tonnes.

Outlook

The new iron ore benchmark price came into effect in January 2005 for all but one of Portman's Chinese customers. For that one customer and for its Japanese customers, it came into effect in April 2005. With demand still strong, the outlook for Portman remains favourable. It is ramping up production and it expects that by the end of 2005, or early in 2006, production at Koolyanobbing will be at a rate as high as 8.0 million tonnes per year, with Cockatoo Island producing at around 1.2 million tonnes per year. However, the company has conceded that it faces skill shortages and rising expenses, and the capital costs of boosting Koolyanobbing output have been higher than expected, putting pressure on the company's dividend payouts. Even if Koolyanobbing is operating at its new full capacity at the end of 2005, the company doubts that its transportation infrastructure will be fully ready then. At mid-2005, the company held ore reserves of approximately 92 million tonnes, and it maintains an active exploration program. Cleveland-Cliffs has announced that it will not move to full acquisition of Portman. The two companies have said they are evaluating several major iron ore projects, with a view to joint development.

PMM Year to 31 December	2003	2004
Revenues ($mn)	145.3	195.4
EBIT ($mn)	21.5	44.3
EBIT margin (%)	14.8	22.7
Gross margin (%)	35.6	42.8
Profit before tax ($mn)	24.1	46.0
Profit after tax ($mn)	16.9	32.8
Earnings per share (¢)	9.8	18.9
Cash flow per share (¢)	14.7	24.3
Dividend (¢)	8	4.5
Percentage franked	75	100
Interest cover (times)	~	~
Return on equity (%)	11.6	20.4
Half year to 30 June	**2004**	**2005**
Revenues ($mn)	97.9	159.8
Profit before tax ($mn)	23.4	58.4
Profit after tax ($mn)	17.2	41.1
Earnings per share (¢)	9.9	23.4
Dividend (¢)	4.5	0
Percentage franked	100	~
Net tangible assets per share ($)	0.92	1.21
Debt-to-equity ratio (%)	11.8	~
Current ratio	1.8	2.5

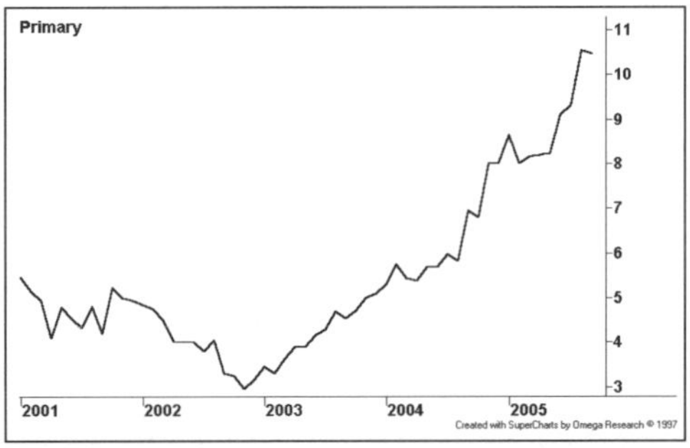

www.primaryhealthcare.com.au

Primary Health Care Ltd

Share price ($)	10.32
12-month high ($)	10.38
12-month low ($)	5.80
Market capitalisation ($mn)	1222.0
Price-to-NTA-per-share ratio	85.4
5-year share price return (% pa)	17.3

Sector: Health care	Company	Sector
Price-earnings ratio (times)	41.1	28.0
Dividend yield (%)	2.4	1.7

Sydney-based Primary Health Care manages 24 medical centres (which are staffed by more than 800 general practitioners), in NSW, Victoria and South Australia. It also operates a small pathology business in NSW. Early in 2005, it acquired Australia's largest medical software company, Health Communication Network (HCN).

Latest business results (June 2005, full year)

The company's continuing growth produced another strong result. The major contribution came from Primary Health Care's 21 medical centres established before 2004, helped by an increase in medical fee rebates. There was also an initial contribution from three new centres opened during the year, one in Adelaide and the company's first two in Victoria. There was an 11.3% increase in patient attendances. Pathology revenues rose 8%, but profits were up just 6% due in part to the costs of interstate expansion, along with higher prices for consumable supplies. The company did not record as a significant item a $2.5 million profit made on the sale of shares in Independent Practitioner Network, following an unsuccessful takeover bid for that company. Primary Health Care also announced that, had it applied the new International Financial Reporting Standards, its after-tax profit would have been around $38.7 million.

Outlook

Primary Health Care is a leading participant in the continuing consolidation of the private medical sector in Australia. It claims that its model of aggregating individual doctors' practices into large medical centres provides medical practitioners with capital from the sale of their business, along with a substantial increase in gross annual income in their first year of working in the company's centres. Because of the considerable cost savings derived from operating large medical centres (as opposed to individual practices), along with the company's continuing drive to boost efficiencies, it is able to offer very competitive pricing to patients. It plans to open seven new centres by June 2006, and expects to operate a total of 40 by 2007. The HCN acquisition gives the company access to more than three-quarters of Australia's GPs, who use the Medical Director software developed by that business. Primary Health Care is working to enhance HCN's products, including a new version of Medical Director.

PRY Year to 30 June	2004	2005
Revenues ($mn)	150.4	190.6
Medical centres (%)	60	55
Pathology operations (%)	40	32
Health technology (%)	0	6
EBIT ($mn)	32.4	49.4
EBIT margin (%)	21.5	25.9
Profit before tax ($mn)	26.6	44.2
Profit after tax ($mn)	18.0	27.9
Earnings per share (¢)	17.7	25.1
Cash flow per share (¢)	38.6	49.0
Dividend (¢)	17.5	25
Percentage franked	100	100
Net tangible assets per share ($)	0.19	0.12
Interest cover (times)	5.6	9.6
Return on equity (%)	9.4	10.8
Debt-to-equity ratio (%)	46.6	26.8
Current ratio	1.4	0.7

Pro Medicus Ltd

Share price ($)	1.15	
12-month high ($)	1.42	
12-month low ($)	0.70	
Market capitalisation ($mn)	108.5	
Price-to-NTA-per-share ratio	9.5	
4-year share price return (% pa)	6.5	
Sector: Health care	**Company**	**Sector**
Price-earnings ratio (times)	20.9	28.0
Dividend yield (%)	3.7	1.7

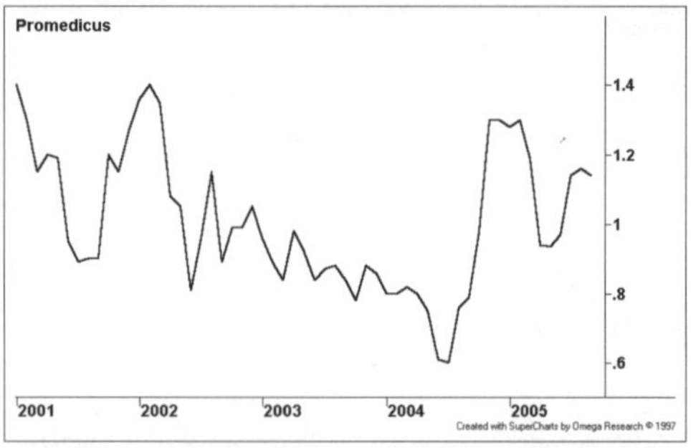

www.promedicus.com.au

Melbourne-based Pro Medicus, established in 1983, provides software and internet services to the medical profession. Its Pro Medicus Practice Management System is a software package designed to manage the administration of a clinic. Its pioneering promedicus.net network allows Australia's first secure internet delivery of diagnostic results and is now used by over two-thirds of Australian GPs. It has entered the GP clinical desktop market with the acquisition of software technology that is being marketed as ProMed Clinical. The company is also at the forefront of digital imaging technology for medical applications.

Latest business results (June 2005, full year)

In the most successful year in the company's history, Pro Medicus achieved powerful expansion in its sales and profits. There was continuing strong growth in the promedicus.net network, with over 19 000 doctors now registered to use it, and with a 13.7% rise during the year in the number of transactions carried, to 2.7 million. The company also experienced an increased uptake by private and public radiology practices of its digital imaging products. A large part of the growth came from Canada, where the company enjoyed success with a $2.6 million digital radiology contract.

Outlook

Pro Medicus has strong positions in several niche markets with high levels of profitability and very attractive growth prospects. It is working to maximise its success with the promedicus.net online network by extending its use to non-radiology providers, a trend it anticipates will accelerate. It also intends to use its relationship with the doctors using promedicus.net to promote its other products and services. It expects good growth domestically for its digital imaging products, and it sees enormous scope overseas. It hopes to leverage its Canadian contract into further sales across the country and sees Alberta—which has announced a $189 million radiology digital imaging program—as offering particular potential. Late in 2004, the company announced a three-year, $10 million agreement with Agfa HealthCare, giving Agfa exclusive rights to market its digital imaging products and its Pro Medicus Practice Management software in the rapidly growing private imaging centre market in North America. With no debt and more than $10 million in cash holdings, Pro Medicus is also to looking to Europe for further expansion opportunities.

PME Year to 30 June	2004	2005
Revenues ($mn)	7.9	10.3
EBIT ($mn)	4.5	7.2
EBIT margin (%)	57.3	69.7
Profit before tax ($mn)	5.0	7.7
Profit after tax ($mn)	3.6	5.5
Earnings per share (¢)	3.6	5.5
Cash flow per share (¢)	3.7	5.6
Dividend (¢)	3.5	4.25
Percentage franked	100	100
Net tangible assets per share ($)	0.11	0.12
Interest cover (times)	~	~
Return on equity (%)	32.8	46.0
Debt-to-equity ratio (%)	~	~
Current ratio	7.6	6.9

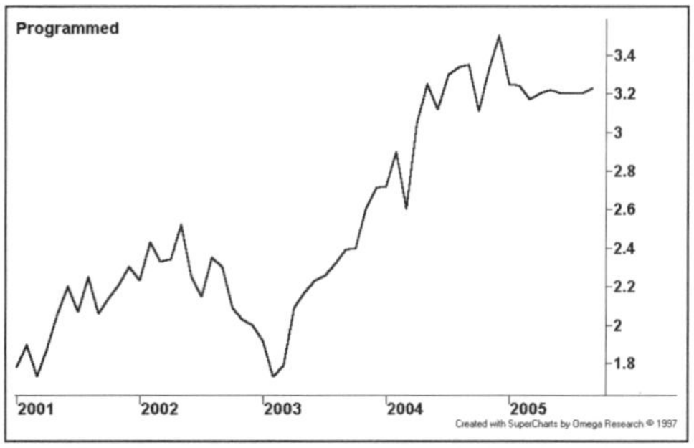

www.pmsltd.com.au

Programmed Maintenance Services Ltd

Share price ($)	3.16	
12-month high ($)	3.52	
12-month low ($)	2.80	
Market capitalisation ($mn)	221.6	
Price-to-NTA-per-share ratio	2.0	
5-year share price return (% pa)	19.2	
Sector: Industrials	**Company**	**Sector**
Price-earnings ratio (times)	12.1	16.2
Dividend yield (%)	4.7	3.6

Melbourne-based Programmed Maintenance Services was established in 1951 to provide painting services to commercial clients. Today it has 5500 clients on long-term contracts, covering 60 000 buildings and properties throughout Australia and New Zealand. Services have expanded from painting to a wide variety of building and property maintenance work. Its Barry Bros. Specialised Services subsidiary is involved in drain and sewer-system maintenance work. The company has entered the UK market with the acquisition in 2000 of the long-established Whittle Painting Group.

Latest business results (March 2005, full year)

For the seventh straight year, the company recorded growth of more than 10% in both revenues and profits, thanks to the continuing enhancement of its product offerings and its moves abroad. The mainstay domestic property maintenance business—responsible for more than two-thirds of total turnover—saw sales revenues up nearly 14%, with EBIT up 3%, constrained by wet weather during the Christmas period when much school painting is scheduled. The small Barry Bros. sewer and drain maintenance business enjoyed an excellent year, with sales up 11% and EBIT soaring 23%. New Zealand business notched up a further strong performance. Though only 14% of company sales, New Zealand contributes fully one-third of total profit. The United Kingdom saw sales continue to grow—up nearly 17%—and with EBIT surging from $0.2 million to $1.1 million. A successful turnaround of the loss-making Manchester business meant that all six British branches were profitable.

Outlook

Programmed Maintenance Services has pioneered the concept of long-term commercial maintenance programs—initial refurbishment followed by regular preventative maintenance—offering building owners a cost-effective way to maintain the standard of buildings by spreading their costs over the life of a contract. It is now offering its clients some 40 different services, and over five years its dependence on Australian painting operations has declined from 56% of turnover to 42%. Domestically, the company continues to grow. The Barry Bros. division has expanded its operations to Tasmania and South Australia, and has made some particularly large investments in new equipment. The company has high hopes for the UK, with notably strong growth continuing in maintenance programs for schools and other institutional structures.

PRG Year to 31 March	2004	2005
Revenues ($mn)	190.6	217.8
EBIT ($mn)	26.6	29.9
EBIT margin (%)	13.9	13.7
Profit before tax ($mn)	24.0	26.7
Profit after tax ($mn)	16.3	18.1
Earnings per share (¢)	23.9	26.1
Cash flow per share (¢)	33.9	37.8
Dividend (¢)	12	15
Percentage franked	50	71
Net tangible assets per share ($)	1.46	1.60
Interest cover (times)	10.4	9.1
Return on equity (%)	17.1	16.4
Debt-to-equity ratio (%)	40.7	39.9
Current ratio	3.1	3.0

Publishing and Broadcasting Ltd

Share price ($)	15.46	
12-month high ($)	17.58	
12-month low ($)	13.40	
Market capitalisation ($mn)	10 462.9	
Price-to-NTA-per-share ratio	2.5	
5-year share price return (% pa)	6.8	
Sector: Consumer discretionary	**Company**	**Sector**
Price-earnings ratio (times)	20.0	24.2
Dividend yield (%)	3.4	1.2

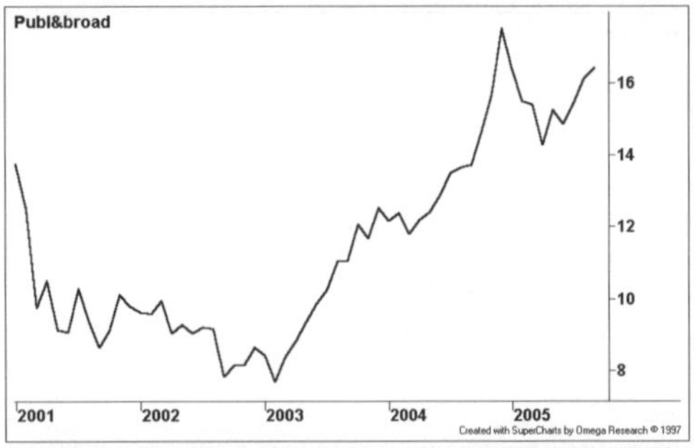

www.pbl.com.au

Publishing and Broadcasting (PBL), controlled by Kerry Packer and his family, operates television's Nine Network as well as Melbourne's Crown Casino and Perth's Burswood casino. It also owns Australian Consolidated Press, which publishes many of Australia's best-known magazines, including *The Australian Women's Weekly*, *Woman's Day*, *Cleo* and *The Bulletin*. It owns the Ticketek ticketing agency, as well as 25% of Foxtel cable television, 50% of the Premier Media Group (formerly Fox Sports), 50% of the ninemsn internet service, 33.3% of Sky News Australia, 25% of the SEEK online jobs service and 50% of Hoyts Cinemas.

Latest business results (June 2005, full year)

Sales and profits rose, thanks in particular to the company's casino business. There was strong growth at Crown and the inclusion of ten months of trading at Burswood, and the gaming division saw revenues up 26%, with EBIT growing by 8%. The magazines business also achieved good growth, due to healthy economic conditions in both the Australian and New Zealand markets. Revenues rose 11% and EBIT was up 17%. Total advertising revenues were up 17%, with circulation revenues rising 6%. However, the company's television operations were hit by strong levels of competition. Continuing strength in advertising pushed this division's revenues up 4%, but EBIT was down 4%. The Ninemsn business reported an excellent 56% profit rise, with SEEK and Premier Media Group also in profit. PBL recorded a $28.2 million after-tax loss on its share in Foxtel.

PBL Year to 30 June	2004	2005
Revenues ($mn)	2874.1	3320.6
Gaming (%)	39	44
Television (%)	28	26
Magazines (%)	24	24
EBIT ($mn)	726.0	772.5
EBIT margin (%)	25.3	23.3
Gross margin (%)	7.6	10.1
Profit before tax ($mn)	620.4	649.1
Profit after tax ($mn)	484.0	514.6
Earnings per share (¢)	73.1	77.3
Cash flow per share (¢)	92.8	100.8
Dividend (¢)	43	52
Percentage franked	100	100
Net tangible assets per share ($)	5.95	6.24
Interest cover (times)	6.9	6.3
Return on equity (%)	12.2	11.8
Debt-to-equity ratio (%)	25.3	38.8
Current ratio	1.5	1.7

Outlook

PBL enjoys powerful profitability from its three core activities of gaming, television and magazines, and these have the potential to continue to bloom while the economy remains firm. The company also continues to move into new businesses, some with quite exciting long-term prospects. It has launched a joint venture with Melco International Development of Hong Kong to build a major casino and resort complex at Macau. It has initiated a venture with Hearst Corporation to develop opportunities in the British magazine market. It has acquired the management rights to the SuperDome stadium in Sydney. The introduction of digital services is boosting Foxtel, which now has 1.8 million subscribers, and its loss contracted sharply in the second half of the June 2005 year, suggesting that it is on the road to profit.

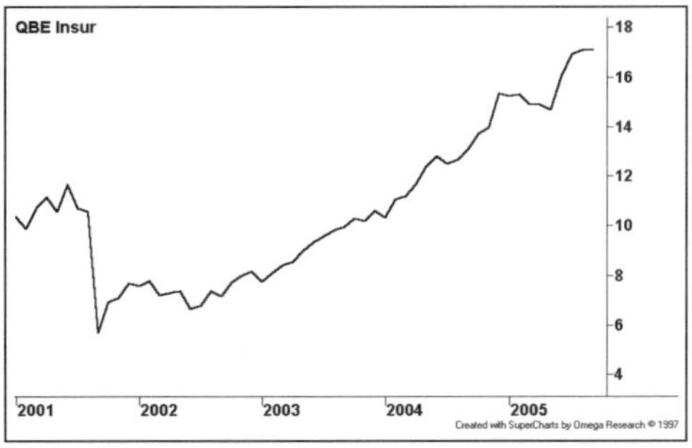

www.qbe.com.au

QBE Insurance Group Ltd

Share price ($)	17.09
12-month high ($)	17.14
12-month low ($)	12.08
Market capitalisation($mn)	13374.0
Price-to-NTA-per-share ratio	3.8
5-year share price return (% pa)	19.1

Sector: Financials	Company	Sector
Price-earnings ratio (times)	14.5	14.3
Dividend yield (%)	3.2	4.5

Sydney-based QBE—founded as North Queensland Insurance Company in 1886—is one of Australia's best-regarded insurance companies, specialising in general insurance and reinsurance. It has expanded globally via operations in 39 countries, and over three-quarters of its business comes from abroad, with particular strength in Europe. It has become the second-largest underwriter at Lloyd's of London.

Latest business results (June 2005, half year)

Booming financial markets, rising premiums and a series of acquisitions helped power QBE to another strong rise in profits. All operating divisions produced improved insurance profits, and 37 of the 39 countries in which the company operates produced underwriting profits. The result was assisted by a lower than expected frequency of claims and by acquisitions made in the second half of 2004, principally the purchase of ING's 50% interest in the QBE Mercantile Mutual joint venture. Reinsurance costs decreased from 22% of gross earned premium to 19%, thanks to synergies from acquisitions and the restructuring of QBE's British operations. Net investment income rose from $132 million to $337 million. On a regional basis, QBE Insurance (Europe) saw after-tax profit soar 76% to $164 million, the Lloyd's division was up 58% to $120 million, while Australia edged up 2% to $138 million. The result was the first under the new international financial reporting standards, and QBE restated its June 2004 results, with profits a little higher than previously.

Outlook

QBE has made a stunning recovery from the traumas of September 11, which forced the global insurance industry into a period of intense rationalisation. It has divested itself of underperforming businesses, acquired more than a dozen other insurers over 18 months, raised premiums and tightened claim conditions. QBE continues to seek further acquisitions worldwide, and has indicated it could spend $250 million on buying out smaller insurers in the second half of 2005. It maintains a low exposure to equity markets, and it will benefit from any rise in US interest rates. However, it is also affected by international currency fluctuations. The company has announced that it does not expect Hurricane Katrina in the US to have a large impact on its business.

QBE Year to 31 December	2003	2004
Net earned premium ($mn)	6036.0	6781.0
Profit before tax ($mn)	765.0	1080.0
Profit after tax ($mn)	572.0	820.0
Earnings per share (¢)	89.5	117.8
Dividend (¢)	42	54
Percentage franked	23	50
Return on equity (%)	18.3	21.2
Half year to 30 June	**2004**	**2005**
Net earned premium ($mn)	3114.0	3506.0
Profit before tax ($mn)	429.0	675.0
Profit after tax ($mn)	343.0	491.0
Earnings per share (¢)	47.2	64.6
Dividend (¢)	24	33
Percentage franked	50	50
Net tangible assets per share ($)	3.48	4.47
Debt-to-equity ratio (%)	9.7	5.5
Current ratio	1.2	1.4

Rebel Sport Ltd

Share price ($)	2.22	
12-month high ($)	3.27	
12-month low ($)	1.90	
Market capitalisation ($mn)	163.5	
Price-to-NTA-per-share ratio	2.0	
5-year share price return (% pa)	29.5	
Sector: Consumer discretionary	**Company**	**Sector**
Price-earnings ratio (times)	10.5	24.2
Dividend yield (%)	4.5	1.2

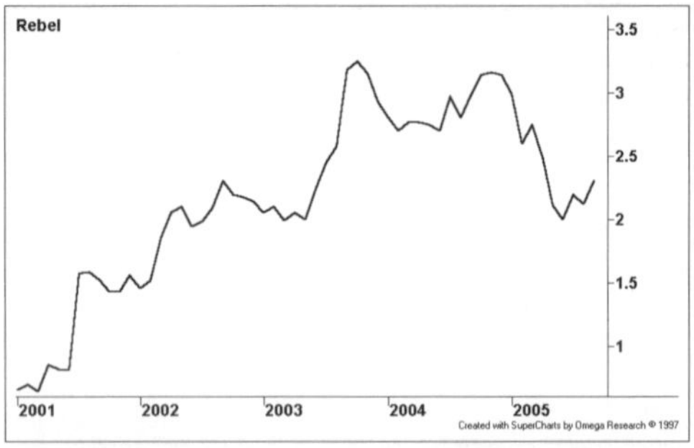

www.rebelsport.com.au

Rebel Sport, one of Australia's leading sporting goods retailers, began trading as a single store in Sydney's west in 1985. It has grown into a large chain of retail outlets across Australia and also manages the small Glue chain of 'athleisure' stores, which sell fashionable sporting and leisure wear. Harvey Norman Holdings owns a majority of Rebel Sport's equity. At the end of August 2005 the company operated 57 Rebel Sport stores and nine Glue stores.

Latest business results (July 2005, full year)

In an environment of slowing consumer spending, total retail sales rose 3.8%, though on a like-for-like basis the rise was just 0.8%, and profits fell. Reduced athletic footwear sales were a major contributor to the sluggish result, and the figures were also affected by strong business in the July 2004 year in connection with the Rugby World Cup. In addition, the company's business was affected by increased wage expenses and set-up costs for a new head office and for the new Rebel Direct operation. The Glue business was hurt by delays in opening two new stores, which led to inventory build-up and the necessity to dispose of surplus stock out of season at reduced prices.

Outlook

Rebel Sport has been engaged in a major three-year restructuring of its business, with the particular aim of changing from a head office-driven operation to one where major decisions are made at the store level. This has involved some large expenses, including a degree of senior staff turnover. However, the result is a reduced cost base, no net debt and more than $22 million in net cash holdings. Nevertheless, the company would likely be affected by any significant slowdown in consumer spending. In addition, sports retailing is to some extent influenced by fashion trends, including the success of national sports teams and individuals. The company has launched its new Rebel Direct division to concentrate on the development of own-brand products. Rebel Direct will also build a new business supplying team wear and sporting apparel to schools, clubs and other organisations. The company believes the Soccer World Cup and Commonwealth Games will provide a good boost to 2006 business. It plans to open eight new Rebel Sport stores during the July 2006 year and one new Glue store.

REB Year to 2 July*	2004	2005
Revenues ($mn)	305.4	316.9
EBIT ($mn)	24.5	22.4
EBIT margin (%)	8.0	7.1
Gross margin (%)	35.9	35.4
Profit before tax ($mn)	25.4	23.6
Profit after tax ($mn)	18.2	16.3
Earnings per share (¢)	23.7	21.2
Cash flow per share (¢)	36.0	35.2
Dividend (¢)	10	10
Percentage franked	100	100
Net tangible assets per share ($)	1.02	1.13
Interest cover (times)	~	~
Return on equity (%)	25.0	19.8
Debt-to-equity ratio (%)	~	~
Current ratio	2.2	2.7

*3 July 2004

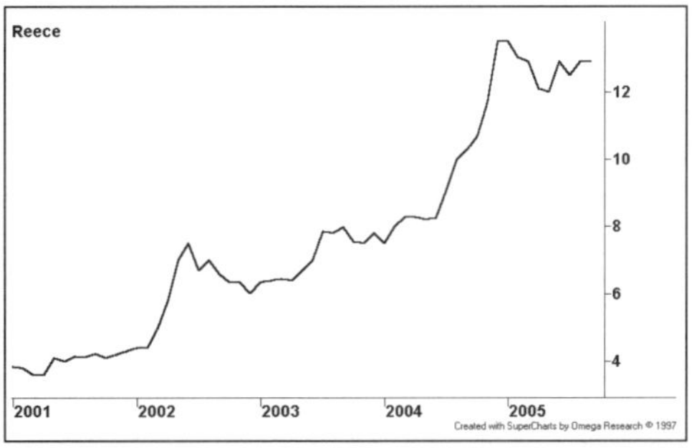

www.reece.com.au

Reece Australia Ltd

Share price ($)	12.85	
12-month high ($)	13.70	
12-month low ($)	9.15	
Market capitalisation ($mn)	1284.8	
Price-to-NTA-per-share ratio	3.9	
5-year share price return (% pa)	32.0	
Sector: Industrials	**Company**	**Sector**
Price-earnings ratio (times)	17.0	16.2
Dividend yield (%)	3.0	3.6

Melbourne-based hardware wholesaler Reece Australia traces its origins back to 1919, when Harold Reece started selling plumbing supplies from the back of a truck. It has gradually expanded from its Victorian roots, with notable growth coming from the acquisition of the Plumbing World and Bridglands chains. Today it is one of the country's leading suppliers of plumbing products, with 236 stores and showrooms nationwide, and it has also expanded into related fields. Its four operating divisions are plumbing and bathroom, Reece HVAC (heating, ventilation, air conditioning), industrial and irrigation. It also operates a National Training Centre in Melbourne, for plumbers wishing to enhance their technical and business skills. The controlling Wilson family own more than 75% of the company's equity.

Latest business results (June 2005, full year)

The continuing strength of the domestic economy helped Reece enjoy an excellent result, with sales and profits up strongly, and ahead of the company's own forecasts, despite a softening of the housing market. All four company divisions realised growth. The company's emphasis on inventory management and cost control showed great success, with profits growing at a faster rate than sales. Reece opened 20 new stores during the period.

Outlook

Reece is heavily geared to the housing and renovations market, and, with a softening trend evident, the company has not been prepared to make a forecast for the June 2006 year. In particular, it has noted that it faces the problem of rising salaries and materials costs, and that managing expenses will be a particular challenge during the year. In addition, the plumbing supplies market is becoming increasingly competitive. Nevertheless, Reece remains a conservatively managed company that occupies a central position in the hardware supply business. It sells mainly to plumbers and builders, though does some retail business as well. It continues to open new stores, and with no debt and around $46 million in cash holdings it is also interested in growth by acquisition. It has launched a series of specialised stores and services to meet evolving needs, including Reece Irrigation for the landscape and agricultural supply industries, Reece Projects for larger residential developments, Reece Gas for customers working with domestic and commercial gas appliances and evaporative cooling systems, and Reecedesign for architects and interior designers.

REH Year to 30 June	2004	2005
Revenues ($mn)	871.8	1009.6
EBIT ($mn)	88.1	107.5
EBIT margin (%)	10.1	10.6
Gross margin (%)	26.8	27.2
Profit before tax ($mn)	89.1	108.5
Profit after tax ($mn)	61.5	75.3
Earnings per share (¢)	61.8	75.6
Cash flow per share (¢)	72.3	86.4
Dividend (¢)	28	38
Percentage franked	100	100
Net tangible assets per share ($)	2.82	3.27
Interest cover (times)	~	~
Return on equity (%)	23.5	24.8
Debt-to-equity ratio (%)	~	~
Current ratio	1.9	2.0

Rinker Group Ltd

Share price ($)	14.95	
12-month high ($)	15.30	
12-month low ($)	7.96	
Market capitalisation ($mn)	13552.9	
Price-to-NTA-per-share ratio	5.9	
5-year share price return (% pa)	na	
Sector: Materials	**Company**	**Sector**
Price-earnings ratio (times)	24.1	17.0
Dividend yield (%)	1.4	2.2

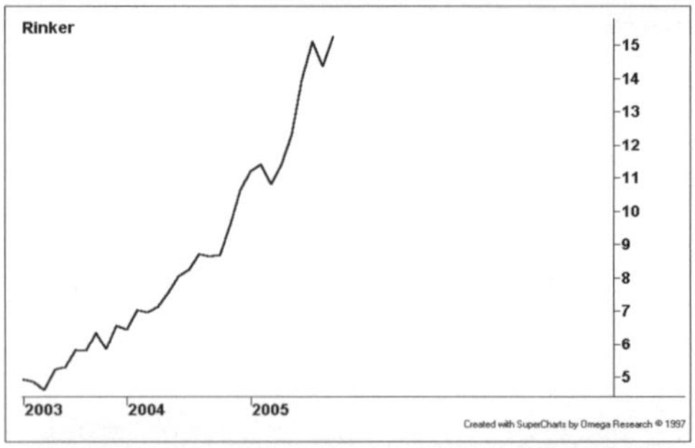

www.rinkergroup.com.au

Sydney-based Rinker Group was part of CSR until it demerged in 2003 (companies demerged from another entity are eligible for inclusion in this book after two years of profits and dividends, instead of the five years that is the rule for all other companies). It is among the world's ten largest manufacturers and distributors of heavy building materials, such as cement, concrete, aggregates and concrete blocks and pipes. It operates through Rinker Materials Corporation in the United States and Readymix in Australia. It is also making moves into China.

Latest business results (March 2005, full year)

Strong construction markets in both Australia and the US handed Rinker an excellent result. Continuing efforts to drive down costs meant that margins were also generally higher, while price increases more than offset higher costs for fuel, freight and raw materials. Rinker Materials sales—about three-quarters of total company turnover—were up 16% in US dollar terms, or 9% in Australian dollars, with EBIT surging 48% in US dollars and 38% in Australian dollars. All product areas were firm, with particular strength in concrete and concrete blocks, thanks to higher demand and double-digit price increases. Readymix domestic sales were up 12%, with EBIT rising 21%.

Outlook

Its strength in the US has seen Rinker become a stock market powerhouse, and it continues to grow. It is a major supplier to the construction markets in Florida and Arizona, where economic growth continues to outstrip the US average. In mid-2005 the company announced that demand remained high, despite a series of price rises, with the result that US profits would likely rise by at least 30% in the March 2006 year. With minimal debt, the company is also looking to expand through acquisition. However, with most of its revenues and costs now US$-denominated, it will from next year report its financial results only in US dollars, and it will be increasingly unable to pay fully franked dividends. In Australia, the company is a beneficiary of continuing spending on major infrastructure projects, and this is helping to offset slowdowns in other construction markets. However, the company is being hurt by rising fuel, raw material and freight costs, and it forecasts flat domestic profits for March 2006.

RIN Year to 31 March	2004	2005
Revenues ($mn)	5339.5	5843.0
EBIT ($mn)	713.3	957.1
EBIT margin (%)	13.4	16.4
Gross margin (%)	41.8	44.2
Profit before tax ($mn)	644.5	913.0
Profit after tax ($mn)	426.8	585.2
Earnings per share (¢)	45.2	62.1
Cash flow per share (¢)	80.8	98.1
Dividend (¢)	14	21
Percentage franked	100	73
Net tangible assets per share ($)	2.01	2.55
Interest cover (times)	10.4	21.7
Return on equity (%)	13.9	18.3
Debt-to-equity ratio (%)	26.4	10.7
Current ratio	1.9	1.8

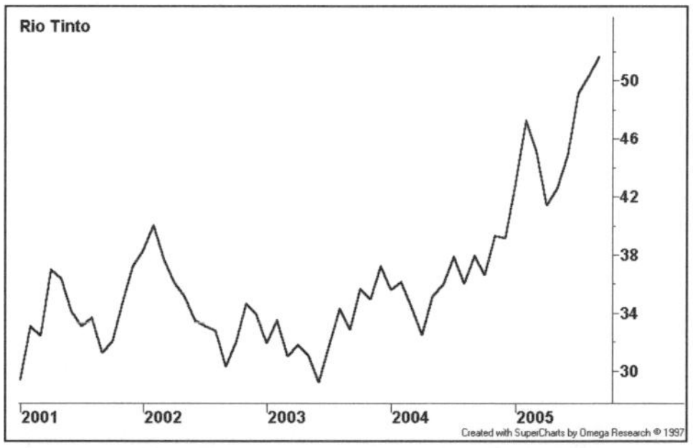

www.riotinto.com

RIO TINTO LTD

Share price ($)	52.74	
12-month high ($)	53.40	
12-month low ($)	35.70	
Market capitalisation ($mn)	23470.2	
Price-to-NTA-per-share ratio	4.8	
5-year share price return (% pa)	18.8	
Sector: Materials	**Company**	**Sector**
Price-earnings ratio (times)	23.7	17.0
Dividend yield (%)	2.0	2.2

British-based Rio Tinto, one of the world's largest mining companies, retains its ASX presence in a dual-listing structure, and continues to pay franked dividends to Australian shareholders. Australian subsidiaries include Coal & Allied Industries and Energy Resources of Australia, and it has a big stake in Papua New Guinea's Lihir Gold. Among its major products are copper, gold, industrial minerals, iron ore, diamonds and coal, and it is also a large aluminium producer.

Latest business results (June 2005, half year)

The global resources boom handed Rio Tinto another impressive result. The company reported that higher commodities prices boosted the after-tax profit by US$1 billion, while record volumes for most of its products raised the profit figure by US$460 million. The leading contributor to earnings was the company's copper operations, with an after-tax profit of US$834 million (up 112% from the June 2004 half). Iron ore contributed US$681 million, up 165%. The company's energy business—principally coal—contributed US$307 million, up 96%, with US$203 from aluminium, which constituted a 25% rise. Note that Rio Tinto reports its results in US dollars. The figures in the tables on this page are based on Australian dollar figures supplied by the company.

Outlook

Rio Tinto is a prime beneficiary of the booming Chinese economy and that country's surging demand for raw materials, and the company has reported that it continues to experience very strong Chinese demand. In response, it is working to boost output (even at the expense of rising costs) in order to reap the full benefit of high commodity prices. The company said it believed that low inventories and the time lag in raising output would keep markets tight in the medium term. For the long term, it has a large stream of new projects, including the recent purchase of a 50% stake in the $1.5 billion Hope Downs iron ore project in Western Australia. This is expected eventually to boost the company's iron ore production by some 20%. The company will also proceed with a $1 billion mineral sands project in Madagascar and a $250 million upgrade of mineral sands processing facilities in Canada.

RIO Year to 31 December	2003	2004
Revenues ($mn)	18143.0	19248.0
EBIT ($mn)	3251.8	4628.7
EBIT margin (%)	17.9	24.0
Profit before tax ($mn)	3038.0	4430.1
Profit after tax ($mn)	2133.0	3069.0
Earnings per share (¢)	154.9	222.5
Cash flow per share (¢)	267.3	342.1
Dividend (¢)	89.7	103.82
Percentage franked	100	100
Interest cover (times)	15.2	23.3
Return on equity (%)	17.9	22.7
Half year to 30 June	**2004**	**2005**
Revenues ($mn)	9206.0	12258.0
Profit before tax ($mn)	1959.0	3979.0
Profit after tax ($mn)	1342.0	2710.0
Earnings per share (¢)	97.3	197.4
Dividend (¢)	45.53	50.56
Percentage franked	100	100
Net tangible assets per share ($)	10.02	10.99
Debt-to-equity ratio (%)	42.0	28.8
Current ratio	1.4	1.5

The Rock Building Society Ltd

Share price ($)	4.55
12-month high ($)	4.61
12-month low ($)	3.46
Market capitalisation ($mn)	82.3
Price-to-NTA-per-share ratio	2.2
5-year share price return (% pa)	20.3

Sector: Financials	Company	Sector
Price-earnings ratio (times)	15.7	14.3
Dividend yield (%)	5.2	4.5

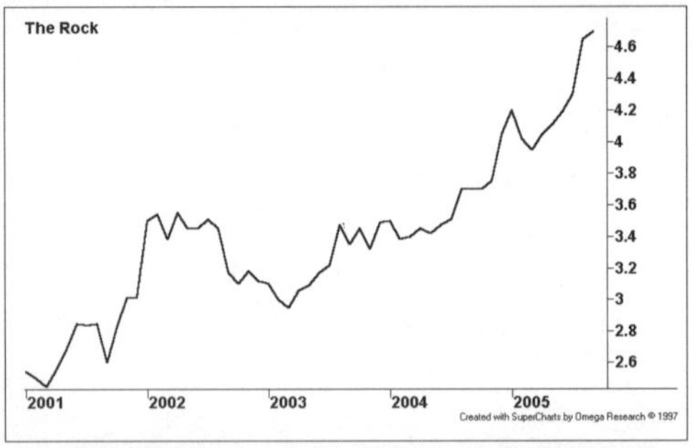

www.therock.com.au

The Rock Building Society was established in 1967 and is based in Rockhampton, Queensland. Its main role has been to take retail deposits and provide housing finance for that state's residents, and it is the leading home lender in central Queensland. It also has a strong presence in the south of the state and a growing business in NSW and Victoria.

Latest business results (June 2005, full year)

In the face of a weakening housing market, the company achieved a solid rise in its profits. Loan approvals actually fell 16% to $320 million, though the year-end loan balance stood at $1.04 billion, up nearly 7% from a year before. Also at the end of June 2005, total deposits stood at $479.4 million, up 7% from a year earlier, and total assets under management were up 9% to $1.26 billion. There was particularly good growth in funds under management, up 37% to $67 million. A deterioration in some of its financial ratios reflected the inclusion in the June 2004 results of a $1.6 million after-tax profit from the sale of the building society's holdings in Cashcard. After a period of decline, the interest margin has been edging up again.

Outlook

The Rock is striving to diversify away from its heavy dependence on home lending. In particular, it has been working to build its financial planning operations and this business — though still small — saw revenues up 52% in the latest results. It is also seeking to expand its insurance and business banking activities, while at the same time boosting the profitability of these businesses. Like most of its rivals it is also seeking to contain costs, particularly staff costs, and was able to restrict personnel expenses to just a 3.6% rise in the June 2005 year. It has completed a restructuring of its operations, including the redesign of its Central Queensland branches, and this is now being expanded to other regions. It is planning further loan products and a new credit card product, and is also reviewing its fee structure. But despite all these initiatives, the bank remains heavily dependent on housing trends and for the time being this market remains sluggish, which could dampen margins and profits.

ROK Year to 30 June	2004	2005
Operating income ($mn)	25.4	25.1
Net interest income ($mn)	8.3	9.4
Operating expenses ($mn)	17.4	18.4
Profit before tax ($mn)	5.6	6.6
Profit after tax ($mn)	3.9	4.6
Earnings per share (¢)	25.3	29.0
Dividend (¢)	20.5	23.5
Percentage franked	100	100
Non-interest income to total income (%)	67.2	62.4
Net tangible assets per share ($)	1.71	2.10
Cost-to-income ratio (%)	68.4	73.4
Return on equity (%)	15.7	13.8
Return on assets (%)	0.9	0.9

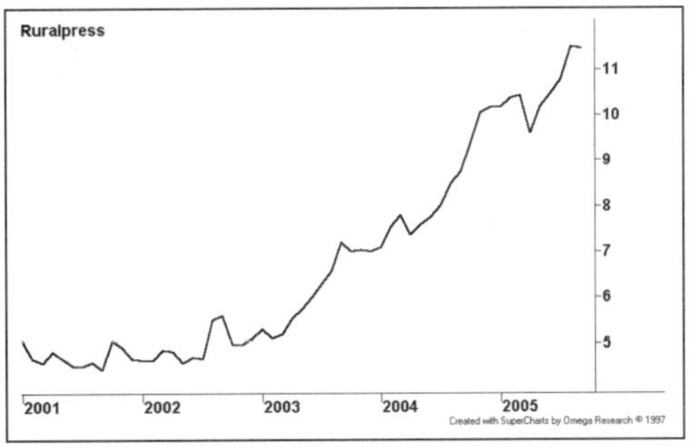

wwww.ruralpress.com.au

Rural Press Ltd

Share price ($)	11.30
12-month high ($)	11.45
12-month low ($)	7.90
Market capitalisation ($mn)	1355.2
Price-to-NTA-per-share ratio	2.0
5-year share price return (% pa)	19.0

Sector: Consumer discretionary	Company	Sector
Price-earnings ratio (times)	11.9	24.2
Dividend yield (%)	4.6	1.2

Rural Press, based in country NSW, was established in 1911 and is today one of the world's leading agricultural publishers, with specialist newspapers and magazines in Australia, America and New Zealand. It also manages a string of regional newspapers—including *The Canberra Times*—throughout Australia. In addition, it operates major printing businesses in all Australian states, and it owns the Star Broadcasting Network, which runs radio stations in South Australia and Queensland. The Fairfax family own more than 50% of the equity.

Latest business results (June 2005, full year)

Rural Press unleashed a big rise in its annual profit, thanks in particular to record advertising revenues at its domestic publications. Australasian publishing saw revenues up 11% to $420 million, with EBIT jumping 19% to $124 million. Advertising volumes grew, despite a slowdown in property advertising, and the company was also able to achieve higher rates. Australasian printing operations boosted revenues 16% to $105 million, with EBIT up 20% to $32 million. The company's American publishing activities recorded a 7% drop in sales to $36 million, with EBIT plummeting 63%. Its broadcasting operations moved from the red into profit, and sales were up 27% to nearly $10 million, due in particular to a strong performance by Ipswich's River 94.9FM station.

Outlook

With its high fixed costs, Rural Press, like other media and printing companies, is a major beneficiary of the continuing strength of the Australian economy. It continues to expand, purchasing six regional publications during the June 2005 year and upgrading five printing presses. Management has said that a $150 million line of credit is available to the company from its banks and it is ready to move quickly if acquisition opportunities present themselves. The company has also expressed its interest in moving into the television business. New management at the company's US operations has initiated a fresh publishing strategy intended to boost business there, though this was not reflected in the latest results. The company announced in late August that business in the first seven weeks of the new financial year was slightly ahead of the previous year. The prospect that the government might ease the country's cross-media ownership laws has placed media companies in the spotlight, and could help support the share price.

RUP Year to 30 June	2004	2005
Revenues ($mn)	509.5	564.6
EBIT ($mn)	137.6	162.1
EBIT margin (%)	27.0	28.7
Profit before tax ($mn)	128.8	152.5
Profit after tax ($mn)	87.1	112.9
Earnings per share (¢)	78.3	95.1
Cash flow per share (¢)	95.2	110.6
Dividend (¢)	39	51.5
Percentage franked	100	100
Net tangible assets per share ($)	5.39	5.52
Interest cover (times)	15.8	16.9
Return on equity (%)	13.8	17.0
Debt-to-equity ratio (%)	22.2	26.6
Current ratio	1.2	1.5

Santos Ltd

Share price ($)	11.00	
12-month high ($)	11.80	
12-month low ($)	6.50	
Market capitalisation ($mn)	6313.4	
Price-to-NTA-per-share ratio	2.5	
5-year share price return (% pa)	17.9	
Sector: Energy	**Company**	**Sector**
Price-earnings ratio (times)	16.9	17.7
Dividend yield (%)	3.0	1.9

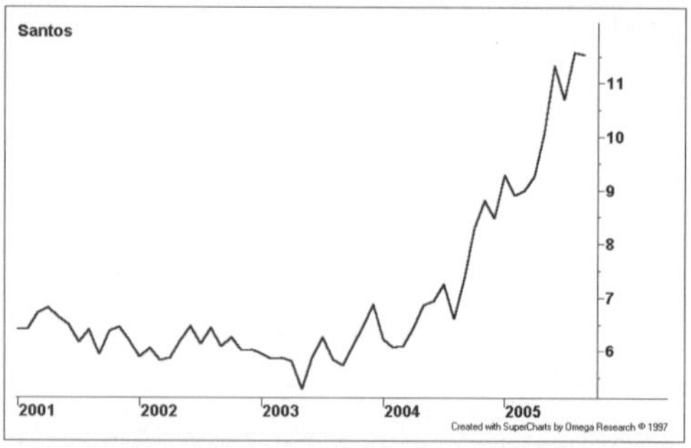

www.santos.com.au

Adelaide-based Santos, established in 1954, is one of Australia's leading independent producers of oil and gas. Most of its output is from the Cooper/Eromanga Basins in central Australia, though it has additional interests in other parts of Australia, as well as in the US, Indonesia and Papua New Guinea. It is a major gas producer, supplying natural gas to all mainland states and territories.

Latest business results (June 2005, half year)

In the midst of soaring oil prices, Santos posted a major increase in profits. Other factors were also at work—the June 2004 result had been badly hurt by the loss of substantial production from a fire at the Moomba Gas Plant, and the new Australian International Financial Reporting Standards had a favourable impact through the partial reversal of impairment write-downs. Total production rose from 21.2 million barrels of oil equivalent (BOE) to 26.3 million, with a particular boost from the company's Mutineer-Exeter oilfield off Western Australia, which came ahead of schedule. The average oil price realised by the company was up 41% and the average condensate price was up 36%.

STO Year to 31 December	2003	2004
Revenues ($mn)	1465.0	1500.9
EBIT ($mn)	463.0	570.9
EBIT margin (%)	31.6	38.0
Gross margin (%)	33.5	30.1
Profit before tax ($mn)	430.9	540.8
Profit after tax ($mn)	327.0	379.9
Earnings per share (¢)	56.0	64.9
Cash flow per share (¢)	146.7	156.7
Dividend (¢)	30	33
Percentage franked	100	100
Interest cover (times)	14.4	19.0
Return on equity (%)	11.0	11.5
Half year to 30 June	**2004**	**2005**
Revenues ($mn)	590.5	1019.5
Profit before tax ($mn)	124.2	421.9
Profit after tax ($mn)	85.3	289.5
Earnings per share (¢)	12.6	46.9
Dividend (¢)	15	18
Percentage franked	100	100
Net tangible assets per share ($)	3.46	4.33
Debt-to-equity ratio (%)	61.1	50.6
Current ratio	1.2	1.4

Outlook

Santos is in the happy position of having a number of major new projects coming on stream just at the time that oil prices are at record highs, and it forecasts 2005 production of 55 million BOE, up from 47 million in 2004. Oil production at Mutineer-Exeter has already reached 80 000 barrels per day. The Mutineer 11 appraisal well drilled in May 2005 has shown a positive result and two new development wells are to be drilled. The Bayu-Undan liquids project in the Timor Gap has exceeded expectations, with production of over 100 000 barrels per day. At the John Brookes gas field in Western Australia, production was due to start in September 2005. Development work continues at the Casino gas field in the Otway Basin, with production expected to begin in 2006. In addition, the company has embarked on a major exploration program, with a particular focus on the Kutei and East Java Basins offshore Indonesia, the Gulf of Suez in Egypt, the Bonaparte Basin in the Timor Sea and the Carnarvon Basin offshore Western Australia.

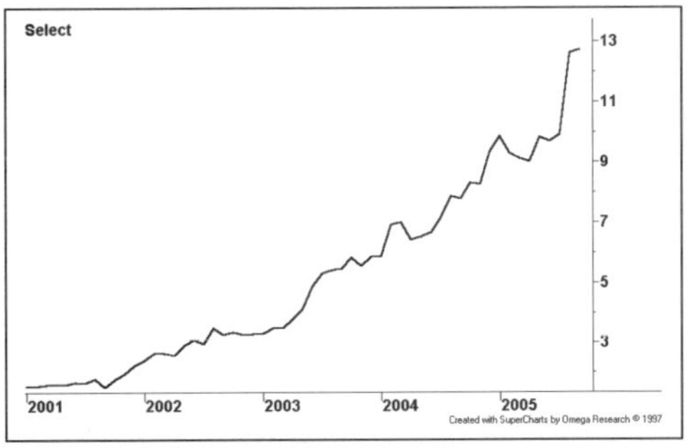

www.selectharvests.com.au

Select Harvests Ltd

Share price ($)	10.50	
12-month high ($)	10.74	
12-month low ($)	7.10	
Market capitalisation ($mn)	412.2	
Price-to-NTA-per-share ratio	6.4	
5-year share price return (% pa)	62.5	
Sector: Consumer staples	**Company**	**Sector**
Price-earnings ratio (times)	18.8	15.6
Dividend yield (%)	4.0	3.3

Melbourne-based Select Harvests is Australia's biggest almond grower and processor. It is responsible for about 40% of national output and is one of the five largest growers in the world. As well as its own almond orchards in Victoria's Sunraysia district, it has a thriving business managing orchards owned by external investors. In addition, it is a leading supplier to Australian supermarkets of processed and packaged nuts, dried fruits and associated products, through the Lucky, Sunsol, Ni-Vit, Meriram and Soland brands. It is selling its small pesticides business.

Latest business results (June 2005, full year)

The company's stunning expansion continued, with the sixth consecutive year of earnings growth in excess of 25%. The almond crop of 6070 tonnes was up 70% from the previous year, and the company was also a beneficiary of lower costs, rising demand and record prices. Revenues from its high-margin almond operations rose 21% to $42.5 million, with EBIT up 44% to $26.3 million, which was nearly 80% of total company profit. Food product sales jumped 49% to $131.4 million, thanks in part to continuing acquisitions (including the Chiquita Nibbles business in September 2004), with EBIT up 19% to $8.1 million. The pesticides business recorded good growth in sales and profits.

Outlook

Select Harvests has had a sensational run of rising profits and this has been reflected in the share price. The company continues to expand at a time when almond prices are at record highs due to a slowdown in global output and increasing demand, as consumers focus on their health benefits. To meet increasing interest in almond orchards as investments, the company planted an additional 4100 acres of investor-owned almond orchards in the June 2005 year, to bring its total under management to 18 100 acres, and it plans a further 6000 acres in the June 2006 year. It is working to build its processed food brands, but faces strong competition from a growing proliferation of cheap home-brand supermarket products. There can also be a time lag in passing on rising nut costs to retailers, which has an impact on margins. Select Harvests has entered into an agreement to sell its pesticides business in October 2005 for $5.7 million, with a pre-tax profit of approximately $4 million.

SHV Year to 30 June	2004	2005
Revenues ($mn)	127.4	178.0
Food products (%)	69	74
Almond operations (%)	28	24
Pesticide products (%)	3	2
EBIT ($mn)	23.8	33.3
EBIT margin (%)	18.7	18.7
Gross margin (%)	28.4	26.1
Profit before tax ($mn)	22.6	32.0
Profit after tax ($mn)	15.2	21.7
Earnings per share (¢)	40.0	55.9
Cash flow per share (¢)	51.4	67.9
Dividend (¢)	26	42
Percentage franked	100	100
Net tangible assets per share ($)	1.35	1.64
Interest cover (times)	19.1	26.3
Return on equity (%)	21.9	25.4
Debt-to-equity ratio (%)	9.6	~
Current ratio	1.7	1.5

Sigma Company Ltd

Share price ($)	9.39	
12-month high ($)	9.74	
12-month low ($)	7.53	
Market capitalisation ($mn)	1335.8	
Price-to-NTA-per-share ratio	15.8	
5-year share price return (% pa)	58.2	
Sector: Health care	**Company**	**Sector**
Price-earnings ratio (times)	22.4	28.0
Dividend yield (%)	2.8	1.7

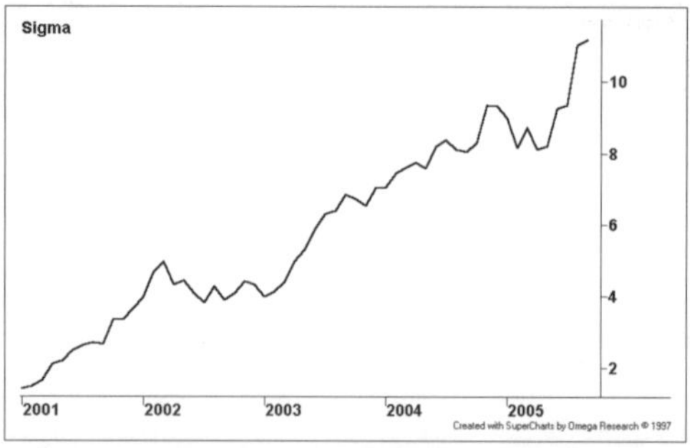

www.sigmaco.com.au

Melbourne-based Sigma, founded in 1912, is Australia's largest pharmaceuticals company. It manufactures more than 500 drugs and medicines, and distributes its products to around 3500 pharmacies nationwide, including to Guardian and Amcal stores. It owns the Herron Group pharmaceuticals business and has announced proposals for a merger with Arrow Pharmaceuticals.

Latest business results (July 2005, half year)

Profits rose strongly again, even after restating the previous half-year result in accord with new accounting standards. The high-margin pharmaceuticals division — responsible for drugs manufacture — saw sales rise less than 5%, but with a 24% surge in EBIT, as the company leveraged its high fixed-cost base to boost margins. The good result came despite having to absorb one-off costs of $2.9 million in relation to the planned closure of the company's manufacturing facility in Croydon in Melbourne. The pharmaceuticals division, though only 16% of total company revenues, contributes more than 60% of total profit. In a tight market, the health care division, which is responsible for drugs distribution, saw sales up nearly 2%, while EBIT rose 6%.

SIG Year to 31 January	2004	2005
Revenues ($mn)	1908.6	2095.8
EBIT ($mn)	83.6	104.8
EBIT margin (%)	4.4	5.0
Gross margin (%)	11.5	11.5
Profit before tax ($mn)	67.3	83.9
Profit after tax ($mn)	44.2	59.6
Earnings per share (¢)	31.4	41.9
Cash flow per share (¢)	44.0	55.7
Dividend (¢)	20	26
Percentage franked	100	100
Interest cover (times)	5.1	5.0
Return on equity (%)	14.7	17.5
Half year to 31 July	**2004**	**2005**
Revenues ($mn)	1021.8	1037.0
Profit before tax ($mn)	39.0	45.2
Profit after tax ($mn)	26.4	31.7
Earnings per share (¢)	19.0	22.6
Dividend (¢)	10.5	14.5
Percentage franked	100	100
Net tangible assets per share ($)	0.43	0.59
Debt-to-equity ratio (%)	55.0	47.4
Current ratio	1.2	1.2

Outlook

Sigma's impressive growth has led to a powerful share price performance. The company itself is forecasting further profit growth of at least 15% in the January 2006 year. For its pharmaceuticals business it expects strong continuing organic growth, along with major benefits from the proposed merger with Arrow Pharmaceuticals, which is Australia's second-largest producer of generic drugs. Sigma has started work on a 30-month, $54 million expansion program for its Dandenong production facility in Melbourne. It expects this to deliver significant cost benefits in coming years, as well as bringing about a big increase in production capacity. The company is also working to cut costs and boost sales in its high-volume, low-margin health care business. It has launched a new retail brand, Amcal Max, with the first pilot store opened in Queensland in August 2005 and a major store roll-out planned from 2006. The larger Amcal Max stores offer pharmacists the opportunity to boost their returns, with a range of retail products added to the traditional mix of drugs and cosmetics.

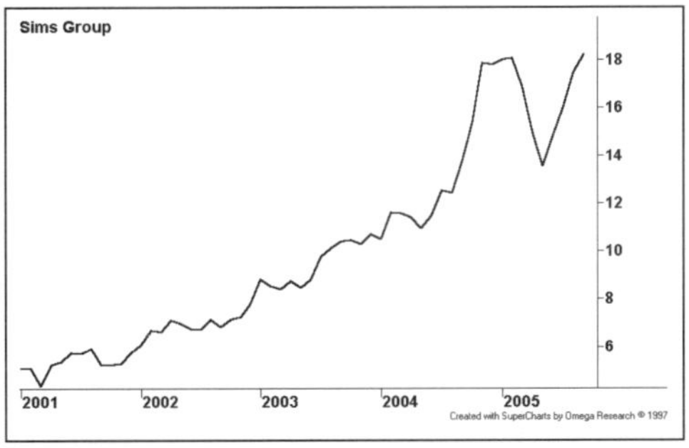

www.simsmetal.com.au

Sims Group Ltd

Share price ($)	17.05
12-month high ($)	19.25
12-month low ($)	11.86
Market capitalisation ($mn)	1506.6
Price-to-NTA-per-share ratio	3.6
5-year share price return (% pa)	30.8

Sector: Materials	Company	Sector
Price-earnings ratio (times)	8.3	17.0
Dividend yield (%)	8.2	2.2

Sydney-based Sims, formerly called Simsmetal, was founded in 1917, and is today Australia's largest metals recycler. It has become the world's largest producer of ferrous scrap metal (which is used in steel making), and a leading producer of non-ferrous scrap, particularly copper and aluminium. Some 55% of revenues and profits come from overseas operations, primarily in America, Britain and New Zealand.

Latest business results (June 2005, full year)

The Chinese economic boom handed Sims another major boost to its business, with sales and profits racing ahead. Overall sales tonnage was up 11%, with shredded production sales up 17%, other processed ferrous sales tonnage up 13% and non-ferrous sales tonnage up 5%. Australian business (45% of company turnover) was up 47%, with pre-tax profit soaring 79%. British sales (29% of turnover) were up 24%, with profits ahead 49%. North America saw sales up 37% and profits surging 71%. North American business is especially profitable, with the region responsible for 23% of company turnover but 35% of total profit.

Outlook

As another Australian beneficiary of the Chinese boom, Sims now sees its immediate fortunes tied in large part to that country's economy. However, with extreme volatility evident in the ferrous metals market, the company must also be astute in the timing of sales. It has reported that the new financial year began weakly, though it expected renewed strength later in the year, with ferrous prices once more on the rise. The company continues to expand. In October 2004, it announced the acquisition of the Dutch-based Mirec group of companies, Europe's leading electronic and electrical equipment recycler. Mirec operates dedicated plants for the recycling of cathode ray tubes from TV and computer monitors, and gives Sims an important base in a market with great potential. In June 2005, Sims announced a major $650 million acquisition of America's Hugo Neu Corporation, which will boost Sims' annual tonnage of recycled metal from five million to nine million tonnes, and make it the world's largest scrap metals recycler, as well as one of America's largest exporters of scrap steel. Under the terms of the takeover, the Neu family will become holders of 26% of the equity in Sims, making them by far the largest shareholders.

SMS Year to 30 June	2004	2005
Revenues ($mn)	1873.9	2565.0
EBIT ($mn)	168.4	280.1
EBIT margin (%)	9.0	10.9
Profit before tax ($mn)	166.6	274.7
Profit after tax ($mn)	112.5	187.9
Earnings per share (¢)	122.6	206.2
Cash flow per share (¢)	155.5	248.8
Dividend (¢)	66	140
Percentage franked	52	57
Net tangible assets per share ($)	4.12	4.78
Interest cover (times)	91.2	52.2
Return on equity (%)	26.6	38.2
Debt-to-equity ratio (%)	4.0	9.9
Current ratio	1.6	1.8

St George Bank Ltd

Share price ($)	26.74
12-month high ($)	27.05
12-month low ($)	20.80
Market capitalisation ($mn)	13 884.5
Price-to-NTA-per-share ratio	3.7
5-year share price return (% pa)	25.0

Sector: Financials	Company	Sector
Price-earnings ratio (times)	17.8	14.3
Dividend yield (%)	4.6	4.5

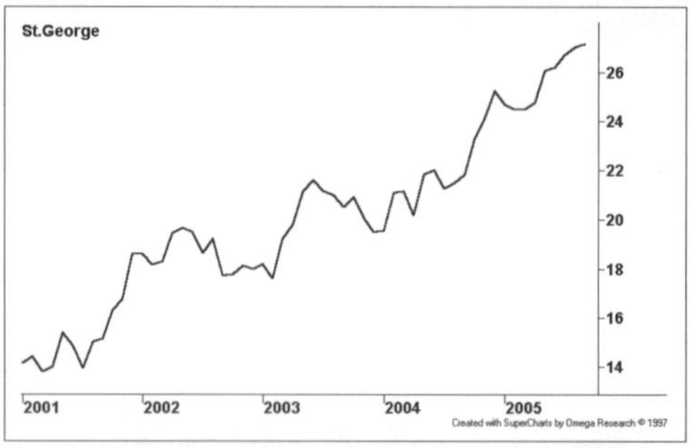

www.stgeorge.com.au

Sydney-based St George, originally a building society founded in 1937, has grown from a series of mergers and acquisitions to become Australia's fifth-largest retail bank. It has its business centred in South Australia (where it is Number One, thanks to its acquisition of BankSA) and in NSW. It also owns the master trust business Sealcorp. In 2005 it sold its Assirt managed funds data and ratings business to Standard & Poor's Australia.

Latest business results (March 2005, half year)

St George achieved another excellent result. Home lending grew 15.1% to $52.8 billion, with commercial lending up 19.5% to $18.8 billion. Retail funds increased 5.5% to $36.8 billion. Healthy cost containment meant that the half-year cost-to-income ratio fell by more than three percentage points from the March 2004 half. Funds under management leapt 23% to $27.8 billion, which includes Sealcorp funds of $20.5 billion. There was a slight deterioration in the bank's interest margin, from 2.74% in the March 2004 half to 2.6%. The bank's wholly owned mortgage insurance provider, St George Insurance, recorded a 64% leap in its after-tax profit to $28 million.

SGB Year to 30 September	2003	2004
Operating income ($mn)	2361.0	2587.0
Net interest income ($mn)	1451.0	1612.0
Operating expenses ($mn)	1170.0	1342.0
Profit before tax ($mn)	978.0	1135.0
Profit after tax ($mn)	658.0	767.0
Earnings per share (¢)	131.0	150.4
Dividend (¢)	95	122
Percentage franked	100	100
Non-interest income to total income (%)	38.5	37.7
Cost-to-income ratio (%)	49.6	51.9
Return on equity (%)	17.5	17.7
Return on assets (%)	1.1	1.2
Half year to 31 March	**2004**	**2005**
Operating income ($mn)	1269.0	1384.0
Profit before tax ($mn)	556.0	660.0
Profit after tax ($mn)	377.0	447.0
Earnings per share (¢)	69.7	86.6
Dividend (¢)	60	67
Percentage franked	100	100
Net tangible assets per share ($)	5.81	7.21

Outlook

St George continues its organic growth strategy, which it believes offers less risk than growth through acquisition and it expects that, despite its own forecasts of a slowdown in home lending activity and a weakening economy, it can still achieve double-digit EPS growth in its September 2005 and 2006 years. It maintains a particular focus on customer service and generally achieves far higher customer satisfaction ratings than most rivals. It is working to streamline its home loan process — 43% of new approvals in the March 2005 half came through home loan brokers — with a new lender program, new incentives and an increase in its lender salesforce. Its wealth management operation is one of the bank's strengths, and this continues to grow, with good business for Sealcorp, which operates the Asgard Master Trust and Wrap services, and for Advance Funds Management. St George continues to expand in Victoria, and is now working to increase its presence in Queensland.

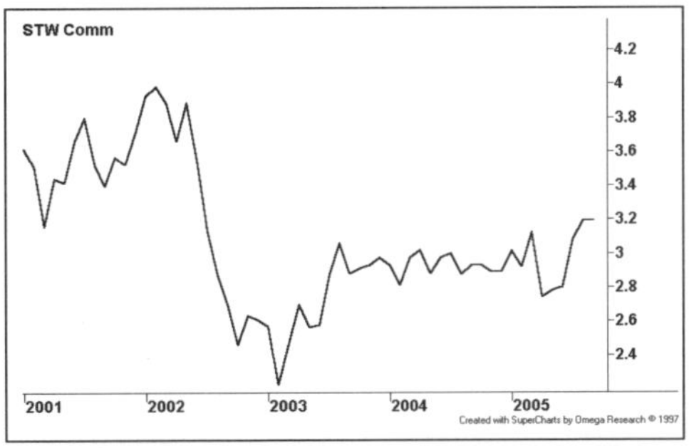

www.stwgroup.com.au

STW Communications Group Ltd

Share price ($)	3.22	
12-month high ($)	3.22	
12-month low ($)	2.66	
Market capitalisation ($mn)	546.5	
Price-to-NTA-per-share ratio	2.8	
5-year share price return (% pa)	8.5	
Sector: Consumer discretionary	**Company**	**Sector**
Price-earnings ratio (times)	23.6	24.2
Dividend yield (%)	4.2	1.2

Sydney-based STW Communications Group, formerly called Singleton Group, was founded by entrepreneur John Singleton, who is the largest shareholder. It is a holding company, owning two-thirds of Singleton Ogilvy & Mather Holdings, as well as a 49% interest in the Australian and New Zealand operations of the advertising company J. Walter Thompson. It also has direct or indirect ownership of over 40 other smaller businesses in such diverse fields as internet design and marketing, ethnic advertising, public relations and direct marketing. It has sold its 20.75% stake in Indonesia's third-largest television network, PT Surya Citra Television.

Latest business results (June 2005, half year)

STW presents its financial results in varying ways, and it can be difficult sometimes to make valid comparisons. The after-tax profit fell, though that largely reflected the sale of the company's Indonesian interests. Excluding this business, the after-tax profit from Australian and New Zealand operations was up 5%. The company also presents its results in another manner. Instead of equity accounting its holdings in numerous smaller companies, it aggregates on a percentage basis its economic interest in their revenues, profits and losses. Using this method, revenues rose 15% to $79.9 million and after-tax profit from Australia and New Zealand was up 14% to $13.9 million. During the half the company acquired 49% interests in Brett Goulston & Associates (direct marketing), I.M. Marketing (advertising), Torque (database management) and Oxygen Learning (training).

Outlook

STW retains a string of blue-chip domestic and international clients, and this underpins its business. Thanks to its holding company structure, it is able to attract rival corporations as clients, each dealing with different arms of the company. It continues to expand, with a rising number of acquired companies providing numerous synergies and cross-selling opportunities. In particular, it sees its marketing services subsidiaries and associates as providing a particular impetus for growth, and it has announced that it expects EPS growth in 2005 of 10% to 15%. Following the loss of several accounts in 2004, the company overhauled its New Zealand operations, with excellent results. It plans a further New Zealand acquisition. Domestically, it plans to establish another major advertising brand during 2006.

SGN Year to 31 December	2003	2004
Revenues ($mn)	32.2	43.2
EBIT ($mn)	26.0	26.5
EBIT margin (%)	80.9	61.3
Profit before tax ($mn)	25.6	24.0
Profit after tax ($mn)	26.0	23.2
Earnings per share (¢)	17.0	13.6
Cash flow per share (¢)	17.2	14.3
Dividend (¢)	13.4	13.4
Percentage franked	100	100
Interest cover (times)	63.8	10.8
Return on equity (%)	13.2	10.8
Half year to 30 June	**2004**	**2005**
Revenues ($mn)	19.2	31.3
Profit before tax ($mn)	11.9	14.1
Profit after tax ($mn)	13.9	12.8
Earnings per share (¢)	8.3	7.3
Dividend (¢)	4.3	4.8
Percentage franked	100	100
Net tangible assets per share ($)	1.01	0.71
Debt-to-equity ratio (%)	9.0	53.2
Current ratio	6.5	1.5

SUNCORP-METWAY LTD

Share price ($)	20.59	
12-month high ($)	20.77	
12-month low ($)	13.85	
Market capitalisation ($mn)	11 364.7	
Price-to-NTA-per-share ratio	3.1	
5-year share price return (% pa)	23.2	
Sector: Financials	**Company**	**Sector**
Price-earnings ratio (times)	13.6	14.3
Dividend yield (%)	4.2	4.5

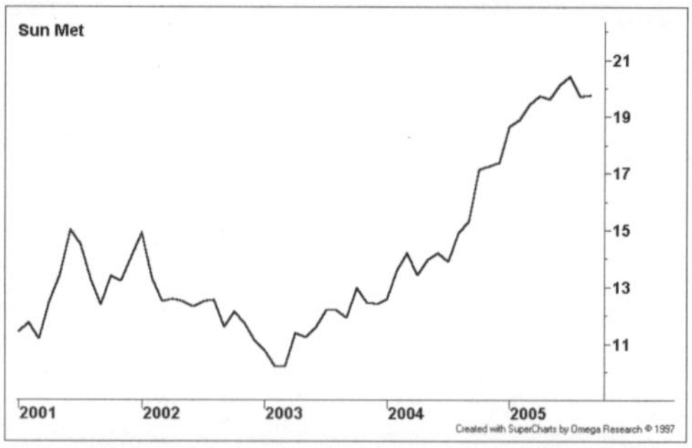

www.suncorp.com.au

Brisbane-based Suncorp-Metway, Queensland's largest company, was formed from the merger of Metway Bank, the Queensland Industry Development Corporation and the insurance company Suncorp. It divides its businesses into three core areas—banking, insurance and wealth management. It is Australia's sixth-largest bank and second-largest general insurance company—the latter under the GIO brand—with some 3.8 million customers.

Latest business results (June 2005, full year)

The bank enjoyed another big jump in profits, with continued strength across all its businesses. Once again, the insurance business was the star, with profits up 40%, driven by strong growth in premium revenue, improved investment income and a favourable claims experience. However, the result was affected by an abnormally high number of storm-related claims in the second half. Banking profits rose 24%, despite a housing slowdown and strong competition for customer deposits. Total lending grew by 15.6%, which the bank said was above the total industry growth rate of 11.8% for the year. Despite a softening of the home loans market, especially in the second half, the bank boosted mortgage receivables by 14.5% to $19.7 billion. The bank was also able to boost its net interest margin from 2.27% to 2.33%. The wealth management business recorded 38% profit growth, or 12.1% when a one-off profit from the sale of management rights was excluded. This division's result was driven largely by strong investment earnings.

Outlook

Suncorp-Metway has become a Queensland powerhouse, with all its businesses in excellent shape. The question now is to what extent it can continue to grow, and the bank has already warned that competition is intensifying in all its markets. In banking, the company expects bad debts to start to rise from their historic lows, and the direction of the housing market is still unclear, as pressure on mortgage rates continues. In insurance, the company is seeing pressure on commercial rates, and it expects its insurance margin—roughly the difference between insurance revenues and insurance claims and expenses—to fall from its present 17.7% to between 11% and 14%. In response, the bank is working to boost the amount of cross-selling business it does between its three areas of operation. It also plans a big interstate expansion of its branch network.

SUN Year to 30 June	2004	2005
Operating income ($mn)	4594.0	5317.0
Net interest income ($mn)	656.0	771.0
Operating expenses ($mn)	3514.0	3937.0
Profit before tax ($mn)	971.0	1292.0
Profit after tax ($mn)	618.0	821.0
Earnings per share (¢)	115.8	151.5
Dividend (¢)	70	87
Percentage franked	100	100
Non-interest income to total income (%)	85.7	85.5
Net tangible assets per share ($)	5.61	6.55
Cost-to-income ratio (%)	76.5	74.0
Return on equity (%)	16.2	19.3
Return on assets (%)	1.5	1.8

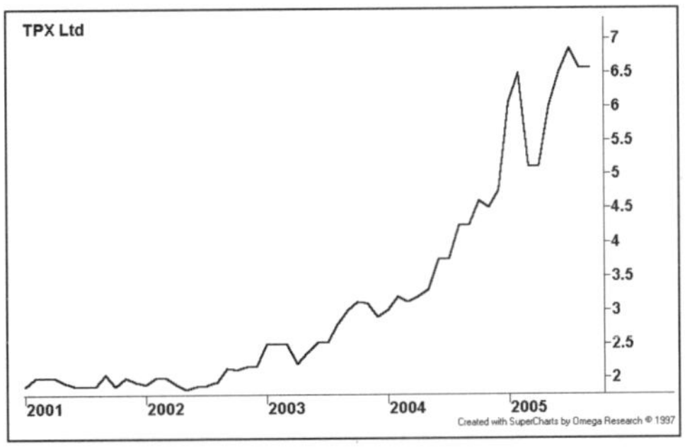

www.tasmanianperpetual.com.au

Tasmanian Perpetual Trustees Ltd

Share price ($)	6.20
12-month high ($)	7.10
12-month low ($)	3.69
Market capitalisation ($mn)	138.8
Price-to-NTA-per-share ratio	7.9
5-year share price return (% pa)	29.4

Sector: Financials	Company	Sector
Price-earnings ratio (times)	26.6	14.3
Dividend yield (%)	3.5	4.5

Tasmanian Perpetual Trustees was formed from the December 2001 merger of Tasmanian Trustees and Perpetual Trustees Tasmania, and maintains a headquarters in Launceston. Both companies had been founded in 1887. It engages in traditional trustee services, such as estate planning, will preparation, estate management and powers of attorney, and also offers a range of financial planning and wealth management services. In addition it runs managed funds and it jointly owns Tasmanian Banking Services, in a fifty-fifty partnership with Bendigo Bank.

Latest business results (June 2005, full year)

The company achieved another good result, continuing the trend of strong performances since the merged company was formed in 2001. In a competitive market, funds under management grew 5% to $1.3 billion. There was a particularly good result from the Tasmanian Banking Services venture, with the company's share of its after-tax profit jumping 80% to $730 000. In addition to the figures in the table on this page, Tasmanian Perpetual Trustees also received a one-off $0.87 million profit (treated as a significant item) from the restructuring of the Tattersall's estate to prepare it for public listing. Tattersall's had its origins in Tasmania and, as part of the process of converting to a public company, it made some significant distributions to its beneficiaries. Tasmanian Perpetual Trustees acts as trustee for many estates and trusts that received this benefit, and thus derived considerable commission income.

Outlook

Tasmanian Perpetual Trustees enjoys a strong reputation in its home state and, together with its Tasmanian Banking Services joint venture, it is a powerful force in Tasmanian finance, with seven branch offices. It services a quarter of all adult Tasmanian residents, and it has more than 5000 business and community clients. It is seen as having particular strength in rural services. The joint venture, Tasmanian Banking Services, is showing excellent growth and, as well as making a strong and growing contribution to Tasmanian Perpetual's profits, it also provides considerable synergies, including four shared branch offices and the ability to gain new clients. In August 2005, it was revealed that New Zealand corporate raider Ron Brierley had sold his 9% stake in Tasmanian Perpetual Trustees to Trust Company of Australia, giving rise to speculation on looming merger or acquisition activity.

TPX Year to 30 June	2004	2005
Revenues ($mn)	15.5	17.8
EBIT ($mn)	6.0	7.1
EBIT margin (%)	38.4	39.7
Profit before tax ($mn)	6.4	7.6
Profit after tax ($mn)	4.3	5.1
Earnings per share (¢)	19.9*	23.3
Cash flow per share (¢)	25.4*	28.5
Dividend (¢)	16.25*	22
Percentage franked	100	100
Net tangible assets per share ($)	0.64*	0.79
Interest cover (times)	~	~
Return on equity (%)	15.9	17.3
Debt-to-equity ratio (%)	~	~
Current ratio	3.8	3.9

* adjusted for a four-for-one share split

Technology One Ltd

Share price ($)	0.59	
12-month high ($)	0.79	
12-month low ($)	0.51	
Market capitalisation ($mn)	183.0	
Price-to-NTA-per-share ratio	6.0	
5-year share price return (% pa)	−12.0	
Sector: Information technology	**Company**	**Sector**
Price-earnings ratio (times)	17.2	34.4
Dividend yield (%)	5.3	1.7

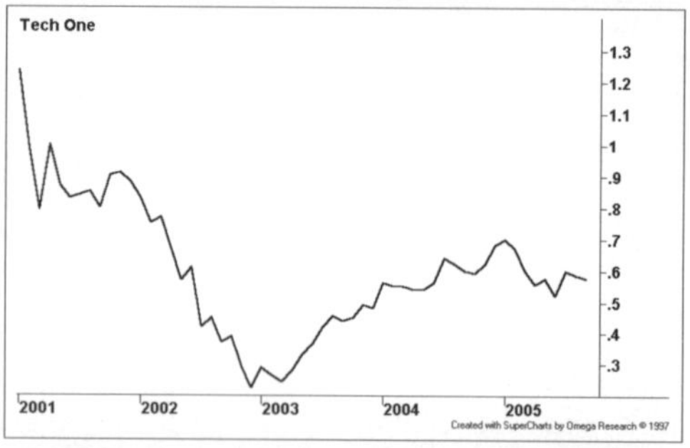

www.technologyone.com.au

Brisbane-based Technology One, founded in 1987, designs, develops, implements and supports financial management and accounting software. It has gained success with its Finance One software product, and enjoys particular strength in local government. Its Student One software is used by many colleges and universities. The company also has a thriving business developing custom software for clients. It operates from ten offices in Australia, Malaysia and New Zealand.

Latest business results (June 2005, full year)

The company recorded satisfactory single-digit growth in sales and profits, a steep drop from the 35% jump in after-tax profit achieved in the previous year. During the year, the company added 83 new clients, and licence fee revenue to new clients was up 17%. This too was a drop from the June 2004 year, when the company added 74 new clients and saw new licence fee revenue up 54%. Research and development spending remained strong at $10.2 million, up 7% from the previous year.

Outlook

Technology One is one of the high-tech companies that listed on the ASX late in 1999, near the height of the dotcom boom. However, unlike virtually all the others, not only has it prospered, it has also managed a record of continuing good profits and dividend payouts. It is a conservatively managed company. It devotes considerable amounts towards R&D and this money is fully expensed as it is incurred, thus providing a realistic picture of its financial position — rather than being capitalised, as is common among many companies. It has built up a strong balance sheet, with more than $22 million in net cash holdings in June 2005, and maintains high dividend payouts to its shareholders. There has been a good reception for the company's next-generation Finance One software product, called Finance One CI (Connected Intelligence). The company is also investigating new applications that will extend the breadth of its products, including customer relationship management, contract management, strategic planning and fleet management. Technology One plans to open an office in the UK early in 2006 and plans to expand throughout Britain over the following four years, believing this offers huge scope for growth. It will also use its British base as a launching pad for moves into other large markets.

TNE Year to 30 June	2004	2005
Revenues ($mn)	50.5	54.4
Service delivery (%)	69	71
Software engineering (%)	27	26
EBIT ($mn)	12.2	13.1
EBIT margin (%)	24.1	24.2
Profit before tax ($mn)	13.1	14.3
Profit after tax ($mn)	9.5	10.3
Earnings per share (¢)	3.2	3.4
Cash flow per share (¢)	3.7	4.0
Dividend (¢)	2.85	3.1
Percentage franked	100	100
Net tangible assets per share ($)	0.09	0.10
Interest cover (times)	~	~
Return on equity (%)	26.1	27.2
Debt-to-equity ratio (%)	~	~
Current ratio	3.4	3.6

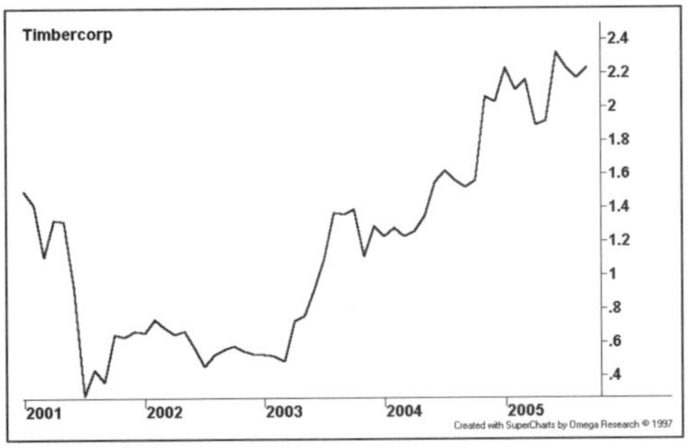

www.timbercorp.com.au

Timbercorp Ltd

Share price ($)	2.17	
12-month high ($)	2.42	
12-month low ($)	1.32	
Market capitalisation ($mn)	531.0	
Price-to-NTA-per-share ratio	2.1	
5-year share price return (% pa)	7.5	
Sector: Materials	**Company**	**Sector**
Price-earnings ratio (times)	11.4	17.0
Dividend yield (%)	2.5	2.2

Melbourne-based Timbercorp, established in 1992, is a prominent agribusiness company. It promotes plantation projects for outside investors, provides finance and manages the properties, receiving recurring annuity-style income—including licence fees, rent and management fees—for its services. The investments are intended for long-term investors and offer the promise of substantial tax benefits, along with potentially high returns. The company's primary plantations are 74 000 hectares of blue gums in the Green Triangle region of Victoria-South Australia and in Western Australia. It also manages a 2700-hectare olive tree plantation—one of the largest in the world—in central Victoria. With Select Harvests it has moved into the almond orchard business, with plantings of more than 3600 hectares. In 2004, it expanded into grape and citrus plantings, and a year later into mango cultivation. It is a substantial shareholder in Select Harvests and in the listed olive oil marketer Piquant Blue.

Latest business results (March 2005, half year)

Profits continued their upward trajectory; although, as is customary, most profit was generated in the company's second half. Annuity-style revenues from existing projects jumped 45% to $56.4 million. New project sales rose nearly 30% to $6.6 million. The company achieved an early sell-out of its 2005 almond, table grape and mango projects.

Outlook

Timbercorp's shares have been stellar performers in recent years as the company continues to expand. In July 2005, it announced that its September 2005 full-year after-tax profit would surge 46% from the previous year to around $60 million. It expected revenues to be up by around 48%, to more than $246 million. This would include annuity-style revenues of more than $120 million (up from $88 million in September 2004), and forecast to rise to more than $150 million in September 2006. It continues to expand. With Select Harvests it plans a major new almond orchard project in Victoria's Sunraysia region. It also plans a big expansion of its olive orchard. It aims to become Australia's largest citrus grower, with 2000 hectares of plantings under management by 2008, up from 355 hectares in 2005. In September 2005, it announced plans to move into avocado production during 2006.

TIM Year to 30 September	2003	2004
Revenues ($mn)	124.8	190.1
EBIT ($mn)	48.6	68.3
EBIT margin (%)	38.9	35.9
Profit before tax ($mn)	44.1	63.6
Profit after tax ($mn)	27.1	41.1
Earnings per share (¢)	12.9	19.0
Cash flow per share (¢)	15.6	22.5
Dividend (¢)	3.5	5.5
Percentage franked	100	100
Interest cover (times)	11.0	14.6
Return on equity (%)	12.9	14.3
Half year to 31 March	**2004**	**2005**
Revenues ($mn)	52.8	82.3
Profit before tax ($mn)	8.8	12.8
Profit after tax ($mn)	5.6	7.6
Earnings per share (¢)	1.7	1.3
Dividend (¢)	0	0
Percentage franked	~	~
Net tangible assets per share ($)	1.03	1.04
Debt-to-equity ratio (%)	53.1	49.9
Current ratio	1.2	1.2

Toll Holdings Ltd

Share price ($)	13.73	
12-month high ($)	14.13	
12-month low ($)	10.38	
Market capitalisation ($mn)	4507.0	
Price-to-NTA-per-share ratio	3.9	
5-year share price return (% pa)	41.3	
Sector: Industrials	**Company**	**Sector**
Price-earnings ratio (times)	20.6	16.2
Dividend yield (%)	1.9	3.6

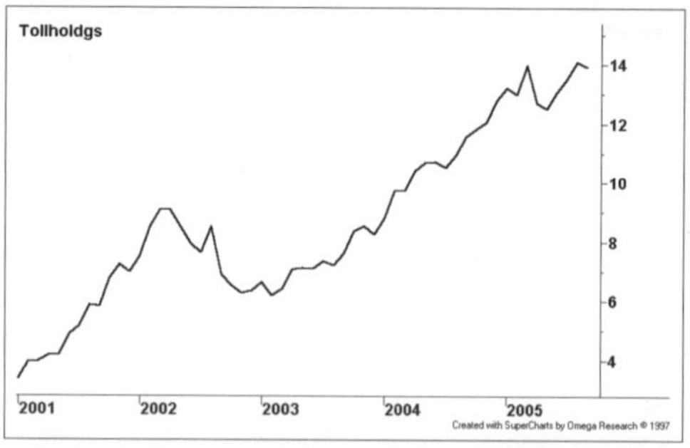

www.toll.com.au

Melbourne-based Toll Holdings was founded in Newcastle in 1888. It is today a giant transportation, warehousing and freight logistics company. It has one million square metres of warehouse space, it manages the ports of Geelong and Hastings and it has moved into rail freight (the Pacific National joint venture with Patrick Corporation). It has also bought New Zealand's Tranz Rail. In August 2005, Toll announced a $4.6 billion hostile takeover bid for Patrick Corporation.

Latest business results (June 2005, full year)

The company's growth continued with another excellent result, powered by further acquisitions. Much of the gain came from the first full year of inclusion of Toll New Zealand, which reported revenues of $626 million and an EBIT contribution of $59.6 million. Excluding Toll NZ, company revenues were up 8%. Toll derives over 40% of its domestic income from the food, beverage and retail sectors and, thanks to the strength of the Australian economy, these businesses continued to deliver excellent returns. There was also strong demand for Toll's services from the automotive sector, which represents a further 10% of domestic revenues. The company's margins continued to improve as a result of significant investment in new depot and warehouse facilities, technology development and integration benefits from past acquisitions. However, there was a significant loss from the company's north Queensland rail-forwarding operation. Pacific National contributed after-tax equity earnings of $51.5 million for the year, up 23% from the previous year, with continuing strong demand for coal transportation.

TOL Year to 30 June	2004	2005
Revenues ($mn)	3271.9	3798.4
Networks (%)	38	36
Logistics (%)	33	31
Toll North (%)	16	17
Toll NZ (%)	13	16
EBIT ($mn)	235.2	281.7
EBIT margin (%)	7.2	7.4
Profit before tax ($mn)	212.1	257.9
Profit after tax ($mn)	168.6	216.6
Earnings per share (¢)	53.3	66.6
Cash flow per share (¢)	89.4	108.8
Dividend (¢)	20.5	26.5
Percentage franked	100	100
Net tangible assets per share ($)	2.97	3.56
Interest cover (times)	10.2	11.8
Return on equity (%)	20.0	18.6
Debt-to-equity ratio (%)	29.0	23.7
Current ratio	1.1	1.0

Outlook

Toll has become a transportation and logistics powerhouse, with rapidly growing businesses and a surging share price. It has already forecast another record profit for the June 2006 year. Its future is now tied to its takeover bid for Patrick Corporation. If successful, Toll would become an $8.6 billion transport and logistics company, with major interests in road, rail, warehousing, ports and aviation, and with only limited competition. Announcing the bid in mid-August, Toll said it had already built up a 4.3% stake in Patrick. It said it believed the acquisition, if successful, would create synergies of at least $50 million annually within two or three years. It said it would reduce Patrick's holding in the Virgin Blue airline operation from 62% to around 10%.

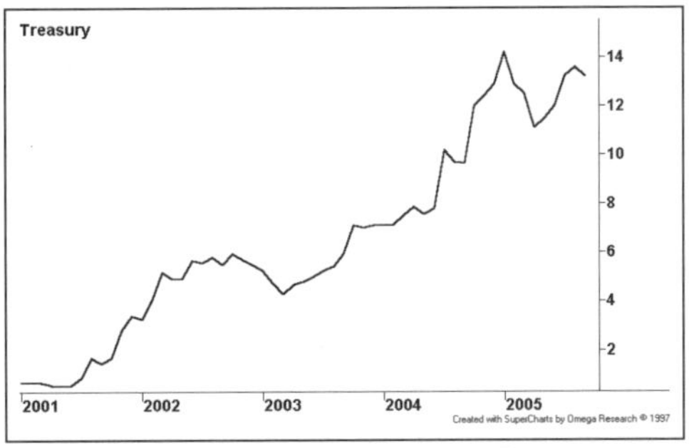

www.treasury-group.com

Treasury Group Ltd

Share price ($)	13.80
12-month high ($)	15.00
12-month low ($)	9.18
Market capitalisation ($mn)	291.1
Price-to-NTA-per-share ratio	10.1
5-year share price return (% pa)	92.5

Sector: Financials	Company	Sector
Price-earnings ratio (times)	23.0	14.3
Dividend yield (%)	2.9	4.5

Melbourne company Treasury Group provides specialist back-office services for boutique fund management companies. Not only does it take a fee for its services—based on the amount of funds under management—but it also takes an equity stake in the companies with which it works. It owns 67% of the equity of Global Value Investors, 50% of Investors Mutual and of Armytage Private, 36% of Orion Asset Management and 35% of Confluence Asset Management.

Latest business results (June 2005, full year)

The booming stock market and the strength of Treasury Group's stable of fund management companies combined to deliver further big increases in revenues and profits. There was a maiden contribution from Global Value Investors, which started operations as a fund manager in February 2005 and which focuses on broad international asset management. At the end of June 2005, funds under management by Treasury's stable of funds totalled $8.67 billion, which was up 68% from a year earlier.

Outlook

Treasury Group has enjoyed huge success since its launch and has become a stock market superstar, with a soaring share price. Thanks to the rapid growth in Australia of the boutique funds management business, the company has had many requests to provide backroom services, and it has been able to select only those fund managers it believes offer the best long-term growth potential. The main risk to its business is that it is heavily dependent on highly talented individuals, and if any of them chose to quit they might be difficult to replace. Much of the company's success has come about through its close ties with Investors Mutual, which was established by renowned fund manager Anton Tagliaferro, a former manager of the famous Perpetual Industrial Share Fund. In July 2005, Treasury Group established Treasury Asia Asset Management, a new boutique fund management business that will focus on Asian equities. Treasury Group has a 47% equity stake in the new company, with the remainder held by staff. During the June 2005 year, Treasury companies launched several new funds that the company believes will drive its next growth phase. They included the IML Diversified Value Fund, the GVI Industrial Share Fund, the TAAM Total Return Fund and the Armytage Special Opportunities Fund.

TRG Year to 30 June	2004	2005
Revenues ($mn)	29.9	44.0
EBIT ($mn)	18.5	31.9
EBIT margin (%)	62.0	72.4
Profit before tax ($mn)	19.3	33.2
Profit after tax ($mn)	6.3	12.5
Earnings per share (¢)	37.2	60.0
Cash flow per share (¢)	38.9	61.5
Dividend (¢)	28	40
Percentage franked	100	100
Net tangible assets per share ($)	0.90	1.37
Interest cover (times)	~	~
Return on equity (%)	45.5	51.1
Debt-to-equity ratio (%)	~	~
Current ratio	2.7	2.9

Troy Resources NL

Share price ($)	2.88
12-month high ($)	3.92
12-month low ($)	2.18
Market capitalisation ($mn)	139.7
Price-to-NTA-per-share ratio	3.5
5-year share price return (% pa)	38.4

Sector: Materials	Company	Sector
Price-earnings ratio (times)	18.2	17.0
Dividend yield (%)	2.3	2.2

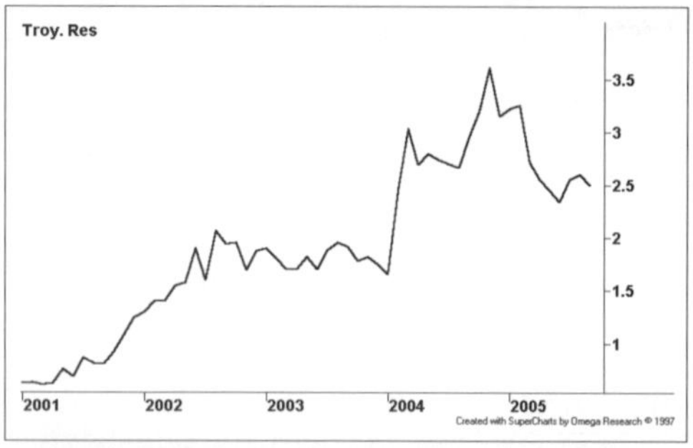

www.try.com.au

Perth-based Troy Resources, founded in 1984, is among the ten largest Australian-owned gold mining companies. It has two gold mining operations—at Sandstone in Western Australia and a 70% holding in the Sertão mine in the state of Goiás in central Brazil.

Latest business results (June 2005, full year)

Revenues and profits fell, as gold production dropped to 71 851 ounces, well down from 122 531 ounces in the previous financial year. This was due to the cessation of activities at the company's Cornishman mine in Western Australia, which had been operated in partnership with Sons of Gwalia. Output was also hit by the winding down of operations at the Bulchina mine at Sandstone. Second-half profitability was affected by start-up delays for the new Lord Nelson mine at Sandstone, due to objections against clearing permits. It was also affected by lower gold production from the Sertão mine, due to a lower average grade, though this was partially offset by higher ore throughput. Nevertheless, the operating cost for Sertão was just $129 per ounce, and it is believed to be one of the lowest cost gold mines in the world. During the year the company incurred exploration expenditure of $6.6 million, up from $4.2 million in the previous year.

Outlook

Troy has two new mines—named Lord Henry and Lord Nelson—in the Sandstone region. Mining began at Lord Henry in April 2005, and was due to commence at Lord Henry in October 2005. These two mines have combined proved and probable reserves of 201 000 ounces of gold, and the company is forecasting 2005–06 gold production of around 100 000 ounces. Also contributing will be the company's newly discovered orebody extension at the Sertão mine, with a probable reserve estimated at 54 200 ounces. Mining of this high-grade deposit began in May 2005. Thanks to the expectation of higher grades and higher production levels at both Sandstone and Sertão, Troy is forecasting a significant increase in profitability in the June 2006 year. Further exploration work continues in Brazil, with the company hopeful of significant new discoveries. In addition, Troy has exploration licences covering one million hectares in Mongolia, and is exploring for gold, coal and uranium.

TRY Year to 30 June	2004	2005
Revenues ($mn)	85.1	54.6
EBIT ($mn)	22.0	15.0
EBIT margin (%)	25.9	27.4
Gross margin (%)	38.5	50.0
Profit before tax ($mn)	22.8	16.5
Profit after tax ($mn)	14.1	8.7
Earnings per share (¢)	25.7	15.8
Cash flow per share (¢)	46.5	31.3
Dividend (¢)	6	6.5
Percentage franked	100	100
Net tangible assets per share ($)	0.69	0.82
Interest cover (times)	~	~
Return on equity (%)	43.8	21.0
Debt-to-equity ratio (%)	~	~
Current ratio	6.8	4.4

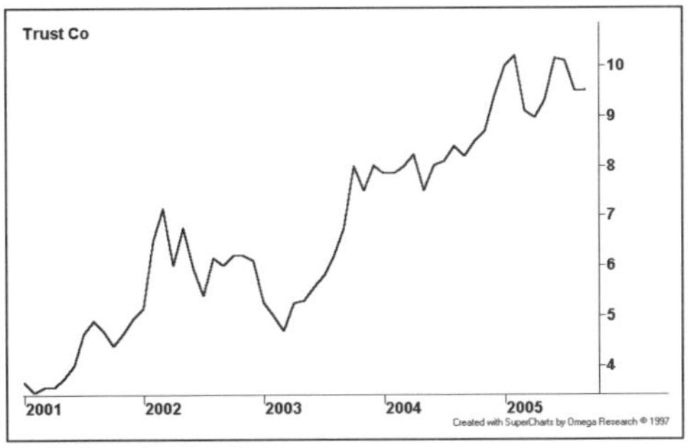

www.trust.com.au

Trust Company of Australia Ltd

Share price ($)	9.70	
12-month high ($)	10.60	
12-month low ($)	7.95	
Market capitalisation ($mn)	313.9	
Price-to-NTA-per-share ratio	4.1	
5-year share price return (% pa)	29.2	
Sector: Financials	**Company**	**Sector**
Price-earnings ratio (times)	22.7	14.3
Dividend yield (%)	3.9	4.5

Melbourne-based Trust Company of Australia was founded in 1885 and is one of Australia's oldest trustee companies. In 2002 it merged with Permanent Trustee Company, which had been established in 1887. Its services include funds management, estates and trusts, financial planning, property and infrastructure custody, superannuation, charitable services, securitisation and structured finance. It has offices in Sydney, Melbourne, Brisbane and Townsville.

Latest business results (February 2005, full year)

The company achieved a sound result, thanks to the strength of the local sharemarket, good cost control efforts and increased revenues from private clients, corporate services and funds management. However, superannuation division revenues fell, following the outsourcing of the company's masterplan product and its DIY super administration. The estates and trusts division also experienced a decline in revenues due to a drop in new estates and the poor performance of the company's Parramatta accounting business. Altogether, corporate services saw assets up 21% to $104 billion, with superannuation assets up 30% to $10.5 billion, and assets essentially flat for both funds management and estates and trusts, at around $1.1 billion for each. Private client funds under administration rose 4% to $750 million.

Outlook

In the wake of its merger with Permanent Trustee, Trust Company of Australia continues to restructure its operations. In particular, it is working to exit itself from businesses that it judges do not offer strategic advantages or operational efficiencies, in order to concentrate on those operations—notably trustee, fiduciary and investment management and advice areas—that it deems will provide the best potential for growth. Thus, it has sold its custody business in equity and fixed asset products to ANZ, and has disposed of its poorly performing Parramatta accounting business. In mid-2005, the company launched a joint venture in securitisation with the Bank of New York. It expects that this venture will enable it to continue to expand its highly profitable securitisation business, with more investment in additional services. In mid-2005, Trust Company of Australia was revealed as the buyer from Guiness Peat of a roughly 9% equity stake in Tasmanian Perpetual Trustees, giving rise to speculation that Trust Company might launch a takeover bid.

TRU Year to 28 February*	2004	2005
Revenues ($mn)	63.9	65.2
EBIT ($mn)	15.9	16.5
EBIT margin (%)	24.9	25.3
Profit before tax ($mn)	16.2	17.0
Profit after tax ($mn)	10.8	13.8
Earnings per share (¢)	33.3	42.7
Cash flow per share (¢)	49.9	59.8
Dividend (¢)	35	38
Percentage franked	100	100
Net tangible assets per share ($)	2.03	2.39
Interest cover (times)	~	~
Return on equity (%)	8.9	11.2
Debt-to-equity ratio (%)	~	~
Current ratio	2.8	3.0

* 29 February 2004

United Group Ltd

Share price ($)	10.35	
12-month high ($)	10.40	
12-month low ($)	5.46	
Market capitalisation ($mn)	1050.5	
Price-to-NTA-per-share ratio	6.0	
5-year share price return (% pa)	65.0	
Sector: Industrials	**Company**	**Sector**
Price-earnings ratio (times)	25.2	16.2
Dividend yield (%)	2.9	3.6

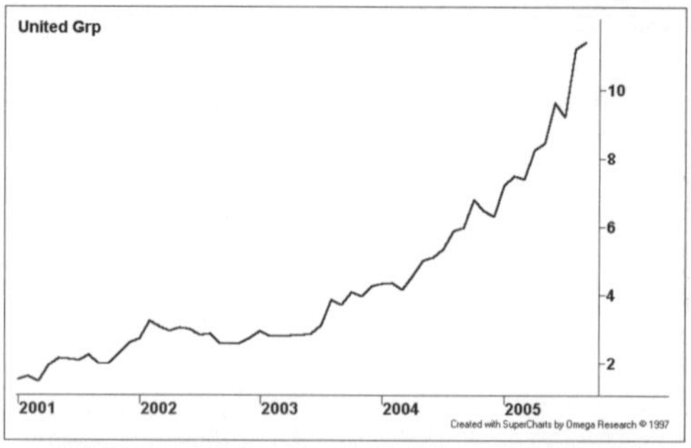

www.unitedgroup.com.au

Sydney-based United Group is one of Australia's leading engineering companies. It specialises in power supply, water and waste management, defence, resources engineering, telecommunications and heavy haulage railways. It groups its activities into four businesses: United Goninan is a leader in railway manufacturing, maintenance and engineering; United KG is engaged in engineering, construction, facilities management and industrial maintenance businesses; United KFPW provides corporate property services; and United Gooder is a New Zealand engineering and construction business.

Latest business results (June 2005, full year)

The company achieved its fourth successive year of profit expansion exceeding 30%, driven largely by organic growth. United Goninan enjoyed an excellent year, with sales up 33% and profits rising 38% thanks to strong increases from both the private and government sectors in rail infrastructure spending. United KFPW saw its turnover more than double, with profits up 69%, and a growing number of major contracts to service government buildings. Profits edged down for United KG, on a 15% sales decline, though this largely reflected the transfer of its facilities management business to United KFPW. However, margins remained low. In New Zealand, the United Gooder division continued its turnaround, with profits up 56% on a 35% sales increase. At the end of June 2005, the company's order book was nearly $4.3 billion, up from $2.3 billion a year earlier.

UGL Year to 30 June	2004	2005
Revenues ($mn)	1076.9	1254.9
Construction & fabrication (%)	47	45
Service & maintenance (%)	42	41
Facilities management (%)	4	8
Business process outsourcing (%)	7	6
EBIT ($mn)	43.9	60.5
EBIT margin (%)	4.1	4.8
Profit before tax ($mn)	38.5	52.9
Profit after tax ($mn)	29.1	43.0
Earnings per share (¢)	29.1	41.1
Cash flow per share (¢)	45.6	57.7
Dividend (¢)	18	30
Percentage franked	100	100
Net tangible assets per share ($)	0.93	1.73
Interest cover (times)	8.1	7.9
Return on equity (%)	17.4	16.9
Debt-to-equity ratio (%)	22.5	~
Current ratio	1.3	1.3

Outlook

United has become a leading beneficiary of a continuing trend of strong infrastructure spending and, with two new acquisitions in mid-2005, it anticipates further growth. The first of these is PREMAS International, Singapore's leading property services company, which was acquired for $45 million. PREMAS has operations in 16 Asian cities, including in China and India, and United now expects property services to become a fast-growing part of its operations. It has also acquired the local transport business of engineering giant ALSTOM, for $267 million, and sees this adding 10% to company EPS in the June 2006 year, with a greatly strengthened presence in the rolling stock supply and maintenance business in Australia and New Zealand. United's own long-term goal is earnings growth of 10% to 15% per year, though it expects to exceed this target in June 2006.

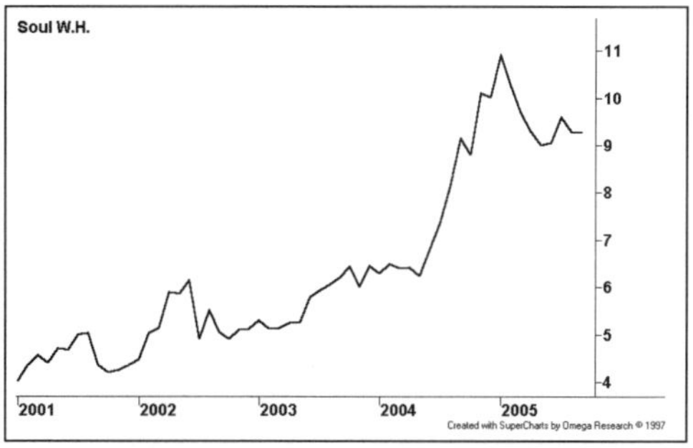

www.whsp.com.au

Washington H. Soul Pattinson & Company Ltd

Share price ($)	9.31	
12-month high ($)	11.40	
12-month low ($)	7.62	
Market capitalisation ($mn)	2200.8	
Price-to-NTA-per-share ratio	2.9	
5-year share price return (% pa)	24.9	
Sector: Financials	**Company**	**Sector**
Price-earnings ratio (times)	14.2	14.3
Dividend yield (%)	2.1	4.5

With its origins as a Sydney pharmacy store opened in 1872, and publicly listed for more than 100 years, Washington H. Soul Pattinson is today a diversified group operating in many businesses—New Hope Corporation (64% owned, and now publicly listed) has coal mining operations in Queensland and Indonesia; SP Telemedia (50% owned, also publicly listed) provides telecommunications services to the Hunter Valley region; and Keith Harris (50% owned, also publicly listed) manufactures juices and fragrances. In addition, the company retains ownership of nine Sydney pharmacies, and it owns 20% of the equity in Australian Pharmaceutical Industries and 29% of nutritional supplement maker Clover Corporation. In a cross-shareholding arrangement designed to forestall takeovers, it owns nearly 50% of the equity of Brickworks, which in turn owns 43% of Soul Pattinson.

Latest business results (January 2005, half year)

Profits fell. However, this was due to some large special profits in the January 2004 half, including a $35 million profit from the Brickworks sale of its investment portfolio and one-off earnings from Soul Pattinson's Indonesian coal business. Excluding these, the company's after-tax profit actually rose 28%. The main contributing factor was the New Hope coal operation, which benefited hugely from accelerating coal prices and demand. The company's investment portfolio also helped boost profits, with a 32.9% return for the half, compared to 18.6% for the benchmark S&P/ASX 300 Accumulation Index. At the end of January 2005 the portfolio was worth $2.6 billion.

Outlook

With the listing in September 2003 of its New Hope subsidiary, Soul Pattinson has largely transformed itself into an investment company. It has also sold, in mid-2004, its wholly owned NBN Television business to its subsidiary SP Telemedia. Much of its fortunes are now tied to its large stake in Brickworks, with a housing downturn clouding the outlook for this business. It will also be greatly influenced by trends in the coal market. It has established a new public company, Souls Private Equity Limited (in which it maintains a substantial shareholding), to house and develop its private equity investments.

SOL Year to 31 July	2003	2004
Revenues ($mn)	340.6	392.9
EBIT ($mn)	131.7	235.3
EBIT margin (%)	38.7	59.9
Gross margin (%)	37.3	33.5
Profit before tax ($mn)	128.8	234.2
Profit after tax ($mn)	88.3	155.9
Earnings per share (¢)	37.0	65.3
Cash flow per share (¢)	49.6	78.9
Dividend (¢)	17	20
Percentage franked	100	100
Interest cover (times)	44.9	217.3
Return on equity (%)	12.6	19.5
Half year to 31 January	**2004**	**2005**
Revenues ($mn)	175.5	238.8
Profit before tax ($mn)	151.2	107.6
Profit after tax ($mn)	98.0	68.9
Earnings per share (¢)	41.1	28.9
Dividend (¢)	8	10
Percentage franked	100	100
Net tangible assets per share ($)	3.03	3.16
Debt-to-equity ratio (%)	11.5	~
Current ratio	1.5	2.7

Wesfarmers Ltd

Share price ($)	40.30	
12-month high ($)	42.45	
12-month low ($)	27.89	
Market capitalisation ($mn)	14 970.5	
Price-to-NTA-per-share ratio	8.9	
5-year share price return (% pa)	31.8	
Sector: Industrials	**Company**	**Sector**
Price-earnings ratio (times)	24.6	16.2
Dividend yield (%)	4.5	3.6

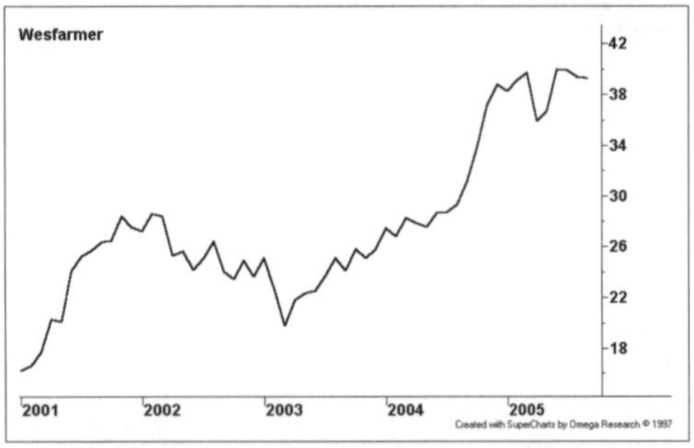

www.wesfarmers.com.au

Perth-based Wesfarmers, founded in 1914 as a farmers' cooperative, is a powerful force in rural business, but it has other major areas of operation as well. It manufactures fertilisers and agricultural chemicals, and it operates the Bunnings and Hardwarehouse chains of hardware stores. It has forestry interests, is a coal miner and a supplier of liquefied petroleum gas (LPG) and is a supplier of industrial safety products. It is also engaged in numerous businesses related to livestock, wool, real estate, insurance and finance. It owns 50% of the investment bank Gresham Partners Group and of the rail transportation company Australian Railroad Group.

Latest business results (June 2005, full year)

Sales and profits were up again. The star was the company's energy business, with profits surging 33% thanks to the company's booming coal operations. Energy was responsible for just 14% of total sales revenues but contributed 31% of EBIT. Hardware sales rose 6%, with profits up 9%, though the company noted a marked slowdown in growth in the second half. The best growth was in New Zealand and Western Australia, with difficult trading conditions in other regions. The company opened ten new warehouse stores. It closed four warehouse stores and five smaller format stores. The insurance business showed buoyant growth, with a boost from lower-than-expected levels of claims. Profits for the industrial and safety equipment division edged down, hurt by poor results in New Zealand and the loss of several domestic sales contracts. Chemicals and fertilisers sales were up 14%, with profits up 4%.

WES Year to 30 June	2004	2005
Revenues ($mn)	7451.5	8047.1
Hardware (%)	46	50
Energy (%)	12	14
Industrial & safety distribution (%)	14	14
Insurance (%)	10	14
Chemicals & fertilisers (%)	6	7
EBIT ($mn)	886.9	951.1
EBIT margin (%)	11.9	11.8
Gross margin (%)	30.3	34.1
Profit before tax ($mn)	832.4	880.3
Profit after tax ($mn)	569.2	618.3
Earnings per share (¢)	151.5	163.9
Cash flow per share (¢)	225.8	237.4
Dividend (¢)	140	180
Percentage franked	100	100
Net tangible assets per share ($)	4.94	4.51
Interest cover (times)	16.3	13.4
Return on equity (%)	16.1	19.3
Debt-to-equity ratio (%)	45.3	55.6
Current ratio	1.5	1.3

Outlook

Wesfarmers has been a very impressive stock market performer, with surging revenues, profits and share price over many years. Most recently it has been a prime beneficiary of the strong coal market, and the company itself forecasts a significant increase in profits in the June 2006 year, based on generally improved conditions for all operating divisions, and the impact of high export coal prices. For the longer term, the company has been actively seeking out growth opportunities, and has stated its desire to expand abroad, possibly through the acquisition of a major offshore energy asset. There has also been speculation that Wesfarmers might try to acquire fertiliser and chemicals company Orica.

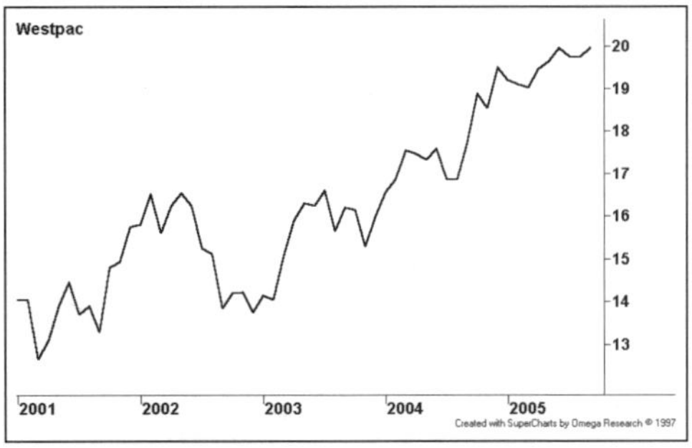

www.westpac.com.au

Westpac Banking Corporation

Share price ($)	19.97	
12-month high ($)	20.13	
12-month low ($)	16.08	
Market capitalisation ($mn)	37374.0	
Price-to-NTA-per-share ratio	2.8	
5-year share price return (% pa)	14.9	
Sector: Financials	**Company**	**Sector**
Price-earnings ratio (times)	14.5	14.3
Dividend yield (%)	4.3	4.5

Westpac, which began trading in 1817 as the Bank of New South Wales, is the smallest of Australia's big four banks, with interests in most areas of financial services. Around 15% of revenues and profit come from New Zealand, where Westpac Trust is one of that country's leading banks. It has moved strongly into wealth management, with the acquisition of BT Financial Group, Rothschild Australia Asset Management and Hastings Funds Management.

Latest business results (March 2005, half year)

Profits rose again, with solid cost control and a good performance by all business units. The core Australian business and consumer banking business saw profits up an excellent 17%, despite slower growth and increased competition. Business lending was up 10%. Institutional bank profits jumped 23%, with particularly strong results from financial markets trading, up 32%, and from client business revenues, up 12%. New Zealand retail banking and wealth management profits were up 8% in local currency. Total NZ lending grew 13%, despite intense competition in the mortgage market. BT Financial Group profits surged 33%, reflecting growing revenues from improved investment ratings and more favourable market conditions. Total funds under management grew 6% to $40 billion, and there was a 48% increase in funds under administration to $27 billion, supported by 43% growth in its wrap products.

Outlook

With its focus on Australia and New Zealand, Westpac continues to work at boosting efficiency across all areas of its operations. It is seeking to improve the productivity of its business and consumer banking salesforce, to better position itself for future growth. It is also launching new products, including the Max-I Direct cash management account which has attracted more than $3 billion in deposits since March 2004. It expects continuing excellent results from its BT wealth management business. In mid-2005 it moved from 51% to 100% ownership of Hastings Funds Management, which offers excellent growth potential through a range of specialised funds. However, the bank will be affected by any economic slowdown, as well as by intensifying competition in many of its business areas.

WBC Year to 30 September	2003	2004
Operating income ($mn)	7330.0	8010.0
Net interest income ($mn)	4344.0	4755.0
Operating expenses ($mn)	3926.0	3940.0
Profit before tax ($mn)	2919.0	3492.0
Profit after tax ($mn)	2183.0	2539.0
Earnings per share (¢)	119.7	137.5
Dividend (¢)	78	86
Percentage franked	100	100
Non-interest income to total income (%)	40.7	40.6
Cost-to-income ratio (%)	53.6	49.2
Return on equity (%)	17.9	17.6
Return on assets (%)	1.1	1.1
Half year to 31 March	**2004**	**2005**
Operating income ($mn)	3878.0	4204.0
Profit before tax ($mn)	1662.0	1884.0
Profit after tax ($mn)	1225.0	1325.0
Earnings per share (¢)	62.1	71.9
Dividend (¢)	42	49
Percentage franked	100	100
Net tangible assets per share ($)	6.43	7.18

Wide Bay Australia Ltd

Share price ($)	8.45	
12-month high ($)	8.70	
12-month low ($)	6.40	
Market capitalisation ($mn)	174.1	
Price-to-NTA-per-share ratio	2.1	
5-year share price return (% pa)	26.7	
Sector: Financials	**Company**	**Sector**
Price-earnings ratio (times)	13.9	14.3
Dividend yield (%)	5.0	4.5

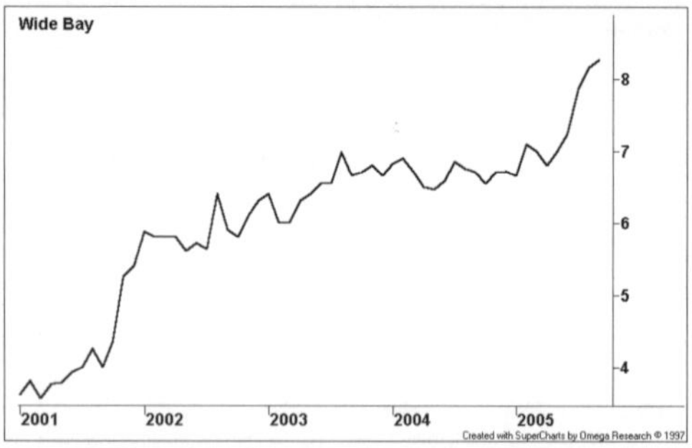

www.widebaycap.com.au

Based in Bundaberg in Queensland, Wide Bay Australia—formerly known as Wide Bay Capricorn Building Society—was founded in 1979 from the merger of two smaller building societies. It is a leading provider of financial services in south-east and central Queensland, with a network of over 30 branches and 80 000 customers, and is one of Queensland's largest non-bank deposit-taking institutions. A 44%-owned subsidiary, Fincom, is marketing automatic teller machine technology and software in Australia and abroad.

Latest business results (June 2005, full year)

In a slowing housing market, the company achieved another excellent result. Loan approvals for the year actually fell 7% to $448.5 million. However, the weaker housing market led to a slowing in the churning that had been experienced over the previous several years, and the total loan book grew 12% to $1.3 billion. Altogether, assets and funds under management were up 11.2% to $1.5 billion. The company's captive lenders mortgage insurance company, Mortgage Risk Management, made another strong contribution.

Outlook

Stringent cost control—the cost-to-income ratio fell significantly in the June 2005 period—and a steady expansion program are helping Wide Bay prosper in a slowing housing market. It opened its first interstate branch in Sydney's Parramatta in 2004, launched a Brisbane branch in August 2005 and planned its initial Victorian branch—in Melbourne's Camberwell—for late in 2005. Wide Bay management expect all these new sites to provide a substantial boost to business, although they concede that it will likely mean that the proportion of loan approvals originating from mortgage brokers will rise from 16.5% to around 25% of the total, placing pressure on margins. Further branches are possible in both NSW and Victoria, as well as on Queensland's Gold Coast. A new electronic loans processing system is expected to achieve significant economies through more efficient management of loan files and processes. It also provides cost savings by allowing a large percentage of loan mortgage documentation to be prepared inhouse. In August 2005, Wide Bay acquired a 25% equity stake in the financial planning firm Financial Technology Securities. It believes this acquisition will strengthen its presence in the financial planning industry and expand the range of services available to its customers.

WBB Year to 30 June	2004	2005
Operating income ($mn)	37.5	41.6
Net interest income ($mn)	26.9	28.9
Operating expenses ($mn)	23.5	24.1
Profit before tax ($mn)	14.0	17.6
Profit after tax ($mn)	9.9	12.4
Earnings per share (¢)	48.7	60.8
Dividend (¢)	34	42
Percentage franked	100	100
Non-interest income to total income (%)	28.1	30.5
Net tangible assets per share ($)	3.94	4.07
Cost-to-income ratio (%)	62.7	57.8
Return on equity (%)	12.3	15.2
Return on assets (%)	1.2	1.4

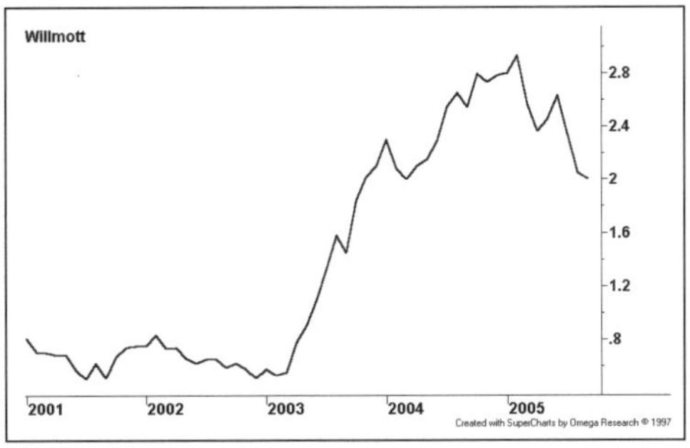

www.willmottforests.com.au

Willmott Forests Ltd

Share price ($)	2.25	
12-month high ($)	3.05	
12-month low ($)	2.11	
Market capitalisation ($mn)	113.6	
Price-to-NTA-per-share ratio	1.0	
4-year share price return (% pa)	45.5	
Sector: Materials	**Company**	**Sector**
Price-earnings ratio (times)	8.5	17.0
Dividend yield (%)	2.7	2.2

Willmott Forests, a fully integrated forestry company based in Melbourne, was established in 1979. It manages more than 24 000 hectares of softwood pine plantations, mainly in the Bombala and Murray Valley regions of south-eastern NSW. It also operates two downstream timber-processing facilities in Bombala, supplying structural, landscape and fencing timber products, with sales concentrated in NSW, ACT and Victoria. Since 1989 it has been offering a series of structured forestry products to investors.

Latest business results (June 2005, full year)

Booming interest in the company's managed investment products delivered Willmott an excellent result. Its Management Investment Scheme income jumped 62% to $49.9 million, with pre-tax profit up 49% to $19.5 million. Timber processing sales rose 43% to $20.6 million. However, this business remained in the red, with the pre-tax loss widening slightly from $0.97 million to $0.98 million. The company reported that weakness in the housing sector, particularly in the key NSW market, led to slower sales than expected and a softening of margins.

Outlook

Willmott Forests occupies a relatively small but secure position in the booming forestry business, and the long-term outlook is excellent. This has been reflected in the share price which has enjoyed a sustained rally, after a period of weakness following its 2000 listing, on concerns that the tax authorities might clamp down on managed forestry schemes. The company is working to develop a stream of further managed investment products. Willmott has a strong presence in the Bombala region, with forest plantations, processing plants and a wharf, and it believes it could boost its holdings to 60 000 hectares. The NSW Government owns 32 000 hectares of plantations in Bombala—processed by Willmott under a ten-year agreement—and there has been speculation that the government might divest itself of this business, with Willmott a strong contender as potential purchaser. The company has been boosting capital spending to overcome problems at its processing mills and has reported that, thanks to equipment upgrades and sound management, production has improved. It is working to expand the market for its products, particularly with moves into Victoria. Nevertheless, it is heavily exposed to the NSW housing market, where the downturn has hit hardest, and this could have a negative impact on its business.

WFL Year to 30 June	2004	2005
Revenues ($mn)	45.3	70.5
Managed investments (%)	68	71
Timber processing (%)	32	29
EBIT ($mn)	6.7	12.5
EBIT margin (%)	14.9	17.7
Profit before tax ($mn)	12.1	18.5
Profit after tax ($mn)	8.4	13.1
Earnings per share (¢)	19.9	26.5
Cash flow per share (¢)	23.3	29.9
Dividend (¢)	4	6
Percentage franked	100	100
Net tangible assets per share ($)	1.27	2.22
Interest cover (times)	~	~
Return on equity (%)	15.1	14.8
Debt-to-equity ratio (%)	30.0	22.7
Current ratio	0.6	1.2

Woodside Petroleum Ltd

Share price ($)	33.38	
12-month high ($)	33.95	
12-month low ($)	17.70	
Market capitalisation ($mn)	21 066.7	
Price-to-NTA-per-share ratio	6.8	
5-year share price return (% pa)	22.3	
Sector: Energy	**Company**	**Sector**
Price-earnings ratio (times)	34.2	17.7
Dividend yield (%)	1.8	1.9

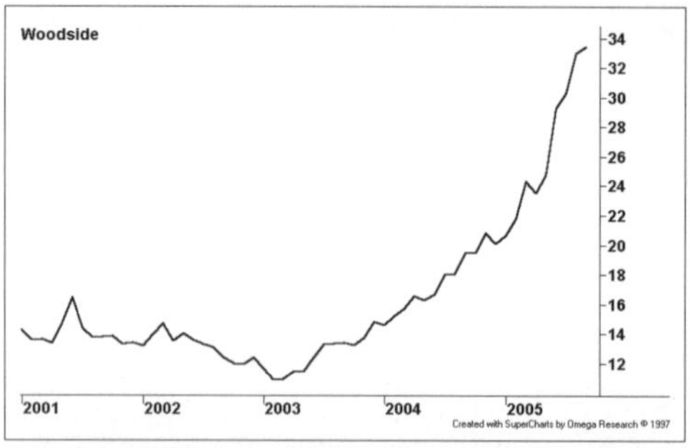

www.woodside.com.au

Perth-based Woodside, founded in 1954, is Australia's largest listed specialist energy company. Its major interest is the North West Shelf project off Western Australia, which supplies liquefied natural gas (LNG) for Asia, natural gas for the domestic market and liquefied petroleum gas, crude oil and condensate for international markets. It also has major exploration and development interests in Western Australia. It is operator of oil and gas discoveries in offshore Mauritania, is a partner in gas and condensate production in Algeria and has exploration interests in the US, Libya, Kenya, Liberia and the Canary Islands. Shell Australia owns 34% of Woodside's equity.

Latest business results (June 2005, half year)

Surging oil prices and strong demand delivered Woodside a powerful gain in its mid-year profit. The result was also helped by the new international accounting standards under which the company was forced to include as profit a $63.7 million after-tax unrealised gain on derivatives that are embedded in some of its contracts. Higher demand meant that sales volumes were up 7.5%. The average oil price of US$49.27 per barrel of oil-equivalent (BOE) was a 40.6% jump from the previous corresponding period, partially offset by a higher Australian dollar. The company expects to produce at least 58 million BOE in 2005, up from 56 million BOE in 2004.

WPL Year to 31 December	2003	2004
Revenues ($mn)	2059.3	2158.6
EBIT ($mn)	854.2	993.5
EBIT margin (%)	41.5	46.0
Gross margin (%)	61.2	60.2
Profit before tax ($mn)	827.9	972.1
Profit after tax ($mn)	526.7	650.9
Earnings per share (¢)	79.0	97.6
Cash flow per share (¢)	112.5	137.2
Dividend (¢)	46	59
Percentage franked	100	100
Interest cover (times)	32.5	46.5
Return on equity (%)	22.2	23.2
Half year to 30 June	**2004**	**2005**
Revenues ($mn)	994.4	1,231.9
Profit before tax ($mn)	541.2	740.3
Profit after tax ($mn)	351.0	512.2
Earnings per share (¢)	52.6	76.8
Dividend (¢)	27	35
Percentage franked	100	100
Net tangible assets per share ($)	4.49	4.94
Debt-to-equity ratio (%)	13.3	14.0
Current ratio	2.3	1.9

Outlook

Woodside has a 20-year supply agreement (which started in 1989) with eight Japanese electric power and gas companies to supply 7.5 million tonnes annually of LNG, and this underpins profits. Its business will receive a boost from a $25 billion contract to supply China's Guangdong Province with three million tonnes of North West Shelf LNG annually for 25 years from 2006, and a $2 billion expansion of its LNG facilities will be completed in 2008. The company has greatly accelerated its global oil exploration activities, with the aim of lifting total output to 80 million BOE in 2007 and 140 million in 2010. It sees particular potential in Africa and the Gulf of Mexico, and is believed to be investigating the possibility of involvement in exploration ventures in Iraq.

Part II: the tables

Tables index

A Market capitalisation

B Revenues

C Year-on-year revenues growth

D EBIT margin

E Year-on-year EBIT margin growth

F After-tax profit

G Year-on-year EPS growth

H Return on equity

I Year-on-year return on equity growth

J Debt-to-equity ratio

K Current ratio

L Price-earnings ratio

M Price to NTA-per-share ratio

N Dividend yield

O Year-on-year dividend growth

P Five-year share price return

Q Non-interest income to total income

R Cost-to-income ratio

S Return on assets

TABLE A

Market capitalisation

A company's market capitalisation is determined by multiplying the share price by the number of shares. To be included in this book a company must be in the All Ordinaries Index which comprises the 500 largest companies by market capitalisation.

	$mn
BHP Billiton	72750.7
National Australia Bank	49241.3
Commonwealth Bank	47728.8
ANZ Banking	40369.2
Westpac Banking	37374.0
Rio Tinto	23470.2
Woodside Petroleum	21066.7
Wesfarmers	14970.5
Macquarie Bank	14403.4
St George Bank	13884.5
Rinker Group	13552.9
QBE Insurance	13374.0
Coles Myer	11753.0
Suncorp-Metway	11364.7
Publishing & Broadcasting	10462.9
AXA Asia Pacific	7979.1
Australian Gas Light	6511.0
CSL	6465.6
Santos	6313.4
Origin Energy	5883.4
Toll Holdings	4507.0
Boral	4074.4
Fairfax (John) Holdings	4030.7
Patrick Corporation	3918.9
Computershare	3902.5
Leighton Holdings	3763.1
Foodland	3174.3
Billabong International	2874.6
Harvey Norman	2845.4
Australian Stock Exchange	2681.3
Perpetual Trustees Australia	2664.6
CSR	2394.3
Washington H. Soul Pattinson	2200.8
Cochlear	2155.3
Metcash	1757.6
Downer EDI	1723.9
Sims Group	1506.6
Australand Property	1492.6
Brickworks	1490.1
Bendigo Bank	1432.7
Rural Press	1355.2
Flight Centre	1344.3
Sigma	1335.8
Reece Australia	1284.8
Adelaide Bank	1279.6
Primary Health Care	1222.0
Gunns	1214.0
Bank of Queensland	1169.4
Corporate Express	1128.0
Coates Hire	1113.0
Adelaide Brighton	1076.2
United Group	1050.5
David Jones	957.0
Incitec Pivot	923.2
GWA International	879.4
Great Southern Plantations	874.6
Hills Industries	791.3
Portman	695.7
FKP Property	664.0
Alesco	577.2
Cabcharge Australia	564.5
Amalgamated Holdings	551.6
STW Communications	546.5
Timbercorp	531.0
GUD Holdings	496.7
IRESS Market Technology	479.3
McGuigan Simeon Wines	452.3
Colorado Group	435.5
Commander Communications	434.2
OAMPS	412.3
Select Harvests	412.2
Campbell Brothers	410.1
Count Financial	340.9
Pacifica Group	320.2
Monadelphous	317.2
Trust Company of Australia	313.9
Fantastic Holdings	310.5
Fleetwood	302.7
Treasury Group	291.1
AV Jennings Homes	287.3
Funtastic	280.8
K & S	224.3
Programmed Maintenance Services	221.6
Blackmores	221.5
Coffey International	203.8
Housewares International	199.7
ARB	194.4
Infomedia	187.1
CVC	184.8
Gazal	184.8
Technology One	183.0
Central Equity	180.3
Wide Bay Australia	174.1
Oakton	173.3
Rebel Sport	163.5
Collection House	163.3
MaxiTRANS Industries	142.5
Troy Resources	139.7
Tasmanian Perpetual Trustees	138.8
Integrated Group	130.4
Candle Australia	113.9
Willmott Forests	113.6
Pro Medicus	108.5
OrotonGroup	97.9
Angus & Coote	90.1
HGL	87.7
Rock Building Society	82.3
Institute of Drug Technology	76.3
Cellnet Group	68.9
CMI	54.2
Magna Pacific	52.3
Adcorp Australia	45.6

Table B

Revenues

This list ranks the companies in the book according to their most recent full-year revenues figures (operating income for the banks). The figures include revenues from sales and services but other revenues — such as interest receipts and investment income — are not generally included.

	$mn
BHP Billiton	39270.2
Coles Myer	32266.8
Rio Tinto	19248.0
National Australia Bank	13034.0
Commonwealth Bank	11354.0
ANZ Banking	8500.0
Wesfarmers	8047.1
Westpac Banking	8010.0
Metcash	6993.7
QBE Insurance	6781.0
Leighton Holdings	6257.8
Foodland	6026.5
Rinker Group	5843.0
Suncorp-Metway	5317.0
AXA Asia Pacific	4945.0
Origin Energy	4860.6
Boral	4296.7
Australian Gas Light	4058.0
Toll Holdings	3798.4
Macquarie Bank	3749.0
Downer EDI	3724.9
Publishing & Broadcasting	3320.6
CSL	2749.9
St George Bank	2587.0
Sims Group	2565.0
CSR	2367.5
Woodside Petroleum	2158.6
Sigma	2095.8
Harvey Norman	1933.8
Fairfax (John) Holdings	1855.1
David Jones	1769.5
Santos	1500.9
United Group	1254.9
Patrick Corporation	1250.4
Australand Property	1172.6
Incitec Pivot	1107.1
Computershare	1063.5
Reece Australia	1009.6
Corporate Express	982.6
Pacifica Group	872.1
Flight Centre	870.3
Billabong International	843.6
Hills Industries	810.2
Cabcharge Australia	766.5
Adelaide Brighton	696.4
Gunns	668.5
Alesco	632.6
GWA International	626.9
Commander Communications	599.9
Cellnet Group	585.9
Amalgamated Holdings	580.2
Rural Press	564.6
Coates Hire	527.6
Brickworks	485.7
Colorado Group	466.5
Bendigo Bank	452.1
Housewares International	441.0
AV Jennings Homes	436.7
Campbell Brothers	435.6
Integrated Group	395.4
GUD Holdings	394.4
Washington H. Soul Pattinson	392.9
Monadelphous	390.6
McGuigan Simeon Wines	368.1
Perpetual Trustees Australia	342.1
K & S	340.8
Cochlear	318.1
Rebel Sport	316.9
Funtastic	311.3
Great Southern Plantations	309.5
FKP Property	299.7
Bank of Queensland	291.9
Adelaide Bank	282.5
CMI	280.7
OAMPS	280.5
Australian Stock Exchange	279.7
Fleetwood	255.1
Angus & Coote	239.0
Candle Australia	231.8
MaxiTRANS Industries	223.2
Fantastic Holdings	221.0
Programmed Maintenance Services	217.8
Gazal	212.6
Portman	195.4
Primary Health Care	190.6
Timbercorp	190.1
Select Harvests	178.0
Central Equity	171.0
Coffey International	168.5
OrotonGroup	143.6
Blackmores	134.4
Collection House	125.1
HGL	123.1
ARB	114.7
Count Financial	83.5
Willmott Forests	70.5
Trust Company of Australia	65.2
CVC	61.8
IRESS Market Technology	61.1
Infomedia	59.1
Troy Resources	54.6
Technology One	54.4
Oakton	54.0
Treasury Group	44.0
STW Communications	43.2
Wide Bay Australia	41.6
Magna Pacific	36.7
Adcorp Australia	33.8
Institute of Drug Technology	26.5
Rock Building Society	25.1
Tasmanian Perpetual Trustees	17.8
Pro Medicus	10.3

Table C

Year-on-year revenues growth

Companies generally strive for growth though profit growth is usually of far more significance than a boost in revenues. In fact it is possible for a company to increase its revenues by all kinds of means — including cutting profit margins or acquiring other companies — and YOY revenues growth is of little relevance if other ratios are not also improving.

	%
Brickworks	170.5
Monadelphous	76.9
CSL	66.6
Incitec Pivot	61.3
Willmott Forests	55.7
Timbercorp	52.3
Macquarie Bank	52.1
Great Southern Plantations	51.6
Treasury Group	47.3
MaxiTRANS Industries	40.4
Select Harvests	39.8
Funtastic	39.3
Origin Energy	38.0
Sims Group	36.9
Bank of Queensland	36.2
Portman	34.5
STW Communications	34.4
Amalgamated Holdings	31.8
Alesco	31.4
Cellnet Group	31.2
Pro Medicus	30.1
CVC	29.7
Leighton Holdings	29.4
Candle Australia	29.3
Coffey International	28.6
Primary Health Care	26.7
Cochlear	26.0
OAMPS	25.9
Commander Communications	25.2
Billabong International	24.5
BHP Billiton	23.2
Computershare	22.1
OrotonGroup	21.4
ANZ Banking	21.2
Oakton	21.2
Count Financial	21.0
Fantastic Holdings	20.8
McGuigan Simeon Wines	20.4
Adelaide Bank	20.2
CSR	20.1
Downer EDI	19.7
Coles Myer	19.4
Integrated Group	19.4
United Group	16.5
Blackmores	16.2
Toll Holdings	16.1
Australian Stock Exchange	15.9
Perpetual Trustees Australia	15.9
Reece Australia	15.8
Suncorp-Metway	15.7
Coates Hire	15.5
Publishing & Broadcasting	15.5
Washington H. Soul Pattinson	15.3
K & S	15.2
Bendigo Bank	14.7
Tasmanian Perpetual Trustees	14.5
Programmed Maintenance Services	14.2
ARB	14.0
FKP Property	13.6
IRESS Market Technology	13.6
Patrick Corporation	13.6
Hills Industries	13.5
Cabcharge Australia	12.5
Flight Centre	12.4
QBE Insurance	12.3
Campbell Brothers	11.6
Wide Bay Australia	11.1
Rural Press	10.8
Adelaide Brighton	10.4
Fleetwood	10.4
Harvey Norman	10.4
Gazal	10.2
Sigma	9.8
Angus & Coote	9.7
Corporate Express	9.6
St George Bank	9.6
Rinker Group	9.4
Westpac Banking	9.3
Commonwealth Bank	8.2
Wesfarmers	8.0
Technology One	7.8
Collection House	7.4
Rio Tinto	6.1
HGL	5.9
Colorado Group	5.8
Institute of Drug Technology	5.2
Fairfax (John) Holdings	5.1
Woodside Petroleum	4.8
CMI	4.1
AXA Asia Pacific	3.9
Rebel Sport	3.8
Boral	3.5
David Jones	3.4
Gunns	2.9
Santos	2.5
Trust Company of Australia	2.0
National Australia Bank	1.3
Adcorp Australia	0.6
GUD Holdings	0.2
Rock Building Society	–1.3
Australian Gas Light	–2.3
Metcash	–2.5
Housewares International	–3.6
Foodland	–5.6
Pacifica Group	–5.6
GWA International	–6.1
Magna Pacific	–6.8
Infomedia	–15.0
Australand Property	–16.6
AV Jennings Homes	–20.6
Troy Resources	–35.8
Central Equity	–39.3

Table D

EBIT margin

A company's earnings before interest and taxation (EBIT) is sometimes regarded as a better measure of its profitability than the straight pre-tax or post-tax profit figure. EBIT is derived by adding net interest payments (that is interest payments minus interest receipts) to the pre-tax profit. Different companies choose different methods of financing their operations; by adding back interest payments to their profits we can help minimise these differences and make comparisons between companies more valid.

The EBIT margin is the EBIT figure as a percentage of annual sales. Clearly a high figure is to be desired though of course this can be achieved artificially by inflating borrowings (and hence interest payments). And it is noteworthy that efficient companies like some of the giant retailers can operate most satisfactorily on low margins.

The EBIT margin figure has little relevance for banks—whose high interest payments to their customers mean they have virtually no EBIT—and they have been excluded as have the insurance companies.

	%
Treasury Group	72.4
Pro Medicus	69.7
STW Communications	61.3
Washington H. Soul Pattinson	59.9
Great Southern Plantations	56.5
Australian Stock Exchange	51.5
Woodside Petroleum	46.0
Perpetual Trustees Australia	44.9
CVC	44.6
Tasmanian Perpetual Trustees	39.7
IRESS Market Technology	38.8
Santos	38.0
Timbercorp	35.9
Infomedia	35.2
BHP Billiton	30.0
Rural Press	28.7
Magna Pacific	28.1
Troy Resources	27.4
FKP Property	26.1
Brickworks	26.0
Primary Health Care	25.9
Gunns	25.7
Trust Company of Australia	25.3
Technology One	24.2
Rio Tinto	24.0
Institute of Drug Technology	23.7
Cochlear	23.6
Publishing & Broadcasting	23.3
Fairfax (John) Holdings	23.0
Oakton	22.7
Portman	22.7
Billabong International	22.3
Count Financial	20.3
Patrick Corporation	20.2
Coates Hire	19.7
Select Harvests	18.7
Adcorp Australia	18.2
Australand Property	18.2
Willmott Forests	17.7
Collection House	16.8
Australian Gas Light	16.5
GWA International	16.4
Rinker Group	16.4
ARB	16.1
Harvey Norman	15.8
Adelaide Brighton	15.4
HGL	14.9
GUD Holdings	14.7
McGuigan Simeon Wines	14.7
Fleetwood	14.5
Central Equity	14.4
CSL	14.1
Boral	13.7
Programmed Maintenance Services	13.7
CSR	13.6
OAMPS	13.6
Colorado Group	13.4
Blackmores	12.9
Computershare	12.9
Origin Energy	12.7
Amalgamated Holdings	12.4
Wesfarmers	11.8
Fantastic Holdings	11.5
Flight Centre	11.2
Sims Group	10.9
Reece Australia	10.6
Pacifica Group	10.3
Incitec Pivot	10.2
OrotonGroup	9.5
Coffey International	9.1
K & S	9.1
AV Jennings Homes	9.0
Campbell Brothers	8.9
Gazal	8.9
Corporate Express	8.7
Alesco	8.5
Funtastic	8.1
Hills Industries	7.9
MaxiTRANS Industries	7.8
Toll Holdings	7.4
CMI	7.3
Rebel Sport	7.1
Housewares International	6.9
Monadelphous	6.1
Angus & Coote	5.4
David Jones	5.4
Commander Communications	5.2
Sigma	5.0
Leighton Holdings	4.8
United Group	4.8
Cabcharge Australia	4.7
Candle Australia	4.6
Downer EDI	4.6
Integrated Group	4.4
Foodland	4.3
Coles Myer	2.8
Metcash	2.4
Cellnet Group	2.0

Table E

Year-on-year EBIT margin growth

The EBIT (earnings before interest and taxation) margin is one of the measures of a company's efficiency. So a rising margin is much to be desired as it suggests that a company is achieving success in cutting its costs. This table does not include banks or insurance companies.

	%		%		%
Commander Communications	137.9	Monadelphous	13.0	Australian Gas Light	–2.8
CVC	127.7	Angus & Coote	12.6	Computershare	–3.4
Australand Property	63.3	Coffey International	11.0	Hills Industries	–3.7
Washington H. Soul Pattinson	54.9	Woodside Petroleum	10.9	IRESS Market Technology	–3.8
Portman	53.2	Fairfax (John) Holdings	10.1	Fantastic Holdings	–4.0
Leighton Holdings	42.3	GWA International	9.8	Gunns	–4.2
David Jones	41.3	Coles Myer	9.3	MaxiTRANS Industries	–5.1
Colorado Group	38.4	Patrick Corporation	7.8	Boral	–5.3
Origin Energy	35.4	Foodland	7.6	OAMPS	–6.1
K & S	34.3	Collection House	7.5	BHP Billiton	–6.2
Rio Tinto	34.2	Fleetwood	7.5	Harvey Norman	–6.3
Cochlear	31.1	Perpetual Trustees Australia	7.2	ARB	–6.6
Rinker Group	22.6	Rural Press	6.4	Gazal	–6.8
Magna Pacific	22.1	Blackmores	6.2	GUD Holdings	–7.5
Alesco	21.9	Troy Resources	5.7	Timbercorp	–7.7
Pro Medicus	21.5	Cabcharge Australia	5.3	Publishing & Broadcasting	–7.9
Sims Group	21.5	Reece Australia	5.3	OrotonGroup	–11.2
Santos	20.4	Metcash	3.8	Rebel Sport	–11.8
Primary Health Care	20.3	Tasmanian Perpetual Trustees	3.4	Great Southern Plantations	–12.0
Willmott Forests	19.3	Toll Holdings	3.2	CSL	–13.7
Candle Australia	18.7	Downer EDI	2.8	Adcorp Australia	–15.0
United Group	18.3	CSR	2.0	Integrated Group	–17.0
Incitec Pivot	17.7	Oakton	1.9	Infomedia	–17.2
Treasury Group	16.8	Trust Company of Australia	1.7	Funtastic	–18.9
FKP Property	16.5	CMI	0.5	Housewares International	–19.1
Campbell Brothers	15.7	Technology One	0.2	Amalgamated Holdings	–24.1
Count Financial	15.3	Adelaide Brighton	–0.2	STW Communications	–24.2
Coates Hire	14.6	Select Harvests	–0.2	Flight Centre	–26.2
Sigma	14.2	Institute of Drug Technology	–0.6	McGuigan Simeon Wines	–27.0
Australian Stock Exchange	13.7	Wesfarmers	–0.7	Cellnet Group	–39.8
Billabong International	13.6	Central Equity	–1.3	Brickworks	–40.7
Corporate Express	13.6	Programmed Maintenance Services	–1.5	AV Jennings Homes	–49.5
HGL	13.5	Pacifica Group	–1.6		

TABLE F

After-tax profit

This table ranks all the companies according to their most recent full-year after-tax profit.

	$mn
BHP Billiton	7958.9
Commonwealth Bank	3991.0
National Australia Bank	3935.0
Rio Tinto	3069.0
ANZ Banking	2815.0
Westpac Banking	2539.0
Macquarie Bank	823.0
Suncorp-Metway	821.0
QBE Insurance	820.0
St George Bank	767.0
Woodside Petroleum	650.9
Wesfarmers	618.3
Coles Myer	616.5
Rinker Group	585.2
AXA Asia Pacific	540.0
Publishing & Broadcasting	514.6
Australian Gas Light	386.8
Santos	379.9
Boral	376.8
CSL	296.9
Origin Energy	266.0
Fairfax (John) Holdings	252.6
Toll Holdings	216.6
Leighton Holdings	205.4
CSR	200.8
Patrick Corporation	188.4
Sims Group	187.9
Harvey Norman	171.4
Washington H. Soul Pattinson	155.9
Australand Property	145.1
Foodland	142.7
Billabong International	125.4
Great Southern Plantations	124.3
Rural Press	112.9
Perpetual Trustees Australia	111.6
Australian Stock Exchange	108.5
Metcash	104.9
Downer EDI	104.0
Gunns	101.3
Computershare	92.3
Bendigo Bank	87.4
Adelaide Brighton	81.5
Adelaide Bank	80.4
Brickworks	76.0
Reece Australia	75.3
Incitec Pivot	75.0
Flight Centre	67.9
David Jones	65.3
Bank of Queensland	64.5
Coates Hire	63.5
GWA International	63.2
Sigma	59.6
Corporate Express	58.2
FKP Property	54.9
Cochlear	54.5
Amalgamated Holdings	46.2
Pacifica Group	45.0
Colorado Group	44.2
United Group	43.0
Timbercorp	41.1
GUD Holdings	37.8
Hills Industries	36.2
McGuigan Simeon Wines	35.9
Portman	32.8
OAMPS	29.2
CVC	29.0
Primary Health Care	27.9
Alesco	27.6
AV Jennings Homes	27.5
Cabcharge Australia	27.2
Fleetwood	25.1
Central Equity	24.1
Commander Communications	23.6
STW Communications	23.2
Campbell Brothers	21.9
Select Harvests	21.7
K & S	19.9
Housewares International	18.1
Programmed Maintenance Services	18.1
Fantastic Holdings	17.7
Funtastic	16.9
Monadelphous	16.7
IRESS Market Technology	16.3
Rebel Sport	16.3
Infomedia	14.5
Trust Company of Australia	13.8
Willmott Forests	13.1
ARB	12.6
Gazal	12.5
Treasury Group	12.5
Wide Bay Australia	12.4
Count Financial	12.3
Collection House	12.2
Blackmores	11.7
CMI	11.5
MaxiTRANS Industries	11.3
HGL	10.5
Technology One	10.3
Coffey International	10.2
Integrated Group	9.9
Troy Resources	8.7
OrotonGroup	8.4
Oakton	8.3
Angus & Coote	8.1
Magna Pacific	7.3
Candle Australia	7.2
Cellnet Group	6.1
Pro Medicus	5.5
Tasmanian Perpetual Trustees	5.1
Rock Building Society	4.6
Institute of Drug Technology	4.5
Adcorp Australia	4.3

Table G

Year-on-year EPS growth

The earnings-per-share (EPS) figure is a crucial one. It tells you — the shareholder — what your part is of the company's profits for each of your shares. So investors invariably look for EPS growth in a stock. The YOY EPS growth figure is often one of the first ratios that investors look to when evaluating a stock.

	%				
CVC	169.4	CSR	28.1	Amalgamated Holdings	7.0
Commander Communications	123.5	Corporate Express	26.7	Australian Gas Light	6.5
Portman	93.4	Toll Holdings	25.1	Great Southern Plantations	6.5
Monadelphous	90.1	Wide Bay Australia	24.9	Publishing & Broadcasting	5.8
CSL	86.6	Blackmores	24.3	Brickworks	4.6
Leighton Holdings	85.3	Woodside Petroleum	23.6	Hills Industries	4.4
Washington H. Soul Pattinson	76.6	Downer EDI	22.6	Australand Property	4.2
BHP Billiton	72.6	Reece Australia	22.4	Institute of Drug Technology	4.0
David Jones	72.5	Patrick Corporation	21.9	ANZ Banking	2.3
Sims Group	68.2	Fleetwood	21.7	IRESS Market Technology	2.0
K & S	63.7	Perpetual Trustees Australia	21.7	GWA International	1.7
Treasury Group	61.3	Oakton	21.5	Boral	1.3
Macquarie Bank	60.8	Rural Press	21.5	Fantastic Holdings	1.2
Magna Pacific	60.4	Origin Energy	20.2	ARB	0.8
Pro Medicus	53.6	Coates Hire	19.8	HGL	0.7
Commonwealth Bank	53.1	Cabcharge Australia	18.2	Alesco	–0.2
Colorado Group	50.1	Foodland	18.1	National Australia Bank	–0.3
Cochlear	47.4	Fairfax (John) Holdings	17.3	Metcash	–1.1
Timbercorp	47.4	Tasmanian Perpetual Trustees	17.1	AXA Asia Pacific	–1.3
Campbell Brothers	45.9	Computershare	16.0	Harvey Norman	–2.7
Angus & Coote	43.7	Santos	15.9	Pacifica Group	–2.8
Rio Tinto	43.7	MaxiTRANS Industries	14.9	Gunns	–4.5
Primary Health Care	42.1	Westpac Banking	14.9	OrotonGroup	–8.3
Billabong International	41.8	Rock Building Society	14.8	GUD Holdings	–9.0
United Group	41.3	St George Bank	14.8	Rebel Sport	–10.6
Adelaide Brighton	41.2	Incitec Pivot	14.2	CMI	–11.9
Coles Myer	40.7	Collection House	14.1	Adcorp Australia	–15.6
Candle Australia	40.6	Adelaide Bank	13.5	McGuigan Simeon Wines	–15.8
Select Harvests	39.7	Bendigo Bank	12.8	Integrated Group	–17.2
Rinker Group	37.5	Bank of Queensland	12.5	Flight Centre	–17.7
Sigma	33.4	FKP Property	12.3	STW Communications	–19.7
Willmott Forests	33.4	Gazal	11.1	Housewares International	–22.5
Count Financial	33.1	Programmed Maintenance Services	9.1	Central Equity	–28.4
Coffey International	32.8	Technology One	8.2	Infomedia	–29.8
QBE Insurance	31.6	Wesfarmers	8.2	Cellnet Group	–34.3
Suncorp-Metway	30.9	Funtastic	8.1	Troy Resources	–38.5
Australian Stock Exchange	30.4	OAMPS	7.8	AV Jennings Homes	–59.9
Trust Company of Australia	28.2				

TABLE H

Return on equity

Shareholder's equity is the company's assets minus its liabilities. It is in theory the amount owned by the shareholders of the company. Return on equity is the after-tax profit expressed as a percentage of that equity. Thus it is the amount of profit that the company managers made for you — the shareholder — from your assets. For many investors it is one of the most important gauges of how well a company is doing. It is one of the requirements for inclusion in this book that all companies have a return on equity of at least 10% in their latest financial year.

	%
Count Financial	85.3
IRESS Market Technology	51.7
Treasury Group	51.1
Fantastic Holdings	48.2
Pro Medicus	46.0
Australian Stock Exchange	42.8
Blackmores	40.4
Monadelphous	39.0
Sims Group	38.2
BHP Billiton	37.7
Cochlear	36.3
Colorado Group	34.3
Coffey International	34.2
Perpetual Trustees Australia	32.6
Corporate Express	31.1
Infomedia	30.1
Oakton	30.0
GUD Holdings	27.2
Technology One	27.2
K & S	26.4
CVC	26.1
ARB	25.9
Macquarie Bank	25.8
Select Harvests	25.4
Fleetwood	24.9
Reece Australia	24.8
Leighton Holdings	23.6
OrotonGroup	23.5
Woodside Petroleum	23.2
Rio Tinto	22.7
QBE Insurance	21.2
Troy Resources	21.0
Cabcharge Australia	20.6
Billabong International	20.5
Great Southern Plantations	20.5
Portman	20.4
Rebel Sport	19.8
Washington H. Soul Pattinson	19.5
Suncorp-Metway	19.3
Wesfarmers	19.3
Magna Pacific	18.8
Toll Holdings	18.6
Integrated Group	18.4
Funtastic	18.3
Rinker Group	18.3
FKP Property	18.2
Gunns	18.1
ANZ Banking	17.8
St George Bank	17.7
Westpac Banking	17.6
Sigma	17.5
CSR	17.4
Coates Hire	17.3
Tasmanian Perpetual Trustees	17.3
HGL	17.2
Commonwealth Bank	17.1
OAMPS	17.1
Pacifica Group	17.0
Rural Press	17.0
United Group	16.9
Flight Centre	16.7
Programmed Maintenance Services	16.4
Adcorp Australia	16.3
MaxiTRANS Industries	16.2
Coles Myer	15.7
Institute of Drug Technology	15.7
Boral	15.6
Campbell Brothers	15.5
Wide Bay Australia	15.2
David Jones	15.1
Angus & Coote	14.8
GWA International	14.8
Willmott Forests	14.8
Hills Industries	14.6
CMI	14.5
Foodland	14.4
Commander Communications	14.3
CSL	14.3
Timbercorp	14.3
Harvey Norman	14.1
AXA Asia Pacific	14.0
Adelaide Brighton	13.9
National Australia Bank	13.9
Rock Building Society	13.8
Candle Australia	13.7
Computershare	13.7
Gazal	13.6
Adelaide Bank	13.1
Bank of Queensland	13.1
Collection House	13.1
Australand Property	12.9
Incitec Pivot	12.5
Bendigo Bank	12.3
Australian Gas Light	12.2
Amalgamated Holdings	12.1
Downer EDI	12.0
Fairfax (John) Holdings	11.8
Publishing & Broadcasting	11.8
Central Equity	11.7
Santos	11.5
Housewares International	11.4
Origin Energy	11.4
Patrick Corporation	11.3
Trust Company of Australia	11.2
Primary Health Care	10.8
STW Communications	10.8
Alesco	10.6
Cellnet Group	10.6
Metcash	10.5
McGuigan Simeon Wines	10.3
AV Jennings Homes	10.2
Brickworks	10.1

TABLE I

Year-on-year return on equity growth

Company managers have a variety of strategies they can use to boost profits. It is much harder to lift the return on equity (ROE). Find a company with a high ROE figure and one that is growing year by year and the chances are that you have found a real growth stock.

	%
CVC	108.3
Commander Communications	83.5
Leighton Holdings	82.7
Portman	76.1
David Jones	75.7
Monadelphous	67.9
CSL	66.1
Magna Pacific	56.5
Washington H. Soul Pattinson	54.6
Sims Group	43.5
BHP Billiton	42.8
Commonwealth Bank	41.1
Pro Medicus	40.3
Campbell Brothers	37.8
K & S	35.7
Angus & Coote	34.4
Candle Australia	33.9
Rinker Group	31.4
Billabong International	31.2
Adelaide Brighton	30.8
Macquarie Bank	30.5
Coles Myer	29.4
Incitec Pivot	28.5
Cochlear	27.8
Rio Tinto	27.0
Trust Company of Australia	25.3
Count Financial	23.6
Rural Press	23.6
Wide Bay Australia	23.3
Wesfarmers	20.1
Australand Property	19.5
Suncorp-Metway	19.4
Sigma	18.7
Colorado Group	17.2
Downer EDI	16.7
CSR	16.6
Select Harvests	16.3
QBE Insurance	16.2
Primary Health Care	14.9
Gazal	13.9
Oakton	12.4
Treasury Group	12.4
Australian Stock Exchange	11.9
Reece Australia	11.9
Amalgamated Holdings	11.4
Timbercorp	11.2
Cabcharge Australia	10.0
Corporate Express	9.6
Fairfax (John) Holdings	9.5
Foodland	9.2
Tasmanian Perpetual Trustees	9.1
Blackmores	9.0
Fleetwood	8.8
Coates Hire	8.7
Perpetual Trustees Australia	8.6
Collection House	6.6
Reece Australia	5.5
Coffey International	5.2
Santos	5.0
Woodside Petroleum	4.8
Technology One	4.3
Computershare	3.9
FKP Property	3.8
MaxiTRANS Industries	3.7
Bendigo Bank	2.9
Origin Energy	2.4
Pacifica Group	0.8
St George Bank	0.8
Australian Gas Light	0.6
GWA International	0.3
Institute of Drug Technology	–0.1
Patrick Corporation	–1.1
Westpac Banking	–1.6
Willmott Forests	–2.4
Publishing & Broadcasting	–2.9
United Group	–3.2
Alesco	–3.6
Programmed Maintenance Services	–4.2
ANZ Banking	–4.6
Boral	–5.1
Bank of Queensland	–6.4
Adelaide Bank	–6.9
CMI	–6.9
Toll Holdings	–7.0
Funtastic	–8.3
OAMPS	–11.5
ARB	–11.7
Hills Industries	–11.9
HGL	–12.0
GUD Holdings	–12.3
Rock Building Society	–12.3
AXA Asia Pacific	–13.9
Harvey Norman	–15.0
Fantastic Holdings	–15.1
National Australia Bank	–16.3
STW Communications	–18.5
Flight Centre	–19.1
Brickworks	–19.9
Adcorp Australia	–20.0
Rebel Sport	–21.1
McGuigan Simeon Wines	–22.5
Integrated Group	–23.3
Housewares International	–25.2
Great Southern Plantations	–25.6
IRESS Market Technology	–28.1
OrotonGroup	–31.0
Gunns	–31.2
Infomedia	–31.2
Central Equity	–31.8
Cellnet Group	–36.9
Troy Resources	–52.1
Metcash	–53.6
AV Jennings Homes	–63.6

TABLE J

Debt-to-equity ratio

A company's borrowings as a percentage of its shareholder's equity is one of the most common measures of corporate debt. Many investors will be wary of a company with a ratio that is too high. However a company with a steady business and a regular income flow—such as an electric power company or a large supermarket chain—is generally considered relatively safe with a high level of debt whereas a small company in a new business field might be thought at risk with even moderate debt levels. Much depends on surrounding circumstances including the prevailing interest rates. Of course it is often from borrowing that a company grows and some investors are not happy buying shares in a company with little or no debt.

There are various ways to calculate the ratio but for this book the net debt position is used. That is a company's cash has been deducted from its borrowings. For inclusion in this book no company was allowed a debt-to-equity ratio of more than 70%. Some of the companies had no net debt—their cash position was greater than the amount of their borrowings—and so have a zero figure in this table. The ratio has no relevance for banks so they have been excluded.

	%
Adcorp Australia	0.0
Australian Stock Exchange	0.0
AXA Asia Pacific	0.0
Cabcharge Australia	0.0
Candle Australia	0.0
Central Equity	0.0
Colorado Group	0.0
Count Financial	0.0
CVC	0.0
David Jones	0.0
Fantastic Holdings	0.0
Flight Centre	0.0
HGL	0.0
Infomedia	0.0
Institute of Drug Technology	0.0
IRESS Market Technology	0.0
Leighton Holdings	0.0
Magna Pacific	0.0
Monadelphous	0.0
Oakton	0.0
OAMPS	0.0
Perpetual Trustees Australia	0.0
Portman	0.0
Pro Medicus	0.0
Rebel Sport	0.0
Reece Australia	0.0
Select Harvests	0.0
Tasmanian Perpetual Trustees	0.0
Technology One	0.0
Treasury Group	0.0
Troy Resources	0.0
Trust Company of Australia	0.0
United Group	0.0
Washington H. Soul Pattinson	0.0
Angus & Coote	1.1
Fairfax (John) Holdings	1.4
Great Southern Plantations	1.8
Coles Myer	2.0
QBE Insurance	5.5
Corporate Express	7.9
Coffey International	9.2
Sims Group	9.9
Billabong International	10.1
Commander Communications	10.5
Rinker Group	10.7
Woodside Petroleum	14.0
CSL	14.5
Metcash	14.5
Blackmores	16.8
Fleetwood	17.6
CSR	19.7
Incitec Pivot	22.3
Foodland	22.4
Willmott Forests	22.7
Toll Holdings	23.7
FKP Property	26.4
Rural Press	26.6
Brickworks	26.7
Primary Health Care	26.8
Hills Industries	27.1
GUD Holdings	27.7
Rio Tinto	28.8
ARB	29.4
Adelaide Brighton	33.4
Alesco	33.4
OrotonGroup	34.0
Downer EDI	37.5
K & S	37.7
GWA International	38.0
Australian Gas Light	38.2
Gazal	38.2
Funtastic	38.5
Publishing & Broadcasting	38.8
Programmed Maintenance Services	39.9
Patrick Corporation	42.7
Harvey Norman	42.8
Amalgamated Holdings	43.3
McGuigan Simeon Wines	45.7
Housewares International	46.5
Sigma	47.4
Campbell Brothers	48.4
Timbercorp	49.9
Integrated Group	50.5
Santos	50.6
Gunns	53.1
STW Communications	53.2
Collection House	55.0
Wesfarmers	55.6
Boral	56.4
BHP Billiton	56.6
MaxiTRANS Industries	56.7
Cochlear	58.7
Coates Hire	61.3
Australand Property	61.5
CMI	63.5
Pacifica Group	65.8
AV Jennings Homes	65.9
Origin Energy	68.7
Computershare	69.7
Cellnet Group	69.8

Table K

Current ratio

The current ratio is simply the company's current assets divided by its current liabilities. Current assets are cash or assets that can in theory be converted quickly into cash. Current liabilities are normally those payable within a year. The current ratio measures the ability of a company to repay in a hurry its short-term debt should the need arise. Banks are not included.

CVC	36.6
Pro Medicus	6.9
Troy Resources	4.4
IRESS Market Technology	4.3
Magna Pacific	4.3
CSL	4.2
HGL	4.2
Tasmanian Perpetual Trustees	3.9
Australian Stock Exchange	3.8
Technology One	3.6
Cabcharge Australia	3.5
GWA International	3.5
Australand Property	3.4
Institute of Drug Technology	3.4
Housewares International	3.3
McGuigan Simeon Wines	3.0
Programmed Maintenance Services	3.0
Trust Company of Australia	3.0
Central Equity	2.9
Treasury Group	2.9
AV Jennings Homes	2.8
Rebel Sport	2.7
Washington H. Soul Pattinson	2.7
Billabong International	2.6
Funtastic	2.6
Portman	2.5
Colorado Group	2.4
FKP Property	2.4
Perpetual Trustees Australia	2.4
Infomedia	2.3
Fantastic Holdings	2.2
Oakton	2.2
OrotonGroup	2.2
Campbell Brothers	2.1
Gazal	2.0
Reece Australia	2.0
CMI	1.9
David Jones	1.9
GUD Holdings	1.9
Harvey Norman	1.9
Hills Industries	1.9
MaxiTRANS Industries	1.9
Woodside Petroleum	1.9
Count Financial	1.8
Fleetwood	1.8
Rinker Group	1.8
Sims Group	1.8
Angus & Coote	1.7
Candle Australia	1.7
Collection House	1.7
CSR	1.7
Pacifica Group	1.7
Publishing & Broadcasting	1.7
Australian Gas Light	1.6
Alesco	1.5
Blackmores	1.5
Coffey International	1.5
Downer EDI	1.5
Patrick Corporation	1.5
Rio Tinto	1.5
Rural Press	1.5
Select Harvests	1.5
STW Communications	1.5
Boral	1.4
Cellnet Group	1.4
Metcash	1.4
Monadelphous	1.4
QBE Insurance	1.4
Santos	1.4
Adcorp Australia	1.3
Coates Hire	1.3
Cochlear	1.3
Commander Communications	1.3
Flight Centre	1.3
Incitec Pivot	1.3
United Group	1.3
Wesfarmers	1.3
Brickworks	1.2
Corporate Express	1.2
Great Southern Plantations	1.2
OAMPS	1.2
Sigma	1.2
Timbercorp	1.2
Willmott Forests	1.2
ARB	1.1
BHP Billiton	1.1
Coles Myer	1.1
Integrated Group	1.1
K & S	1.1
Computershare	1.0
Fairfax (John) Holdings	1.0
Foodland	1.0
Gunns	1.0
Origin Energy	1.0
Toll Holdings	1.0
Primary Health Care	0.7
Adelaide Brighton	0.6
Amalgamated Holdings	0.6

Table L

Price-earnings ratio

The PER — the current share price divided by the earnings-per-share figure — is one of the best-known of all sharemarket ratios. Essentially it expresses the amount of money investors are ready to pay for each cent or dollar of a company's profits and it allows you to compare the share prices of different companies with widely different profits. A high PER suggests the market has a high regard for the company and its growth prospects; a low one may mean that investors are disdainful of the stock. The figures in this table are based on share prices as of 16 August 2005.

CMI	4.6
CVC	5.5
Great Southern Plantations	6.5
Magna Pacific	6.6
Pacifica Group	7.4
Central Equity	8.1
HGL	8.2
Sims Group	8.3
Willmott Forests	8.5
Adcorp Australia	9.1
Australand Property	9.2
Colorado Group	9.7
K & S	10.4
Rebel Sport	10.5
AV Jennings Homes	10.6
OrotonGroup	10.8
Housewares International	10.9
Angus & Coote	11.1
Boral	11.1
Cellnet Group	11.2
FKP Property	11.2
Timbercorp	11.4
Commonwealth Bank	11.9
Rural Press	11.9
National Australia Bank	12.1
Programmed Maintenance Services	12.1
Amalgamated Holdings	12.2
Gunns	12.2
Incitec Pivot	12.3
CSR	12.4
Fleetwood	12.4
McGuigan Simeon Wines	12.5
MaxiTRANS Industries	12.8
Infomedia	13.0
Integrated Group	13.1
Collection House	13.2
GUD Holdings	13.5
Suncorp-Metway	13.6
GWA International	13.7
David Jones	13.8
Wide Bay Australia	13.9
ANZ Banking	14.0
Gazal	14.0
OAMPS	14.0
Adelaide Brighton	14.2
Washington H. Soul Pattinson	14.2
QBE Insurance	14.5
Westpac Banking	14.5
Adelaide Bank	14.6
AXA Asia Pacific	14.8
ARB	15.0
Candle Australia	15.0
Rock Building Society	15.7
Funtastic	15.9
BHP Billiton	16.1
Fairfax (John) Holdings	16.1
Downer EDI	16.4
Harvey Norman	16.4
Bank of Queensland	16.5
Australian Gas Light	16.8
Bendigo Bank	16.8
Coates Hire	16.8
Macquarie Bank	16.9
Santos	16.9
Institute of Drug Technology	17.0
Reece Australia	17.0
Technology One	17.2
Commander Communications	17.3
Leighton Holdings	17.7
St George Bank	17.8
Fantastic Holdings	17.9
Campbell Brothers	18.1
Troy Resources	18.2
Oakton	18.3
Blackmores	18.6
Monadelphous	18.6
Select Harvests	18.8
Coles Myer	19.2
Brickworks	19.4
Coffey International	19.7
Publishing & Broadcasting	20.0
Origin Energy	20.1
Hills Industries	20.3
Patrick Corporation	20.3
Alesco	20.4
Corporate Express	20.5
Toll Holdings	20.6
Cabcharge Australia	20.7
Pro Medicus	20.9
Flight Centre	21.7
Portman	22.0
Foodland	22.2
Billabong International	22.4
Sigma	22.4
Perpetual Trustees Australia	22.7
Trust Company of Australia	22.7
Treasury Group	23.0
CSL	23.4
STW Communications	23.6
Rio Tinto	23.7
Rinker Group	24.1
Wesfarmers	24.6
Australian Stock Exchange	24.7
United Group	25.2
Metcash	26.1
Tasmanian Perpetual Trustees	26.6
Count Financial	27.1
IRESS Market Technology	29.1
Woodside Petroleum	34.2
Cochlear	39.3
Computershare	40.6
Primary Health Care	41.1

TABLE M

Price-to-NTA-per-share ratio

The NTA-per-share figure expresses the worth of a company's net tangible assets — that is, its assets minus its liabilities and intangible assets — for each share of the company. Intangible assets such as goodwill or the value of newspaper mastheads are excluded because it is deemed difficult to place a value on them (though this proposition is debatable) and also because they might not have much worth if separated from the company. The price-to-NTA-per-share ratio relates this figure to the share price. A ratio of one means that the company is valued exactly according to the value of its assets. A ratio below one suggests that the shares are a bargain though usually there is a good reason for this. Profits are more important than assets.

In some respects this is an 'old economy' ratio. For many high-tech companies in the 'new economy' the most important assets are human ones whose worth does not appear on the balance sheet.

Four companies — Cochlear, Computershare, John Fairfax Holdings and Metcash — with a negative NTA-per-share figure — as a result of having intangible assets valued at more than their remaining net assets — have been omitted from this table.

CMI	0.9
Central Equity	1.0
Willmott Forests	1.0
AV Jennings Homes	1.1
Australand Property	1.3
CVC	1.3
Great Southern Plantations	1.3
Angus & Coote	1.4
HGL	1.4
Amalgamated Holdings	1.5
McGuigan Simeon Wines	1.5
Pacifica Group	1.6
Cellnet Group	1.7
National Australia Bank	1.7
Adelaide Bank	1.8
Bank of Queensland	1.8
Gunns	1.8
Boral	1.9
FKP Property	1.9
Magna Pacific	1.9
GWA International	2.0
Programmed Maintenance Services	2.0
Rebel Sport	2.0
Rural Press	2.0
Brickworks	2.1
CSR	2.1
David Jones	2.1
Timbercorp	2.1
Wide Bay Australia	2.1
Bendigo Bank	2.2
Harvey Norman	2.2
Rock Building Society	2.2
Collection House	2.3
Incitec Pivot	2.3
Commonwealth Bank	2.4
Housewares International	2.4
Publishing & Broadcasting	2.5
Santos	2.5
Adelaide Brighton	2.6
K & S	2.7
Institute of Drug Technology	2.8
Westpac Banking	2.8
ANZ Banking	2.9
Patrick Corporation	2.9
Washington H. Soul Pattinson	2.9
Coates Hire	3.0
Downer EDI	3.1
Suncorp-Metway	3.1
Origin Energy	3.4
OrotonGroup	3.4
Portman	3.4
Colorado Group	3.5
Troy Resources	3.5
Australian Gas Light	3.6
Sims Group	3.6
St George Bank	3.7
Coles Myer	3.8
Hills Industries	3.8
QBE Insurance	3.8
Reece Australia	3.9
Toll Holdings	3.9
Fleetwood	4.0
Gazal	4.0
ARB	4.1
Trust Company of Australia	4.1
Leighton Holdings	4.2
Integrated Group	4.3
Cabcharge Australia	4.4
Macquarie Bank	4.4
MaxiTRANS Industries	4.4
AXA Asia Pacific	4.5
STW Communications	4.5
Campbell Brothers	4.7
Rio Tinto	4.8
Adcorp Australia	4.9
CSL	5.0
Infomedia	5.2
BHP Billiton	5.5
Candle Australia	5.6
Funtastic	5.6
Rinker Group	5.9
Technology One	6.0
United Group	6.0
Flight Centre	6.2
Select Harvests	6.4
GUD Holdings	6.8
Woodside Petroleum	6.8
Monadelphous	7.1
Blackmores	7.7
Tasmanian Perpetual Trustees	7.9
Commander Communications	8.0
Perpetual Trustees Australia	8.2
Fantastic Holdings	8.4
OAMPS	8.7
Wesfarmers	8.9
Australian Stock Exchange	9.5
Coffey International	9.5
Pro Medicus	9.5
Treasury Group	10.1
Foodland	10.2
Oakton	12.3
Corporate Express	14.1
IRESS Market Technology	14.4
Sigma	15.8
Alesco	20.7
Count Financial	21.0
Billabong International	26.4
Primary Health Care	85.4

TABLE N

Dividend yield

Many investors buy shares for income rather than for capital growth. They look for companies that offer a high dividend yield (the dividend expressed as a percentage of the share price). Table N ranks the companies in this book according to their historic dividend yields. Note that the franking credits available from some companies can make the dividend yield substantially higher if you are in an appropriate tax bracket. The figures in this table are based on share prices as of 16 August 2005.

	%
Australand Property	9.6
Adcorp Australia	8.8
Pacifica Group	8.4
Sims Group	8.2
AV Jennings Homes	8.1
Housewares International	7.8
CMI	7.6
Magna Pacific	7.0
OrotonGroup	6.7
FKP Property	6.5
Integrated Group	6.0
GUD Holdings	5.9
Infomedia	5.9
McGuigan Simeon Wines	5.9
GWA International	5.8
Incitec Pivot	5.7
Alesco	5.5
Gazal	5.5
Angus & Coote	5.3
Central Equity	5.3
Commonwealth Bank	5.3
National Australia Bank	5.3
Oakton	5.3
Technology One	5.3
Cellnet Group	5.2
OAMPS	5.2
Rock Building Society	5.2
Colorado Group	5.1
HGL	5.1
David Jones	5.0
Hills Industries	5.0
Wide Bay Australia	5.0
Collection House	4.8
MaxiTRANS Industries	4.8
Boral	4.7
Programmed Maintenance Services	4.7
ANZ Banking	4.6
Candle Australia	4.6
Great Southern Plantations	4.6
Rural Press	4.6
St George Bank	4.6
Institute of Drug Technology	4.5
Macquarie Bank	4.5
Rebel Sport	4.5
Wesfarmers	4.5
Australian Gas Light	4.4
CSR	4.4
Adelaide Bank	4.3
Bendigo Bank	4.3
Campbell Brothers	4.3
Westpac Banking	4.3
Blackmores	4.2
Fairfax (John) Holdings	4.2
STW Communications	4.2
Suncorp-Metway	4.2
Amalgamated Holdings	4.1
Perpetual Trustees Australia	4.0
Select Harvests	4.0
Funtastic	3.9
K & S	3.9
Trust Company of Australia	3.9
Leighton Holdings	3.8
Pro Medicus	3.7
ARB	3.6
Australian Stock Exchange	3.6
Bank of Queensland	3.6
CVC	3.6
Monadelphous	3.6
Adelaide Brighton	3.5
Foodland	3.5
Tasmanian Perpetual Trustees	3.5
Cabcharge Australia	3.4
Coffey International	3.4
Gunns	3.4
IRESS Market Technology	3.4
Publishing & Broadcasting	3.4
Flight Centre	3.2
QBE Insurance	3.2
Coles Myer	3.0
Count Financial	3.0
Downer EDI	3.0
Fleetwood	3.0
Reece Australia	3.0
Santos	3.0
Coates Hire	2.9
Fantastic Holdings	2.9
Treasury Group	2.9
United Group	2.9
Billabong International	2.8
Sigma	2.8
Willmott Forests	2.7
AXA Asia Pacific	2.6
Timbercorp	2.5
Commander Communications	2.4
Corporate Express	2.4
Harvey Norman	2.4
Primary Health Care	2.4
Metcash	2.3
Troy Resources	2.3
Patrick Corporation	2.2
Brickworks	2.1
Washington H. Soul Pattinson	2.1
Cochlear	2.0
Origin Energy	2.0
Rio Tinto	2.0
Toll Holdings	1.9
BHP Billiton	1.8
Woodside Petroleum	1.8
Computershare	1.6
Rinker Group	1.4
CSL	1.3
Portman	1.1

TABLE O

Year-on-year dividend growth

Most investors hope for a rising dividend and this table tells how much each company raised (or lowered) its dividend in its latest financial year.

	%
Commander Communications	200.0
Sims Group	112.1
Monadelphous	90.0
David Jones	83.8
Perpetual Trustees Australia	73.3
Australian Stock Exchange	68.0
FKP Property	66.9
CVC	66.7
United Group	66.7
Select Harvests	61.5
Timbercorp	57.1
Colorado Group	50.0
Magna Pacific	50.0
Rinker Group	50.0
Willmott Forests	50.0
Billabong International	43.4
Primary Health Care	42.9
Treasury Group	42.9
Amalgamated Holdings	42.3
Great Southern Plantations	40.0
Patrick Corporation	39.8
Computershare	37.5
Alesco	36.4
Reece Australia	35.7
Tasmanian Perpetual Trustees	35.4
Downer EDI	32.4
Rural Press	32.1
Macquarie Bank	32.0
OrotonGroup	30.4
Sigma	30.0
Toll Holdings	29.3
Count Financial	28.6
QBE Insurance	28.6
Wesfarmers	28.6
St George Bank	28.4
Woodside Petroleum	28.3
Candle Australia	27.8
Campbell Brothers	27.3
Blackmores	26.1
Adelaide Brighton	25.0
GUD Holdings	25.0
Oakton	25.0
Programmed Maintenance Services	25.0
Suncorp-Metway	24.3
IRESS Market Technology	24.0
Housewares International	23.8
CSL	23.7
Cabcharge Australia	23.6
Australand Property	23.5
Wide Bay Australia	23.5
K & S	22.7
Funtastic	21.4
Pro Medicus	21.4
Publishing & Broadcasting	20.9
Adelaide Bank	20.5
Brickworks	20.0
Coffey International	19.3
OAMPS	18.0
Washington H. Soul Pattinson	17.6
Bank of Queensland	16.2
Rio Tinto	15.7
Coates Hire	15.4
Corporate Express	15.4
Origin Energy	15.4
AXA Asia Pacific	14.6
Rock Building Society	14.6
Collection House	14.3
Gazal	14.3
Institute of Drug Technology	14.3
MaxiTRANS Industries	14.3
Boral	13.3
Foodland	12.9
Bendigo Bank	12.5
Fairfax (John) Holdings	12.1
Coles Myer	11.5
Angus & Coote	11.1
Fleetwood	11.1
Leighton Holdings	11.1
ARB	10.5
Westpac Banking	10.3
Integrated Group	10.0
Santos	10.0
CSR	9.1
Technology One	8.8
Trust Company of Australia	8.6
Troy Resources	8.3
Commonwealth Bank	7.7
Fantastic Holdings	6.8
Hills Industries	6.7
ANZ Banking	6.3
Australian Gas Light	5.0
HGL	4.7
Adcorp Australia	3.8
BHP Billiton	2.4
National Australia Bank	1.8
Cochlear	1.3
AV Jennings Homes	0.0
CMI	0.0
Gunns	0.0
GWA International	0.0
McGuigan Simeon Wines	0.0
Rebel Sport	0.0
STW Communications	0.0
Pacifica Group	–4.7
Central Equity	–7.7
Infomedia	–10.5
Harvey Norman	–13.3
Metcash	–13.6
Flight Centre	–17.2
Cellnet Group	–39.1
Portman	–43.8

Table P

Five-year share price return

This table ranks the return to investors from a five-year investment in each of the companies in the book. It is the accumulated return which means it incorporates not only capital gain but also reinvested dividends bonus stock and rights issues.

	% pa
Treasury Group	92.5
United Group	65.0
Select Harvests	62.5
Metcash	61.2
Coffey International	59.5
Sigma	58.2
Monadelphous	56.8
FKP Property	46.6
Willmott Forests*	45.5
GUD Holdings	44.7
Gunns	43.1
Portman	42.4
Fleetwood	42.3
MaxiTRANS Industries	42.3
Adelaide Brighton	41.9
Funtastic	41.8
K & S	41.3
Toll Holdings	41.3
Boral	38.8
Troy Resources	38.4
Commander Communications*	37.1
Count Financial*	35.6
Foodland	35.1
Billabong International	34.9
AV Jennings Homes	34.0
Origin Energy	33.8
Colorado Group	33.0
Alesco	32.5
Coates Hire	32.5
OAMPS	32.1
Reece Australia	32.0
Wesfarmers	31.8
Sims Group	30.8
Fantastic Holdings	29.9
CSR	29.6
Rebel Sport	29.5
Tasmanian Perpetual Trustees	29.4
Trust Company of Australia	29.2
Wide Bay Australia	26.7
Adelaide Bank	26.6
Angus & Coote	26.3
Brickworks	25.5
St George Bank	25.0
Washington H. Soul Pattinson	24.9
ANZ Banking	24.9
Australian Stock Exchange	24.8
Downer EDI	24.4
Leighton Holdings	24.0
Campbell Brothers	23.9
IRESS Market Technology*	23.6
Suncorp-Metway	23.2
Bendigo Bank	22.6
Macquarie Bank	22.5
Amalgamated Holdings	22.3
Woodside Petroleum	22.3
Bank of Queensland	22.1
Blackmores	21.9
Great Southern Plantations	21.6
Hills Industries	21.5
BHP Billiton	21.1
Patrick Corporation	20.6
Cabcharge Australia	20.3
Rock Building Society	20.3
David Jones	19.7
OrotonGroup	19.5
Housewares International	19.5
Programmed Maintenance Services	19.2
Integrated Group	19.2
QBE Insurance	19.1
Rural Press	19.0
Rio Tinto	18.8
GWA International	18.5
ARB	18.4
Oakton	18.2
Santos	17.9
Perpetual Trustees Australia	17.9
Australand Property	17.5
Primary Health Care	17.3
CVC	17.0
AXA Asia Pacific	16.6
HGL	15.7
Westpac Banking	14.9
Gazal	13.9
McGuigan Simeon Wines	12.9
Australian Gas Light	12.8
Corporate Express	12.6
Commonwealth Bank	12.1
CMI	11.4
Cochlear	11.0
Coles Myer	11.0
Central Equity	9.6
National Australia Bank	9.1
STW Communications	8.5
Magna Pacific	8.1
Timbercorp	7.5
Candle Australia	7.1
Publishing & Broadcasting	6.8
Pro Medicus*	6.5
Fairfax (John) Holdings	3.5
CSL	1.3
Computershare	–2.5
Flight Centre	–3.9
Cellnet Group	–4.2
Pacifica Group	–6.0
Harvey Norman	–6.2
Adcorp Australia	–7.8
Institute of Drug Technology	–10.7
Technology One	–12.0
Collection House*	–15.5
Infomedia	–21.4

* Four-year share price return

TABLE Q

Non-interest income to total income

The final three tables rank the banks only. Most of the banks are working to diversify away from their traditional lending business into other operations such as insurance and funds management. This table ranks them according to their success showing how much of their income derives from non-interest sources.

	%
Macquarie Bank	90.1
Suncorp-Metway	85.5
Rock Building Society	62.4
Commonwealth Bank	47.5
National Australia Bank	44.8
Westpac Banking	40.6
ANZ Banking	38.2
Bendigo Bank	37.9
St George Bank	37.7
Bank of Queensland	37.2
Wide Bay Australia	30.5
Adelaide Bank	10.8

TABLE R

Cost-to-income ratio

All the banks are working to reduce their high costs. The cost-to-income ratio—expressing costs as a percentage of operating income—is one of the measures commonly used by analysts to ascertain their success.

	%
ANZ Banking	47.4
Westpac Banking	49.2
Commonwealth Bank	51.5
St George Bank	51.9
Adelaide Bank	53.6
Wide Bay Australia	57.8
Bank of Queensland	63.4
National Australia Bank	66.9
Macquarie Bank	69.0
Bendigo Bank	71.7
Rock Building Society	73.4
Suncorp-Metway	74.0

TABLE S

Return on assets

Banks have large assets and the return on assets ratio—profits as a percentage of total assets—is another popular measure of their efficiency.

	%
Macquarie Bank	1.8
Suncorp-Metway	1.8
Wide Bay Australia	1.4
Commonwealth Bank	1.3
ANZ Banking	1.2
St George Bank	1.2
Westpac Banking	1.1
National Australia Bank	1.0
Rock Building Society	0.9
Bank of Queensland	0.8
Adelaide Bank	0.7